ZAMBIA
THE FREEDOM STRUGGLE
AND THE AFTERMATH

SYLVESTER M. CHISEMBELE
01.03.1930 – 05.02.2006

ZAMBIA
THE FREEDOM STRUGGLE AND THE AFTERMATH

*The Personal Story of Freedom Fighter
and Leader Sylvester Mwamba Chisembele*

BY

SOPHENA CHISEMBELE

Axminster
Devon, UK
2016

ZAMBIA -- THE FREEDOM STRUGGLE AND THE AFTERMATH
The Personal Story of Freedom Fighter and Leader
Sylvester Mwamba Chisembele

Published by: Sylsop Books

Copyright © 2016, Sophena Chisembele

All rights reserved. No part of this may be reproduced, stored in a retrieval system of transmitted, in any form or by any means, electronic, mechanical, photocopying or otherwise, without the prior written permission of the publisher.

ISBN: 978-0-9934095-0-9

Printed and bound in UK

First Edition: 2016

Author: Sophena Chisembele

Every effort has been made to trace and acknowledge copyright holders, but if any have inadvertently been overlooked, the publisher will be pleased to make the necessary arrangements at the first opportunity.

Cover: The Litunga of the Barotse, Mbikusita Lewanika II, Cabinet Minister, Sylvester Chisembele and Mrs S. Chisembele - Kuomboka Ceremony, 1970.

In memory of my parents and my husband

Table of Contents

Foreword   xi
Acknowledgements   xiii
Map of Zambia   xiv
List of Illustrations   xv
List of Acronyms   xvi

PART ONE: The Freedom Struggle 1948–1964

1 (1948 – 1959)   1
    Backdrop
    On the way to emancipation
    Actions and consequences
    State of Emergency

2 (1960 – 1964)   29
    British VIP visits
    Broken promises
    Independence achieved

PART TWO: The Kaunda Era 1965–1991

3 (1965 – 1969)   59
    Early days
    Personal relationships
    Intrigues and repercussions

4 (1970 – 1972)   99
    Chisembele in Barotseland
    Committee of 14
    Bans; arrests; suspensions and changes
    New alliances and new parties

5 (1973 – 1977)   119
    One Party State
    General Election; Luapula stands firm
    Chisembele in Eastern Province
    Tension and underground campaigns
    Detentions and aggravations
    Chisembele in Copperbelt

6 (1978 – 1979)   133
    Presidential challengers outmanoeuvred
    General Elections veto in use
    Chisembele excluded from Cabinet
    A word on our farming programme

7 (1980 – 1983)   147
    Deaths in England and Zambia
    Chisembele's last Commonwealth
      Parliamentary Conference
    General Elections; prominent leaders ousted
    Chisembele retires
    Kaunda adopts IMF measures

PART THREE: Retirement Onwards 1983 — 2009

8   Some words on youth and character of Chisembele   161

9 (1984 – 1990)   175
    Food riots shock Kaunda
    Instability, detentions and extreme measures

    IMF relations severed
    Country moves towards anarchy
    Calls for Multi-Party Elections

The Chiluba Years: 1991-2001

10 (1991 – 1995)   187
    Multi-party politics re-introduced
    Historic Election brings change
    Euphoria and hopeful beginnings
    Disillusion and disappointment
    Rumours of "Zero Option" coup plot
    State of Emergency

11 (1996 – 1999)   199
    Kaunda seeks to regain control
    General Elections
    Kaunda barred; UNIP boycott elections
    MMD retain power
    "Captain Solo" coup attempt and repercussions
    Chiluba and Kaunda face citizenship challenge

12 (2000)   209
    Kaunda steps down from UNIP presidency
    Chisembele farm illegally removed
    Chiluba "regrets psychological torture …"

The Mwanawasa Years: 2001 – 2009

13 (2001 – 2003)   217
    Chiluba's third term bid fails
    Chiluba appoints Mwanawasa successor
    General Elections Mwanawasa wins
    EU Observers fail to sanction Election results
    MMD in disarray; leaders split

    Chiluba's immunity from prosecution removed
    Chisembele submits claim to British Government
      for atrocities committed during the struggle
    Mung'omba Constitution Commission

14 (2004 – 2005)   231
    Chisembele brings compensation claim on
      British Government before the ECHR
    Mwanawasa and government officials face
      corruption allegations
    Chisembele refuses Independence Day honour
    Chisembele submits paper to Mung'omba
      Constitution Commission

15 (2006 – 2009)   255
    Traumatic death of Chisembele
    Mwanawasa and Kaunda argue over neglect of
      freedom fighters
    General Elections
    Mwanawasa wins and riots follow result
    Death of Mwanawasa
    Family matters and departure from Zambia

Appendix A   "Luapula Province's Contribution to   281
                   Political Independence and Democratic
                   Governance" by Valentine W.C. Kayope
Appendix B   Part autobiography Sophena Chisembele   293
Chapter Notes   305
Footnotes   315
Index   329

Foreword

Chisembele has penned, perhaps, one of most pertinent books on the political history of Zambia. The best catch-phrase for the work as a whole should appropriately be termed, "She was there before, during and after the reconstruction of the territory we now proudly call Zambia." In this regard alone, Chisembele is a vetted pioneer of the creation of the nation of Zambia. But this book is not about her. It is not about the late Sylvester Mwamba Chisembele and his activism as one of the most formidable Zambian political freedom fighters. It is not about Zambia, either. It is about all and everything Zambian – its people, their political struggles and the present and future of the nation's young democracy. It is a book for all of us – Zambians at home, abroad and all those with interest in the development of the Zambian political process.

I first became acquainted with the story of Sylvester Chisembele in Toronto, Canada through sheer inadvertency. Dickson Eyoh, a professor of African Studies at the University of Toronto had bequeathed a collection of papers and newspaper cuttings to Dr. Munyonzwe Hamalengwa, a prominent Zambian-Canadian lawyer and author. These materials became a significant part of my book, *Zambia – Struggles of My People*. But unlike my book which only gives a cursory view of Chisembele's story, in *Zambia – The Freedom Struggle and the Aftermath*, Chisembele his surviving wife, gives us a holistic dissertation of the life and agitation that were lived and spent for the formation of the nation of Zambia. She is cogent, historically correct as well as poignant.

Like many inquisitive Zambian authors and thinkers, I have always bemoaned the lack of a finishing eulogy to the Zambian freedom saga. When I read this work, I immediately knew that, finally, the missing piece in the Zambian historical chess has been found. This book will make it clear that the story of Zambia is a celebration of men and women other than only Kenneth Kaunda, who have gone incognito. It is the narration of great sacrifices of men like Chisembele who gave all to the cause of freedom.

Yet, the story of Chisembele is one that transcends the assumption of self-rule by the Zambian government after 1964. In the context of Zambia celebrating its 50 years of independence, Chisembele's book is a reminder that true independence is hard to acquire. In his life, Chisembele had continued to seek for true independence including when in the first decade of the 2000s he canvassed for reparatory compensation from the British Government against the atrocities he and others had suffered during the struggle for independence. In this vein, too, Chisembele is an epitome of vigilance and conscience with regards to the future relationships between the former colonial masters and what has become of the territories they looted and impoverished, territories like Zambia.

I recommend *Zambia – The Freedom Struggle and the Aftermath*, to all, and especially to those wishing to understand and learn about the neglected history of the Zambian people.

Charles Mwewa,
Professor of Legal Studies, B.A. Law, B.A. English; DipBM
Author: Zambia – Struggles of My People
Toronto, Canada

Acknowledgements

My thanks are due to several people who have very kindly given me their time and assisted me in specific ways to complete this book. In particular, I would like to thank The Hon. Valentine W.C. Kayope for his contribution and the support he gave to me in the first years after my husband's death, as well as personal friends, Michael and Beryl Barr, Shelley and Nini Mehta and the contacts that I made during the course of writing this book, for their encouragement and advice.

MAP OF ZAMBIA

List of Illustrations

1. Sylvester Chisembele, Lusaka 1961
2. Michael and Salome Chisembele with sons, Joseph and Sylvester
3. Sylvester Chisembele visiting chiefs during early days on campaign
4. Freedom Fighters from Northern Rhodesia in China, 1962
5. Return from China via Tanzania, 1962
6. Mrs S. Chisembele, Cabinet Minister, Sylvester Chisembele, The Litunga Mbikusita Lewanika II, Petitions Court Hearings, Mongu, 1970
7. Sylvester Chisembele and Mrs Sophena Chisembele, - Opening of Parliament - 1975
8. Sylvester Chisembele arriving in Chipata, Eastern Province, 1975
9. Chisembele, Reuben Kamanga, Alex Shapi and President Kaunda - Copperbelt Rally 1978
10. Fr. Jan Wessels, M.Afr. farm visit 1981, Chisamba
11. Archbishop James Spaita visit 2005, Lusaka

List of Acronyms

ACC	Anti-Corruption Commission
ANC	African National Congress
AFC	Agricultural Finance Company
BBC	British Broadcasting Corporation
BHC	British High Commission
BSAC	British South Africa Company
ECHR	European Court of Human Rights
FDD	Forum for Democracy & Development
FFTUZ	Federation of Free Trade Unions of Zambia
FNLA	National Front for the Liberation of Angola
IMF	International Monetary Fund
M.Afr.	Missionaries of Africa
MCC	Member of the Central Committee of UNIP
MMD	Movement for Multi-Party Democracy
MPLA	Popular Movement for the Liberation of Angola
PF	Patriotic Front
RST	Roan Selection Trust Group
UNCHR	United Nations Commission on Human Rights
UNIP	United National Independence Party
UNITA	National Union for the Total Independence of Angola,
UNZA	University of Zambia
UPND	United Party for National Development
UPP	United Progressive Party
UTH	University Teaching Hospital
ZANC	Zambia African National Congress
ZCTU	Zambia Congress of Trade Unions
ZDC	Zambia Democratic Congress
ZESCO	Zambia Electricity Supply Co.
ZNBC	Zambia National Broadcasting Corporation
ZHRC	Zambia Human Rights Commission
ZNBS	Zambia National Building Society

PART ONE

The Freedom Struggle
1948 – 1964

Chapter 1
1948 – 1959

1948 – 1950

Sylvester Mwamba Chisembele was born in Fort Rosebery, Luapula Province, Northern Rhodesia (now Mansa, Luapula Province, Zambia) in 1930. His parents had migrated from Mporokoso, Northern Province, at the turn of the twentieth century. They settled in Fort Rosebery, a location described in a Northern Rhodesian RST *Horizon* article in the early 1960s as: *"a town steeped in colonialism; an outpost of British rule; and an administrative centre for a remote part of Northern Rhodesia"*.

At the age of 12, Sylvester Chisembele entered the Lubushi Seminary in Northern Province, run by the Catholic White Fathers, where he was educated and was training for the priesthood. In 1948, he was asked to leave the Seminary because his questions and attitude concerning the second-class status of Africans were considered a disruptive influence on other students.

After leaving the Seminary, although still a youth of 18, he was proving to be a capable businessman. Within the following two years he had established a profitable trading venture supplying finger millet to local traders, but the bulk of the produce he traded was to the Copperbelt and in order to achieve continuity he traded on a contract basis. The produce he supplied came from various districts in the Luapula and Northern Provinces. Apart from trading in grains, he also established fishing camps on the Nganda and

Personal Story of Sylvester M. Chisembele

Sosa beaches on the western shores of Lake Bangweulu in Fort Rosebery District, trading as "Mikwau Fishing Nets", the catch from this venture, too, he supplied locally and to the Copperbelt.

Branching out still further, he then obtained a plot in Fort Rosebery on which he constructed two sizeable buildings; one he used for a bakery and the other for a restaurant. Soon after he purchased a motorcycle which gave him ease of movement to control his various enterprises. He was moving towards purchasing a second-hand lorry so that he would not need to hire vehicles as he was doing.

Chisembele's enterprises were growing fast and his activities had become noticed by the District Commissioner. There was another Fort Rosebery trader, a white settler called Steincamp, who was also trading grains to Kitwe in the Copperbelt Province. Chisembele was keenly and vigorously competing with this trader and had impacted on his business, which up to that time had been a virtual monopoly. Collusion between Mr Steincamp and the District Commissioner introduced a period of unscrupulous harassment.

He was using hired trucks to transport the grains to the Copperbelt, but now roadblocks would appear, seize the truck on fabricated charges, arrest Chisembele and the driver, and confiscate the grains which were then offloaded into a police warehouse. The driver and truck would be released and subsequently sent on to the Copperbelt, empty. Chisembele would later be brought before the magistrate and released, but the damage had already been done because he would have to start the process to deliver the grains over again, the cost of the lorry hiring was lost and further expenses incurred. The grain trading venture was systematically brought to its knees.

The victimisation enraged and distressed Chisembele, so much so, that he knew he would have to actively fight towards removing the colonialists from the country and make sure that indigenous people took back their rights and their land. The grain trading business folded, the fishing camps and the bakery with its restaurant were put under the supervision of his brothers, and he entered the freedom struggle for independence from the colonial power, Britain, becoming a full-time committed freedom fighter.

He joined the African National Congress [ANC]. This nationalist party was originally named "Northern Rhodesian African Congress" and was formed in 1951. The party was shortly afterwards re-named the "African National Congress", Harry Mwaanga Nkumbula was the President of this fledgling political party. Later in 1953, Kenneth Kaunda served as the Secretary General. Although there was a presence of the ANC in Luapula Province, it was initially low-key and insignificant in that it had made little impact on the population of the province.

1951 – 1956
For decades there had been discussions among the white settler leaders, the British Government, the administrators of the territories of Northern and Southern Rhodesia and Nyasaland, of a possible grouping together. In September 1951, a preliminary conference was arranged and held at Victoria Falls to discuss, yet again, a scheme to form a Federation of Central African States. This conference was attended by the Secretary of State for the Colonies, Labour MP James Griffiths, and representatives of the three colonial territories. A statement was issued at the end of this conference confirming agreement, in principle, for the formation of a Federation of the three territories, but although no concrete decisions were taken, it was agreed that there would be no amalgamation of the three territories without the consent of the black African population.

A few months later in November there was a change of government in Britain when the Conservative Party gained control. The new Secretary of State for the 75 Colonies, Oliver Lyttelton, made a statement in the House of Commons on 21 November 1951 voicing the approval and support of the British Government for the formation of a Federation of Central African States, provided certain safeguards were in place which they considered relevant. Discussions were taking place to consider a form and structure for this proposed Central African Federation among the Colonial Office, the overseers of the British protectorates of Nyasaland and Northern Rhodesia; the Governors of these two Protectorates; and the Prime Minister of the self-ruling colony of Southern Rhodesia, Godfrey Huggins. However, the scheme was not supported or agreed by the black African majority of the three territories or, for that matter, by all Members of Parliament in the UK. The overwhelming majority of the black Africans and Chiefs in these territories bitterly opposed any plan or suggestion of a Federation.

The statement of approval made by the British Secretary of State for the Colonies in the House of Commons, appeared ambiguous, for the Secretary of State talked of his support and approval of the formation of a Federation, but during the same parliamentary debate also spoke of the necessity to safeguard the protectorate status of Northern Rhodesia and Nyasaland, so that no amalgamation of the three territories could take place without the consent of the black majority in these territories. The subtle difference between the words 'federation' and 'amalgamation' not readily understandable in this context, but apparently meaning that a black African majority acceptance was not necessary for a Federation to be formed, which would be white dominated and in effect largely in control of the lives of the populace, but was necessary for any changes which a white minority Federation Government might propose which would affect the position of Britain as the superior power. Thus giving the overall impression that ownership of the territories was more important than the inhabitants. In the same debate the previous Secretary of State, James Griffiths, questioned reports of the Southern Rhodesian Governor coming to London to hold discussions with the Government and he emphasised that discussions without black Africans present would fail.[1]

In March 1953 the Secretary of State, Oliver Lyttelton presented Command Papers on the proposals for the formation of a Central African Federation to the House of Commons, followed by a second reading in the House on 24 March 1953 when the proposals on the Central African Federation were approved. This followed lengthy discordant discussions in the House of Commons and notwithstanding objections and the strong opposition to the imposition of such a grouping by black Africans in Northern Rhodesia and Nyasaland. Subsequently, the Secretary of State for the Colonies presented a Bill before Parliament. On 6 May 1953, the Rhodesia and Nyasaland Federation Bill was presented for a second reading and having passed through the House of Commons and then the House of Lords it was forwarded for Royal Assent.[2]

Under the Constitution of the imposed Federation, the seat of political power was in Salisbury, Southern Rhodesia, but the wealth of the Federation was seated in the mines of Northern Rhodesia. In the unicameral Federal Assembly, there was a total representation of 35 members of which elected constituency members were 14 from Southern Rhodesia, 8 from Northern Rhodesia and 4 from Nyasaland. Of the electorate for Northern Rhodesia, 14,588 were Europeans and three were Africans! There were an additional three members for each of the three territories, but

---

[1] Hansard, HC Deb 21 November 1951 vol 494 cc392-7.
[2] Hansard, HC Deb 24 March 1953 vol 513 cc658-801, HC Deb 06 May 1953 vol 515 cc407-30.

only in Southern Rhodesia were these additional three members elected, in Northern Rhodesia and Nyasaland the additional three were appointees.

In Northern Rhodesia one of the main advocates for Federation was Roy Welensky the leading white politician in Northern Rhodesia who was an incoming settler from Southern Rhodesia; he was intent on maintaining white minority rule. The same year that the Federation came into being, Roy Welensky was given a knighthood and was now called Sir Roy Welensky. Although not all of the white population was in total favour of the Federation, their disquiet was purely from the economic viewpoint.

Around the time of the formation of the Federation of Rhodesia and Nyasaland an amusing satirical poem was written, believed to have been by Gervas C.R. Clay, who at that time served in Northern Rhodesia as part of Her Majesty's Overseas Civil Service [HMOCS]. The poem "Cuckoo in the Nest" was a skit, recited to the rhythm of "The Lion and Albert", a song made famous by Stanley Holloway in the early 1930s. Whilst the sentiments expressed were humorous, they were also indicative of the views held by Europeans north of the Zambezi:

There's a place known as NORTHERN RHODESIA
That's noted for fresh air and sun;
It's got a big belt made of copper
That must weigh at least fifty ton.
And thanks to this copper, the country
Is one of the richest on earth;
It has to be --- local shopkeepers
Charge ten times what anything's worth!
   Now just across the Zambezi River
Lies another Rhodesia called SOUTH
Where folk so messed up their finances
They've been living for years hand to mouth.

Zambia – The Freedom Struggle and the Aftermath

Till one day a bright lad called Huggins
Said, "I've thought of a trick we can play
On the show up north of Zambezi
So that most of their brass comes our way.
  "We'll tell them we're having to wind up estate
And South Africa's taking us over
Unless they're prepared to outbid old Malan -
If they fall for it, lads, we're in clover!"
"But first we must find some young fellow up there
Who'll see that our tale's put across
A lad who'll agree, for suitable fee,
To talk the hind leg off a hoss."
  So they sent for a chap called Welensky
Who hadn't much of a brain, but was tough;
And told him their tale, over a pint of old ale,
And he swallowed it, ready enough.
Next they drew up a grand Federation,
Which was read out on 8 o'clock news,
And agreed by a big referendum,
Of all those who had nothing to lose.
  N.R. had a scheme called Kafue,
Which was passed with pre-Fed guarantees,
So they changed it all to Kariba
With Coyne, and the greatest of ease.
When all was signed, sealed and delivered,
They told folks in North, "Clear off home!
We've just the right fellows to rule this new State,
For we've made such a mess of our own!" [3]

When the Federation of Rhodesia and Nyasaland was enforced in 1953 Chisembele was already a political activist. That year a ban was issued on political activities in areas where people were questioning why they were under the rule

---

[3] "The Lion and Albert" and "Cuckoo in The Nest", courtesy Robin B. Clay.

of colonialists and three chiefs in Fort Rosebery District, Luapula Province namely, Senior Chief Milambo Chilyapa, Chief Mulakwa and Chief Kasoma Bangweulu were deposed, banished and taken captive and they were restricted in other districts outside the province. In Nyasaland (Malawi) Chief Philip Gomani who was old and sick, but strongly opposed to the Federation was deposed, deported and he died in a foreign country a few months after his banishment. In spite of the ban on politics Chisembele and his friend and colleague, Alex Shapi, continued their activities and used Chisembele's restaurant as a venue for political organisation. Within the next two years, he and his colleagues established a firm ANC base in Fort Rosebery and were spreading out successfully to all other districts in the province.

By 1956 the Colonial District Commissioner was uneasy and concerned at Chisembele's continuing political activities and his influence that had brought the rapid growth of the ANC movement in Luapula Province. The Commissioner alleged that people in the province were being steered to violence and communism. There were serious attempts made to invoke the support and assistance of Fr. Rene-Georges Pailloux, Prefect of Fort Rosebery Catholic Church, to wipe out and prevent the spread of nationalist activism. The warnings of the District Commissioner, A.C. North, resulted in wrong reports reaching the Prefect, conveyed by the White Fathers at Lubwe Mission, that Sylvester Chisembele had influenced the indigenous, influential Catholic church leaders at Lubwe Mission, Samfya, namely, Sylvester Muchengwa and Protasio Kamayanda, to turn the people against the Church.

When this information reached Fr. Pailloux, his response was to rush to Lubwe Mission to prevent what he had been told was the spread of atheism through a communist doctrine. Fr. Pailloux held a special Service at Lubwe Mission, as usual fully attended by people crammed inside and outside the

Church. During the homily he strongly condemned communism and warned the congregation that if they followed this path and became members of the ANC they would be excommunicated from the Church. In spite of the fact that Fr. Pailloux was well respected and admired by the people of the Luapula Province, the issue at stake was so important that the congregation rejected and even challenged the priest's words saying that if excommunication was the price of struggling for freedom, then they would accept it because nothing was going to stop them from joining the ANC in the fight for freedom and independence.[4] (*Fr. Pailloux was appointed Bishop of Fort Rosebery in 1961. The White Fathers are now named Missionaries of Africa [M.Afr.]*).

Fr. Pailloux after holding Mass returned to Fort Rosebery and attended a meeting with the District Commissioner, whose reaction on hearing the report was to call a big public rally in Chief Mwansakombe's area in Samfya. The District Commissioner, A.C. North, after addressing the crowds for an hour on the danger to them of the activities and the evil intentions of the ANC, asked if anyone had anything to say. Chisembele stood and was allowed to speak, which he did refuting one by one the accusations made by the District Commissioner, but scared by the cheering that greeted Chisembele's words and fearing the reaction of the crowds the Senior Security Officer, Belman, pulled a gun on Chisembele, the District Commissioner ordered him to put the gun away, but it was too late, the incident caused pandemonium and a stampede. People were hurt, in particular, the most vulnerable, the children and women.

The District Commissioner had arranged a similar public rally for the following day at Chief Chitambo's Nawabungwa. Chisembele immediately sent word to Sylvester Muchengwa,

---

[4] Folder "Documents Submitted to ECHR 29.4.04" - Claim Reports 1-5 p 2; Chisembele "Struggle History note", scan.

Personal Story of Sylvester M. Chisembele

a prominent personality and respected leader of the Catholic Church in Samfya, telling him to arrange with the district ANC leaders, Protasio Kamayanda and Ba Chimanya, a challenge and to prepare answers to the allegations the District Commissioner would make against the ANC. He informed Sylvester Muchengwa that he would cycle over as soon as he could in order to be present. Chisembele arrived towards the end of the rally, they, the ANC officials, had made a tremendous victory and the crowds were jubilant. Within an hour, District Commissioner A.C. North had all four men arrested and detained.

After three weeks detention in Fort Rosebery prison, Chisembele and his colleagues were brought before the magistrate, another position held by North. Chisembele was charged with addressing a public meeting, causing a disturbance and inciting people to violence. Chisembele pointed out to the magistrate that he himself had invited him to speak and that the disturbance was caused by his Security Officer, Belman. The magistrate, North, would not listen to reason and he sentenced all four men to nine months imprisonment with hard labour. Chisembele immediately appealed to the High Court. He was transported, in chains, on the back of a truck together with his three colleagues to Ndola's Bwana Mkubwa prison in the Copperbelt Province where they were incarcerated. The group were not released from the prison until they had served in full the sentences imposed upon them. The Appeal against conviction was not heard in the High Court until after the sentence of nine months had passed so that the acquittal then granted was hollow and meaningless.[5]

For its importance and historical interest, I quote Chisembele's report on this incident:

---

[5] Ibid. Fn.4 Folder "Documents Submitted to ECHR 29.4.04" - Claim Reports 1-5 p 3.

Zambia – The Freedom Struggle and the Aftermath

Politics in Fort Rosebery were banned at the imposition of Federation in 1953 in areas where people were critical against Federation and three of our Chiefs from Fort Rosebery were banished and restricted to other districts.

I established a strong ANC base in Fort Rosebery and then I spread out to Samfya and started organising branches. I cycled to Lubwe Mission to visit Sylvester Muchengwa, who in turn organised Protasio Kamayanda, these were leading personalities in the area and were most respected and at the same time were leaders in the Catholic Church. As a result, ANC started spreading very fast.

The local white priests began worrying at the impact and influence the ANC was fast acquiring. They contacted Bishop Pailloux in Fort Rosebery informing him that the Congress movement was not only gaining ground, but its influence had started being felt and it was being propagated by the top Catholic Church leaders in the Mission, meaning Sylvester Muchengwa and Protasio Kamayanda.

When the Bishop received the report in the beginning of 1956 he was scared that the people in Lubwe Mission had turned communist, so he made a special trip to Lubwe Mission and strongly condemned communism and warned the people, especially Christians, that anyone who is a member of ANC is at the same time a Communist and as a result would be excommunicated.

Bishop Pailloux was terribly shocked and shaken by the instant response to the contrary from the congregation in the Church, when the people replied that, 'you have no right to stop us from struggling for freedom, if you do not want us to be members of African National Congress then just excommunicate us, you will remain with your Church buildings and we will be fighting for freedom through ANC'; the people referred to the Eucharist and said 'they can hang they are not even sweet (tatwaba utwakuta lowa)' and that remark caused a big laughter in the Church, the Bishop had no choice, but to denounce the people in the Church that 'I thought you people were true Christians now I have proved that you are not'.

The Bishop's mission failed lamentably to prevent the influence of the ANC growing. When the Bishop returned to Fort Rosebery he reported the matter to the District Commissioner, North.

The District Commissioner decided to go to Samfya sub-Boma and arranged to hold 2 big rallies against the ANC: one rally in Chief Mwansakombe's area and the other in Chief Chitambo's area, all in Ng'umbo district. At that time, I had already been 3 weeks in the area. I was with Alex Shapi in Mwansakombe's village, Shapi's own home village; we were organising the Congress Movement in the area.

On the appointed day, the District Commissioner from Fort Rosebery arrived with his Senior Security Police Officer, Belman, Boma messengers, Chiefs' kapasus (messengers) and a few African clerics. The District Commissioner had called a big public rally in Mwansakombe's village and many people came from surrounding villages. The rally was very big and well attended and the District Commissioner started by warning people not to be misled by dangerous people calling themselves leaders of ANC because these people were bringing nothing to the area but troubles and would destroy the peace.

The District Commissioner went on for an hour, denouncing ANC and then after his public Address, he asked the gathering if they had anything to say. The people were just seated quiet, and then he asked Alex Shapi if he had anything to say, Shapi replied he had nothing to say. Then he asked me if I had anything to say. I said that I had and he then allowed me to stand up and reply. I said the ANC is not here to bring troubles to the people; it is here to awaken the people to rise up and fight for their freedom with a policy of non-violence against the British Rule which has been imposed on us against our will. I said colonialism, as well as slavery, has been *rejected all over the world wherever it imposed its ugly face. I said 'you, District Commissioner, when your ancestors not long ago were colonized by the great Roman Empire, your ancestors had struggled against that foreign rule until you were free; so if it was sweet for your ancestors to struggle and die for their freedom, it is sweet and right for us in Northern Rhodesia to organise ourselves against the foreign rule which you are heading here'.*

Hearing such a reaction, it cheered the people and they started to shout 'down with imperialism, British Government go back to England' at this juncture the Senior Security Police Officer stood up and pulled his revolver pointing it at me as I was addressing the people. Seeing a revolver all the people rose up, some covered me as I am a short man, and there was instant commotion and pandemonium. North ordered Belman to put his revolver away, but it was too late; people were running across each other. There was a stampede on old and young. That was the end of the meeting.

The District Commissioner and his entourage left for Chief Chitambo where he had arranged to have a similar meeting the following day. So what I did was to write a letter to Sylvester Muchengwa informing him what had happened and asking him to organise themselves that very night and arrange to make a showdown in Chief Chitambo's Nawabungwa where District Commissioner North was going to address another big public rally. I told him that I would be cycling to the meeting in the morning.

Ba Sylvester Muchengwa did exactly what I told them and arranged that he, Ba Kamayanda and Ba Chimanya would answer to the allegations of the District Commissioner against ANC. My colleagues followed to the letter so that the District Commissioner North's mission lamentably failed like his friend Bishop Pailloux. It was a victory to the ANC and that action helped ANC spread and grow.

Personal Story of Sylvester M. Chisembele

When I arrived at the meeting it was about to end and it was just jubilation for our victory. An hour later the District Commissioner announced our arrest: Sylvester Muchengwa, Protasio Kamayanda, Ba Chimanya and me. We were confined at the Senior Chief Mwewa for three days and then we were taken to Fort Rosebery prison. After being detained in prison for three weeks, we were taken to the Magistrate Court No.1 and tried by the District Commissioner, North, who sentenced us to 6 to 9 months' imprisonment.

We appealed to the High Court and after we had been 3 months in Fort Rosebery Prison we were transferred to Ndola Bwana Mukubwa prison in the Copperbelt, where we spent another 6 months serving the sentences. Our Appeal was not heard until almost at the end of our prison sentences. A case which we won, but we had already served the sentences. This was one of the many occasions when I was arrested and imprisoned for no reason but purely for the cause of the political struggle based on non-violence.

The Catholic Church in Luapula had been given false cause instigated by the Provincial Commissioner to question the intentions of the freedom fighters and the priests had been brought into an unpleasant situation. But not all the White Fathers believed or accepted the warnings from the colonial administration that Sylvester Chisembele was bringing disunity to the Church with a nationalist campaign which, in effect, produced violence and atheism. There was, for example, one young priest, Fr. James Spaita, who had been to Lubushi Seminary and had been a fellow student with Dominic Chisembele, a younger brother of Sylvester, who years later, speaking at the Funeral Mass for Sylvester Chisembele on the 9th of February 2006 at St Ignatius Church, Lusaka, now as His Grace the Archbishop of Kasama, told the congregation of the early days during the struggle when he would, at night, type out letters for Sylvester who kept up an active campaign by correspondence internationally as well as within Northern Rhodesia.[6]

Another ex-Seminarian who actively participated in this way was Christopher Chiwama. He had also been a fellow student at Lubushi Seminary. Chiwama on leaving the Seminary joined the colonial civil service and on being transferred to Fort Rosebery joined the struggle. He was later employed by the Catholic Mission Fathers from whom he purchased an old typewriter. Although he was not a full-time activist he played a vital role in the campaign carried out by correspondence. He used his typewriter, again for safety by night, to keep up the string of letters which Chisembele sent out including a series of Demands for home rule to the British Government in London.

Because of the onslaught of these letters, which did not cease throughout the struggle period, the District Commissioner ordered an investigation. The typewriter used by Chiwama was old and it had a distinctive French typeface. Intelligence officers questioned the White Fathers who admitted that they had sold an old unwanted machine to Chiwama. When word of the investigation by the intelligence service came through to the leadership, Chiwama, forewarned, surrendered his typewriter to the party which Chisembele then secreted initially in a party office in Kabuta village. Police summoned Chiwama and he was interrogated by police, but eventually released because no proof against him could be found. Subsequently, the colonial administration aware that it had lost control and unable to stem the tide of nationalism that had spread throughout the province, torched nationalist party offices housing equipment and records; everything within was destroyed.[7]

---

[6] David C. Mulford, "Zambia The Politics of Independence" (Oxford University Press, 1967). p 163.
[7] CMS Chiwama, history note, April 2011, scan.

Personal Story of Sylvester M. Chisembele

In November 1956 a new Prime Minister of the Federation of Rhodesia and Nyasaland was in place, Sir Roy Welensky who was an Afrikaner hardliner of Dutch and Jewish ancestry. He had many friends in the British Conservative Government of the day, but equally there were sceptical members of the UK Parliament particularly in the Labour Party who were not convinced by his policies and statements, among them the Labour member, Hon. James Callaghan, who was quoted in the House of Commons as saying that *"Sir Roy Welensky was an angel over here but an ogre in his own country"*.[8]

Sir Roy Welensky's base was in Northern Rhodesia and he remained the Federal Prime Minister until the end of December 1963 when the Federation of Rhodesia and Nyasaland ceased to exist. When on 24 October 1964 Northern Rhodesia officially became Zambia, the struggle for independence at last successful, Sir Roy Welensky was reported to have made a statement that he was not prepared to live in a country where they (black Africans) were in control and he followed through on this by moving back to Southern Rhodesia, where he tried but failed to enter the political ruling class there. He disappeared from Zambian political circles, although he did make a trip back to Zambia for he was present at the Zambian Opening of Parliament in 1973 which I also attended.

1957 – 1959

The indigenous people had little part in their governance, in fact, they were virtually voiceless. In a debate in the House of Commons in June 1957 the future Prime Minister of Great Britain, then in opposition, James Callaghan, speaking on proposed changes to the Federal Assembly in the Constitution of the Federation of Rhodesia and Nyasaland, stated that the Labour Party had from the onset believed that universal adult

---

[8] Hansard HC Deb 27 November 1958, vol 596, cc563-697.

suffrage should determine the nature of the arrangements which were to be made. He further stated that it was for all the people of those territories to determine what should be the final form of the constitutional arrangements under which they were to live. He was responding to statements made by the Colonial Secretary, Alan Lennox-Boyd, which included an affirmation of his admiration and friendship with Sir Roy Welensky and his support, in principle, for intended changes in the Federal Assembly which Sir Roy Welensky had told him would increase the membership of the Federal Assembly from 35 to 59, of this number 12 would be allocated to Africans, an increase of 6. However, these additional six African members covering the three territories of Northern Rhodesia, Southern Rhodesia and Nyasaland would be subject to election by a multi-racial electorate. The support of the Colonial Secretary for the proposed changes was challenged by James Callaghan whose view was that in practice it could reduce the African presence if the qualitative franchise was fixed in such a way that the majority of Africans would be excluded from the process. [9]

The territory of Northern Rhodesia consisted of eight provinces: namely, Luapula, Northern, Western, Central, Eastern, Southern, North Western and Barotseland. Barotseland, home of the Lozi people, was as the norm traditionally ruled by a Paramount Chief and his Kuta (Parliament); this province was distinctive in that in 1901 Paramount Chief Lubosi Lewanika had entered into a separate treaty with the British Crown granting the Barotse certain particular protective rights. In October, 1958 the Governor of Northern Rhodesia, Sir Arthur Benson, decreed that insofar as Barotseland was concerned for future elections the African members would no longer be chosen by the African Representative Council, but would be chosen by the

---

[9] Hansard, HC Deb 04 June 1957 vol 571 cc1085-211.

members of Barotseland Provincial Council, the nineteen members of the Barotse Kuta and all Barotse on the voters roll. However, the Barotse when asked to provide nineteen names refused, stating that they did not wish to be represented in the Federal Parliament or in the Legislative Council. The Barotse were determined not to be part of any future Dominion or Government controlling the whole country, and thereby run the risk of appearing to agree to changes which would affect the protectorate status they had entered into with the Crown in 1901. This was a delicate issue and the British Resident Commissioner, Gervas Clay, had a difficult time convincing the Northern Rhodesia Secretariat. However, the Commissioner's advice was heeded and he received a telegram to say that the Governor agreed that the decree be altered to say that *"nineteen members of the Barotse if they wish"* may vote. The members of the Barotse Kuta were very pleased when this information was relayed to them, calling the Commissioner 'mutusi' meaning 'the helper', a name that they had previously given to him.[10]

With so little prospect of any say in the administration of their lives, or sign of any possible move to universal franchise which would surely bring independence, the political awareness campaign continued to grow very fast throughout the Luapula Province. Resentment, especially among the young men and women, was widespread, fuelled by the daily humiliations ordinary people suffered. Although on the surface the daily life of people in the villages and towns went on much as it had for decades, the restrictions on their movements and the mental state of inferiority which the administration and the settlers tried to inflict upon them caused deep-seated grievance. The picture painted by the administration and settlers to the outside world of a happy,

---

[10] The Hon. Mrs Betty Clay, Diary 25th October 1957, scan, courtesy of Robin B. Clay.

grateful native people overjoyed to have the superior white individual governing them, was a complete myth. The whole system was one-sided ... the incomers took and the indigenous gave. The few schools and clinics which were available for the use of Africans were not provided by the colonial government, but by the Churches. The wealth of the land once exploited went overseas and nothing remained of benefit in as far as the indigenous people were concerned.

Chisembele, the ANC Provincial General Secretary for Luapula Province, was a victim of an assassination attempt in 1958, organised by the colonial authority, when two security officers waylaid and beat him so badly that his right eardrum was shattered. This attempt on his life left him with partial hearing in one ear and recurring headaches that were to stay with him for the rest of his life. Villagers ran to his assistance and saved his life. The villagers refused to take him to the hospital fearing that he would be killed and in any case there was no qualified doctor to provide treatment for the native people and so he was taken to his parents' home where he lay prostrate for three weeks. The assassins were identified by villagers to be security men, but no action was taken on the perpetrators. The District Commissioner, Col. Middleton, was accused of ordering the assassination which he publicly denied and fearing repercussions he immediately arranged the transfer of the security men involved to another province within Northern Rhodesia. Such incidents served to strengthen and swell the numbers joining the struggle for home rule. Chisembele and the leaders throughout Luapula paid a heavy price for their success in mobilising people to join the struggle; they underwent beatings, arrests and imprisonment many times. Non-office-bearing people were not immune, they also suffered harassment both mental and physical.

Later in that year of 1958, Chisembele was called to go to Lusaka for discussions with Harry Mwaanga Nkumbula, the

Personal Story of Sylvester M. Chisembele

ANC party President, who wanted to tour the Luapula Province. A programme was arranged for Nkumbula and meetings had been prepared for him throughout the province.

When party President, Nkumbula, accompanied by Chisembele, arrived at Chembe, the point of entry into Luapula Province after crossing the Luapula River, crowds were waiting to receive him. But Nkumbula greatly disappointed them by his refusal to get out of the vehicle to acknowledge their welcome. Chisembele had to climb on the roof of the vehicle to greet the people and tell them that the party President was unwell. Later during this disastrous visit, even though he was assured by Chisembele that the overwhelming support of the province would ensure a successful tour, Nkumbula was too fearful of the British provincial administration and refused to get out of the vehicle to greet the crowds who came out to see him. This continued throughout the tour, Nkumbula would not greet the crowds without first being driven to the police station for clearance, just to be told that he did not need a permit to greet people.

In one sense, Harry Nkumbula had grounds for his apprehension during this fateful tour of Luapula, for the province and its leadership was militant and so effective that the colonial authority feared that province above all others.

Luapula was notorious for arrests and imprisonments, making it the province most avoided by other national leaders. The province was renowned for being fiercely independent and the most highly organised. The Luapula leadership was known as fanatically committed to the nationalist cause.

At one point fearing the influence and militancy of Luapula Province, Nkumbula announced that he had dismissed Chisembele and Shapi because they had embezzled party funds. This ludicrous accusation did nothing but help quicken the end of the ANC as the national party for freedom. The historian David Mulford in his book "Zambia the Politics of Independence" referring to this particular Luapula tour stated:

> *The 'Luapulans' were easily the most volatile, militant, and independent of A.N.C.'s cohorts ... Nkumbula arrived in Fort Rosebery on 18 September for a visit which must have been one of the least successful tours of his career.*

Shortly after this failed, fateful visit a decision was taken to form a breakaway party the Zambia African National Congress [ZANC]. ANC was the national party but as events had shown it was too weak a vehicle to speed up the attainment of independence. Behind the scenes, there was a considerable amount of in-fighting within the ANC hierarchy and the organisation and its effectiveness was weak. At the time of this breakaway in the latter half of 1958 Kenneth Kaunda was the Secretary General of the ANC.

The crossover was seamless and virtually total as far as Luapula was concerned, because the province was politically united with a committed full-time leadership which demonstrated on many occasions a remarkable degree of local authority with a capacity for independent action. Initially, there were pockets of diehard ANC remnants but these were completely subdued and Luapula became overwhelmingly ZANC, which was later to become United National Independence Party [UNIP] in that all branches of ANC became ZANC and then UNIP.

Kenneth Kaunda was selected as President of the newly formed party, ZANC/UNIP. Kaunda's parents had come originally from Nyasaland (Malawi) and had settled in the Northern Province. His wife, Betty, came from Malambo District, Fort Jameson (now Chipata) in the Eastern Province. The newly formed party had its strongest foundation in the Bemba-speaking areas of Luapula, Northern and Copperbelt Provinces and the fact that Kenneth Kaunda had a cross-

Personal Story of Sylvester M. Chisembele

border-provincial background was a possible consideration in his selection as party President, with the need for the new party to capture the full support of all other provinces, especially those not yet fully committed to the freedom struggle. From early times the Eastern Province with its porous border with Nyasaland (Malawi) resulted in many cross-border family unions, including the Kaundas. However, at the same time it could be considered a disadvantage in that Kenneth Kaunda was not considered by all to be a true national for it was said that he had been born in Nyasaland. In fact, his appointment at the initiating conference as party President was not wholeheartedly supported, with delegates at this conference having in mind that the leadership would be revisited at an appropriate time.

When ZANC was proscribed, the decision was made to take over UNIP which was a small localized party in Kabwe, Central Province, whose President was Mainza Chona. Chona had also previously been a member of the ANC. Chona agreed to give way for Kaunda to take over the presidency of UNIP which then embraced all ZANC's national structures. At that time Kenneth Kaunda was a professed egalitarian and in those initial stages he showed no sign that he would deviate from the path of democracy as subsequently he did.

The colonial authorities were masters in the practice of misinformation and on one occasion when Chisembele was in Lusaka, Kenneth Kaunda, then living in Chilenge Compound, asked Chisembele to go for a walk with him to Matero. But on the way Kaunda instead took him to the office of the Chief Secretary where three officials of the Northern Rhodesian Government were waiting for them. With no prior warning or information, Chisembele was grilled about rebellion in Luapula and told that security reports received were of people in Luapula rioting and of the destruction at Chembe where the pontoon was burnt down.[11] The vital Chembe pontoon was the only method available of crossing the Luapula River connecting Luapula Province with the Copperbelt via the Pedicle Road running through the Belgian Congo (later named Zaire and now Democratic Republic of the Congo). Kenneth Kaunda aware of the pre-expressed colonial allegations, was himself in doubt on being told that parts of Luapula were in anarchy. Chisembele had to convince both the colonial authority and Kenneth Kaunda that the reports were pure lies and nothing more than fabrication. Control in the province was firmly held by the Luapula UNIP leadership, there had been no riots and the Chembe pontoon was intact and functioning as usual. This sort of misinformation was a tactic used to cover and justify unlawful actions carried out by the colonial administration.

The Governor-to-be of Northern Rhodesia, Sir Evelyn Hone, flew to Samfya on 4 March 1959 to hold a meeting with Chisembele who was summoned from Senior Chief Kalasa Mukoso's chiefdom in a remote part of Samfya where he was politically organising; a few days after this meeting a State of Emergency was declared on 12 March. Sylvester Chisembele wrote the following on the initial implementation of this State of Emergency:

I was touring Kawambwa and Mwense districts in February 1959 as Provincial General Secretary for Luapula Province in the newly formed Zambia African National Congress Party (ZANC). In March, I was touring Samfya District and on the 3rd March 1959 I received an urgent message from Fort Rosebery from the Provincial Commissioner, E.C. Thomson, for Luapula Province, informing me that the Chief Secretary, Sir Evelyn Hone, will be flying from Lusaka to Samfya

---

[11] "Chembe Pontoon" circa 1959, photograph courtesy Ian Singer.

tomorrow Wednesday, the 4th March 1959 and he will meet you in the office of the District Secretary in charge of the Samfya sub-Boma at 10.00 hours. When I received this message I interrupted my tour programme as I was in the interior rural part of the Samfya District, and came back to Samfya sub-Boma.

The following day I met the Governor-to-be, Sir Evelyn Hone in the office of the Senior District Secretary in charge of Samfya sub-Boma. The meeting was cordial and straightforward, very different from the meetings I usually had with the Provincial Commissioner. The discussion was based on the general security situation in the province. At the meeting, it was agreed that I would be allowed, and all our district political leadership, to address public meetings.

I continued with my tour programme of Samfya District and started holding public meetings throughout my tour in the district without Government interference.

On the 11th March 1959 Wednesday, I received another message from Fort Rosebery sent by the Senior Provincial Commissioner, Thomson, asking me to cut my tour programme in Samfya District and return back to Fort Rosebery and he urged me to report in Fort Rosebery before 18.00 hours the latest because he wanted to meet me in his office at 8 hours in the morning of the 12th March 1959.

I cut short my tour programme as a result of this message from the Provincial Commissioner, Thomson, and cycled back. Before 18.00 hours we were in Fort Rosebery and I went straight to my premises in the suburbs.

In the middle of the night about 12.30 a.m., I heard a very big bang with a big shout, thus: 'open the door – POLICE'. Then I awoke everybody and told them to dress up as it sounded like a State of Emergency. I hesitated to open the door to allow everybody to dress while the Police were forcing the doors banging and shouting at the same time.

Zambia – The Freedom Struggle and the Aftermath

As I opened the door three white security officers pushed into the building and began to call my name. I replied that 'I am here' then immediately I was surrounded by three white security officers pointing their revolvers at me. They showed me a warrant of arrest and started reading the warrant signed by the Governor to me. I was informed a State of Emergency has been declared. The rest of the Party officials and other members were taken to the next room.

Security Police armed with guns surrounded my two buildings, with long batons, revolvers and some African Security Police were holding tiller lamps. The security officers, some had come from Lusaka, had lined up from my premises to the Police Headquarters. After reading the warrant of arrest from the Governor, Sir Arthur Benson, they took me to a station-wagon. Two white plain clothes security officers sat in the front seat and turned their faces to me pointing their revolvers at me. Two other white officers were in the middle seats, one on my left and the other on my right, pointing their revolvers at me and three other white officers were in the back. I was ordered by shouts not to touch anything, a paper, a book or anything and not to talk. I was told that I should not ask anything or else they would shoot me.

We drove straight to Chembe, accompanied by another Land Rover full of Fort Rosebery Police, then we drove back to Fort Rosebery; then we drove straight to Samfya and then we drove back to Fort Rosebery; and then we drove straight to Chipili and then as we were driving back again to Fort Rosebery it dawned. This time we drove to my father's house and the Security shouted to my father to bring my suitcase. When my father started asking why, what is happening, they pointed guns at him, slapped him around the face and shouted 'bring the suitcase'.

It was already past 6 a.m. and we drove to the airstrip in Fort Rosebery. A plane landed around 7 a.m. Doors opened

Personal Story of Sylvester M. Chisembele

and several armed uniformed security officers appeared at the door. I was alone with the security officers in the station-wagon. They pushed me out of the vehicle, then picked me up and threw me into the plane. I saw some of my fellow freedom fighters from other provinces within.

We flew to Ndola and were put together with other detainees. We were then flown in small groups to Mongu. Four of us were flown to Kalabo District: Dingiswayo Banda, Lawrence Mulenga, Mutunda and me where we were restricted.

The authorities starting revoking the restriction orders, one by one and by the end of September the other three were released, and I was left alone in an old building which was in the middle of the bush and it had no doors to close. At the end of December on the 31st, the Kalabo District Commissioner called me to his office and informed me that the Governor, Arthur Benson, had revoked my restriction order.

I was put in a canoe which took me to Mongu crossing the Zambezi. In Mongu the District Commissioner called me. I did not find any of my friends, who were restricted in Mongu. Officials in the District Commissioner's office said that the restriction orders of my friends, Messrs Simon Kapwepwe, Justin Chimba and Nephas Tembo had been revoked sometime back, nobody was left, all had been released he informed me. I asked does it mean I was left alone in the whole province and I was told yes. When I asked why, I was told that it was because restriction orders were only revoked by the Governor in Lusaka.

Officials from the District Commissioner's office put me on a lorry which took me to Lusaka where I was given papers to state that I was a 'freeman' and also given the documents entailed for my journey back to Fort Rosebery. I left by bus and arrived in Fort Rosebery on the 8th of January 1960. [12]

---

[12] Ibid. Fn. 4 Folder "Documents Submitted to ECHR 29.4.04" - Claim Reports 1-5 pp 13, 4.

Zambia – The Freedom Struggle and the Aftermath

Questions were raised in the British House of Commons on the legality of the detention and rustication of African political leaders and trade union officials in Northern Rhodesia where the Governor had said that the reason for the arrest and rustication was because they were involved in an alleged plot to spread chaos through Northern Rhodesia, and in the case of the trade union officials for a strike which had taken place three years earlier. Several Labour Party Members of Parliament expressed their disquiet, among them Fenner Brockway, Member for Eton and Slough and Stephen Swingler, Member for Newcastle-under-Lyme, who said that as no actual charges had been brought against detainees, they were denied the right to answer those charges in a Court of Law. He went on to say that *"in the case of some of those whom the Government have claimed to rusticate in Northern Rhodesia, the Government have been acting illegally and unconstitutionally for several years"*.[13]

The political prisoners with whom Chisembele was grouped were taken to a remote area in Barotseland, somewhere in Kalabo District.[14] I do not know whether as a result of a hunger strike or through negotiation, but at some later stage during the detention, when the release of some prisoners had started, the inmates were allowed a certain limited freedom of movement and used this to surreptitiously visit nearby villages to continue the freedom campaign *(when some years later in 1970 we were stationed in Mongu, several people told me of the time when Chisembele held in restriction had still managed to come to their village to talk to them about the struggle for freedom).*

The British Resident Commissioner during this period was Gervas Clay. Robin Baden Clay, his son, wrote me the

---

[13] Hansard HC Deb 15 May 1959 vol 605 cc1571-91.
[14] Postcard received in detention, September 1959, scan.

Personal Story of Sylvester M. Chisembele

following anecdote which, for interest, I quote with his permission:

I do recall one anecdote of his. As Resident Commissioner, Barotseland, he was responsible for detainees sent to the province to keep them out of trouble. On one occasion, some threatened a hunger strike. His response was to forbid them any water at all, for any purpose, not even for washing. It was pointed out to them that they were on "hunger" strike, which did not prevent them from drinking. Instead of water, they were provided with unlimited quantities of milk. A person can survive for only a few days without water, but for an almost unlimited time on just milk. Thus they held to their hunger strike, but came to no harm.

Chapter 2
1960 – 1964

1960 – 1964
When in January Chisembele was released from restriction in Barotseland, he went first to Lusaka where he remained for some days in consultation with fellow leaders and then he returned to Fort Rosebery (Mansa) and found that during his absence, under the orders of the District Commissioner, Col. Middleton, his buildings had been demolished and all his property, equipment, books, documents and records were gone. This was a serious setback both politically and personally, but was overcome and served only to fuel the anger of the people and guarantee the continuing progress in the organising of resistance in the province.

In this month of January, shortly before Chisembele returned to Luapula, the British Prime Minister, Harold Macmillan, Conservative MP for Bromley, who was making a tour of African Commonwealth States, came to Northern Rhodesia. He held talks in Lusaka with African leaders before travelling on to South Africa. The Litunga of Barotseland, Sir Mwanawina Lewanika III on whom the British had previously bestowed a KBE (Knight Commander of the Order of the British Empire), was present at the talks held in Lusaka. He came with confidence in the assurance given him by the Governor-General of the Federation of Rhodesia and Nyasaland that treaties made between the Federation and Barotseland, backed and witnessed by the British Government, would be honoured.[15] Just over a year earlier, in September 1958, the Governor-General of the Federation, Lord Dalhousie and his wife Lady Dalhousie made an official visit to Barotseland. They were received by the Litunga, at his Lealui capital where in the Kuta (Barotse Parliament) speeches were made during which Lord Dalhousie gave a promise that British treaties made with the Barotseland Protectorate would be kept.[16] The Litunga would later be greatly disappointed.

On arrival in South Africa, the British Prime Minister, Harold Macmillan, on 3 February 1960 addressing the South African Parliament made the historic "Wind of Change" speech which appeared on the surface to be conciliatory towards justice for the indigenous peoples of southern Africa, but the words were not trusted so that when the Monkton Commission came to Northern Rhodesia later in the year, ostensibly to make recommendations to the UK Parliament regarding the Constitution of the Federation and beyond, the Luapula leadership decided that it would organise a boycott. It had no intention that any view put forward to the Commission be deliberately misconstrued leaving room for misinterpretation and thereby used to maintain white rule. The boycott was more successful in Luapula Province than in any other part of the country.

Following the visit of the British Prime Minister, Queen Elizabeth The Queen Mother made an official visit to Rhodesia in May 1960 to open the Kariba Dam spanning the Zambezi River between Northern and Southern Rhodesia. 27,000 people in the Gwembe Valley were displaced to make way for the flooding of the Kariba Lake. A few months before the scheduled visit there were violent protests in

---

[15] "The Litunga, British Prime Minister", January 1960.
[16] "Barotse Kuta", The Litunga, Federation Governor-General and British Resident Commissioner"; The Litunga with Lord and Lady Dalhousie, September 1958 Photographs courtesy Robin B. Clay.

Zambia – The Freedom Struggle and the Aftermath

Lusaka and Gwembe Valley, but this did not deter The Queen Mother.[17]

During this tour, she made a three-day visit to Barotseland where she stayed in the residence of the Commissioner, Gervas Clay and his wife Hon. Betty Clay. The Queen Mother was afforded a lavish welcome. The Paramount Chief, Sir Mwanawina Lewanika III, gave a speech of welcome in the Kuta during which he spoke of the confidence he had in the protected status treaty which existed between Britain and Barotseland.[18]

The following year, the Paramount Chief, Sir Mwanawina Lewanika III, with members of his Kuta made an official visit to London. The party left for the UK on 4 April 1961 and was accompanied by the British Barotseland Resident Commissioner, Gervas Clay. On the aeroplane, an unexpected passenger, who boarded at Lusaka, was Kenneth Kaunda en route to the U.S.A. After several aeroplane stopovers, the party eventually reached London.

The Paramount Chief was afforded a fulsome welcome and the day before the official talks began with the Secretary of State, the Paramount Chief was invited by The Queen Mother to take tea in Clarence House. That evening this was followed by a Government cocktail party given in his honour.

On 12 April the official talks began. A few days later the Paramount Chief together with his Ngambela (chief counsellor) were escorted by Commissioner Gervas Clay to lunch at the offices of the Anglo American Corporation, hosted by Phillip Oppenheimer, cousin of Harry Oppenheimer.

The talks went on for some days and the Paramount Chief together with his entourage was fully entertained throughout

---

[17] "Kariba Dam, 1958" newspaper cuttings, courtesy Robin B. Clay.
[18] "Drum-beat Welcome for The Queen Mother", May 1960; "We Value Status Barotse", The Queen Mother visits Kuta, May 1960, photographs courtesy Robin B. Clay.

the period; he attended several dinner parties given in his honour and was taken to various amusements. A fuller interesting account of this visit written by the Barotse Resident Commissioner, Gervas Clay, is footnoted with the permission of his son Robin B. Clay.[19]

The Litunga made a further trip to London for talks with the First Secretary of State, R.A. Butler, in July 1963, again seeking reassurance that the special relationship between Barotseland and Britain would be protected. Earlier, in 1962 uneasy about the new Constitution being considered for Northern Rhodesia and the status of Barotseland in a new Constitution, the Litunga made representation to the British Government for the desire of his kingdom to become a separate State with its own Constitution. He was given assurance that Barotseland would be protected, although this assurance was tempered by a statement made in the UK Parliament by the Secretary of State, Rab Butler, that a final decision regarding the future of Barotseland would only be taken after discussions between the Northern Rhodesian Government and the Barotseland Native Council.[20]

The misgivings which the Litunga of Barotseland had, even though he had been given several assurances regarding the protected status treaty, were later realised when the treaty was superseded in May 1964. With independence nearing, the British Government drew up a document called "The Barotseland Agreement" with the intention of pacifying and reassuring the Litunga, Paramount Chief Sir Mwanawina Lewanika III, K.B.E., that the status quo as far as governance of Barotseland was concerned would always remain firmly in

---

[19] "Visit of the Paramount Chief & Party to England for Talks with the Secretary of State, April 1961", Gervas Clay, Resident Commissioner, 28 April 1961. NB I am grateful to Robin B. Clay for the use of some footnoted (copyright) material and pictures from his family archives.
[20] HC Deb 21 March 1963 vol 674 cc93-4W; HC Deb 25 July 1963 vol 681 cc218-9W.

the hands of the Litunga and the National Council of Barotseland. But the wording of the Barotseland Agreement was ambiguous, even misleading, in section three paragraph (3) the words *"full consultation with the Litunga and Council"* did not mean "with the permission or agreement of the Litunga and Council" and section four (b) the words *"responsibility for administering Barotse customary land law within Barotseland"* did not mean "executive power over the administration of land rights in Barotseland". And on page six of this Agreement under the heading *"Land"* paragraph (2) stating that the Litunga of Barotseland and his Council shall continue to have the land powers hitherto enjoyed and that the Barotse Native Courts shall have original jurisdiction to the exclusion of any other court in the Republic of Zambia, is completely abrogated by a following paragraph establishing the overall jurisdiction and powers of the High Court of the Republic of Zambia. In other words, the Barotseland Agreement was not worth the paper it was written on.

The fact that this Agreement included a covenant to the effect that the Prime Minister of Northern Rhodesia undertook that the Barotseland Agreement would be reaffirmed by the Government at Independence was, therefore, also meaningless.[21]

However, prior to these future problems, back pre-independence, Chisembele, publicly stated by Kenneth Kaunda to be a brilliant organiser, was making rapid progress, utilising to the full a duplicating machine which he purchased with his own funds. Mulford records in his book "Zambia the Politics of Independence" that:

> *UNIP branch formation was most spectacular in Luapula Province ... and that ... Thus by the time Sylvester*

---

[21] "The Barotseland Agreement 1964" Secretary of State for Commonwealth Relations, May 1964.

Personal Story of Sylvester M. Chisembele

Chisembele, perhaps the most widely known and respected of Luapula's Z.A.N.C. (UNIP) restricted persons, returned to Fort Rosebery on 8th January 1960, bearing a duplicating machine and 1,000 new membership cards, an important advance had been made in Luapula ... Chisembele went around the province establishing branches and sending UNIP membership cards to the district officials he had organised ... between April and December 1960 the total number of UNIP branches registered in the country rose from 28 to 482, of these Luapula Province alone accounted for 305 with an estimated membership of 69,000.

Mulford goes on to state:

A security report from Luapula Province in September drew from the Chief Secretary the comment: 'I don't like the sound of UNIP's ideas – they are learning too fast,' The Governor agreed, and a few weeks later a meeting, which included Roberts*, took place at Government House to discuss the growing threat of nationalist parties. The Governor, replying to questions raised by Roberts about UNIP, expressed the Government's concern over the rapid emergence of UNIP, indicating that it might well become necessary to declare a state of emergency ...[22]

*John Roberts of the white settlers United Federal Party.

The colonial authority planted informers in all districts in Luapula, but most of these if not all were identified and Chisembele instructed all leaders to take no action, but be aware and where possible feed them wrong information. Chisembele implemented a system whereby political prisoners would use the same laws which unjustly imprisoned them to free them and by using the same

---

[22] Ibid. Fn.6 David C. Mulford, "Zambia The Politics of Independence",

government method of infiltration, he managed to recruit and plant activists in the local prisons to take messages and brief prisoners on the grounds that they should use to appeal their sentences. Mulford records that:

> *In Fort Rosebery, government suspicions were aroused by the unprecedented number of appeals which were suddenly received from convicted prisoners at the local prison. As it turned out, one Oscar Mulenga, a clerk at the prison, was identified by Government officials as an ex-ZANC restricted person, planted there by UNIP's provincial Secretary.* [23]

The numbers of people being arrested and imprisoned, suffering beatings and in many cases permanently maimed swelled alarmingly. Even children were not immune from violations, for example, in April 1958 the Labour Party's Barbara Castle raised a question in the British House of Commons regarding the case of a 12 year-old African boy in Lusaka given 22 strokes of the cane for theft which, she said, was a violation of the penal code. She also questioned the barbarous punishment of whipping introduced in Southern Rhodesia for the theft of maize. [24]

When about to start a 'disobedience' campaign which was to be coordinated throughout the province, the method Chisembele used was not to make known the date when an action was to be carried out, but at an appropriately timed meeting to which all district leaders were called, after discussion, he would give out the date and the details; lockdown the delegates for however long was needed and then they would all be allowed to disperse with just enough time to return to their districts and issue instructions to the people. This method of keeping the element of surprise incapacitated

---

[23] Ibid. Fn.6 David C. Mulford, "Zambia The Politics of Independence", p 138.
[24] Hansard HC Deb 03 April 1958, vol 585, cc1377-8.

the ability of the colonial security service to prevent demonstrations by their methods of intimidation and pre-dawn arrests, which were a frequent colonial practice. During this period of lock-down, women activists would prepare and provide food for the delegates. Trusted people would also be sent to the Copperbelt and if it were to be a total, unified operation, the national UNIP leadership would be aware so that a coordinated, country-wide campaign could be mounted.

In Luapula this seemingly heavy-handed approach used by Sylvester Chisembele was accepted as necessary by the grassroots leaders in order to prevent infiltrated informers alerting the colonial authorities and giving them time to organise their armed response. Many people died during this struggle for Zambia's independence, but the death toll would have been far higher had the colonialists been kept aware, through collaborators, of planned dates for campaigns. Figures quoted for the first six months of 1961 alone were given by James Callaghan, Labour Member for Cardiff, South-East, in the House of Commons, of *"over 2,600 arrests made, particularly in Northern Rhodesia. A number of people have been killed"*. James Callaghan gave the estimated figures of between twenty and forty Africans, shot, missing or died in disturbances. The unconfirmed figures given for dead or missing were disbelieved by freedom fighters on the ground, who knew them to be much higher.[25]

The professed main aim of the occupying Government was to 'keep the peace', and to avoid confrontation and bloodshed, but in effect this meant as long as the status quo remained in as far as the seat of power was concerned, which was totally in the hands of the colonialists. In spite of protestations to the contrary, the hold the colonialists had over the lives of the indigenous people was not benevolent, the attraction that the territory of Northern Rhodesia had for the British

---

[25] Hansard, HC Deb 19 October 1961 vol 646 cm366.

Zambia – The Freedom Struggle and the Aftermath

Government and European settlers was purely economic. The mineral resources held the key to their interest. On the Copperbelt the indigenous people were needed for their labour for which they received negligible recompense and had to endure if not actual contempt, then an uncaring indifference which saw those working in private households or businesses living in appalling conditions and in some cases provided with minimal housing. Those working in the mines received meagre payment, for example, miners worked for 5% of the wage paid to white miners of equal skill. Black miners were not allowed to drink in the bars used by their white counterparts, just as their wives and they were not allowed to enter into shops, unless in some cases by the back door, but this restriction made it possible for the drinking shebeens where the black miners congregated for recreation to be also used as venues for political organisation.

Inevitably, there were isolated hotspots of unrest where people, particularly youths, infuriated and angered at the injustices and humiliations that their parents and they suffered were impatient for change, and occasionally an individual took independent action. For example, at one time in Chinsali, Northern Province, an unfortunate white man went into a village where he was challenged to produce a chitupa (identity card) under the rationale that if a villager had to carry a chitupa and have a reason to enter the town of the white man, then he a white man, was not allowed into a village without a chitupa and a reason for being there. He was told that black people were being killed and that he too could be killed. One individual threw a spear at this man which seriously injured him causing his later death. This action was not sanctioned or approved by the UNIP official leadership and it became the subject of a warning freedom song performed by the Butungwa Choir in Luapula Province. Isolated incidents of harm to white individuals did occur and were made much of by the intelligence service but although such incidents on a far higher scale were suffered by Africans these did not receive anything like as much notoriety and usually went completely ignored by the media. However, as far as the freedom fighters were concerned such episodes were generally kept under control by an effective district UNIP leadership and if a dangerous situation arose, then the provincial UNIP leadership would quickly intervene, so that by and large the organisation in Luapula Province, for example, with its unity of purpose and absolute commitment to home rule was kept intact.

In spite of the resistance movement's fundamental policy of non-violence which was accepted and generally observed there was another notable incident where the frustration and resentment of the people boiled over and mass bloodshed threatened. On this occasion, the British Senior Security Officer came to Chisembele's home in Fort Rosebery to ask for his assistance to prevent a dangerous situation that was brewing in Kawambwa District in Luapula Province. The Officer told Chisembele that their security reports were of an imminent threat of killings of expatriates and he asked what Chisembele would do about it. Chisembele responded immediately, for the non-aggression freedom fight was against the British Government and not white people in general. He left immediately for Kawambwa where he found that it was true that some people, infuriated at the injustice and blatant refusal of the colonialists to grant independence, had unilaterally planned an attack on Europeans. Daylight had already faded away by the time Chisembele arrived and he was informed by the local UNIP leadership that people were already surrounding the European compounds, hiding in the bush with pangas (axes) and other weapons ready to attack during the night. The only course left open to him was to walk along the roads and paths with a vehicle headlights shining directly upon him so that he could be recognised, and as he walked he shouted out his name calling on the people to put down their weapons and go home until daytime when he would hold a public meeting. They did disperse and an ugly incident was avoided which would not only have caused bloodshed, but would have given reason and excuse to the colonial authorities for reprisals and the imposition of even more repressive measures on the people.

1961 – 1962

The Federation of the territories of Northern, Southern Rhodesia and Nyasaland was an imposition and none among the nationalist leadership in Nyasaland or Northern or Southern Rhodesia accepted for a moment that it would be allowed to stand. The widespread opposition within all the territories and the determination of the indigenous people to regain their lands and the right to self-rule brought about savage repression from the colonial authorities, mainly represented by the settler communities who made up around 3% of the population.

Although the Federation did not hold the power of a sovereign, independent State, it held a great degree of control over the internal affairs of the three territories. In 1959 the Northern Rhodesian Legislative Council consisted of 30 members, eight ex-officio Government Heads of Department and of the 22 remaining members, eight were Africans and the remainder were Europeans. The election of these representatives, in which the Africans were given a token presence, could hardly be called 'free and fair' when it was not conducted on a 'one man one vote' basis, but with an imposed condition which required a certain minimum financial standing in order to be eligible to vote, thus ensuring that the majority of Africans were excluded from the process.

The lives of the indigenous people were in the hands of the white settler community, who whether or not they saw something wrong in their treatment of the Africans brushed it aside; even Sir Winston Churchill, that most ardent imperialist, on seeing for himself the white settlers' activities in Africa, was stated in the House of Commons by the Labour Member for Rugby, James Johnson, to have written in his book "My Africa Journey" that *"It will be an ill day for the Native Races when their fortunes are removed from the imperial and august administration of the Crown and abandoned to the fierce self-interest of a small population of white settlers"*. This statement of Churchill made the more powerful by the fact that he was so confident in the superiority of white people that during World War II even though the colour bar in the British Services had been lifted, he then issued a directive to Embassies and High Commissions to find *"administrative means"* to reject black volunteers.

The power held by the white settlers can be assessed by a statement made in the House of Commons by Creech Jones, a former Colonial Secretary of State in a Labour Government, in opposition to proposals presented in a Government White Paper on Constitution changes to Northern Rhodesia. He spoke of the moral wrong of the Secretary of State for the Colonies, Alan Lennox-Boyd, transferring his responsibility to that of a minority in the country. He also referred to the Secretary of State, Alan Lennox-Boyd appearing to agree with the Prime Minister of the Federation that in future officials shall look to him, and implement the policy of the Federation; in other words, the handing over by the British Government of control to the white-dominated Federation. In fact this apparent handing of power to the white settler community was just a continuance of the views of the Secretary of State who the year previously had said that *"it would be contrary to the spirit of the Conventions which govern our relations with the Central African Federation if we on this Committee discussed the internal affairs of the Federation"* he further stated that the natural focus of loyalties was to the federal and territorial Governments.[26]

It was and is a claim and boast of the settlers and their descendants that under the rule of the white dominated administration, the territory of Northern Rhodesia was prosperous, peaceful, as near to a 'Garden of Eden' as is possible on earth and that the indigenous Africans were not capable of running a country or able to produce the doctors and skilled manpower needed for such a task. It is true that even by the time that independence was achieved there was an almost total lack of medical personnel and just a handful of African graduates, but what an indictment on those who claimed to be the rightful rulers of a country when they failed to provide even a basic education for the indigenous people whilst at the same time using their labour and land resources to produce the wealth and the comfort for the lifestyle they enjoyed.

In June 1961 in an attempt for a charge of treason to be brought against Sylvester Chisembele, he was arrested and detained together with his deputy, Evans Mulenshi. They were accused of concealing explosives in the thatch roof of their homes. This was an obvious set-up and a complete fabrication. They were held for three weeks in custody pending court appearance for sentencing, but there was a public outcry and intervention by the Catholic parish priest, Fr. Clement Chabu Kasansha. The situation was tense and the District Commissioner fearing riots was forced to release them from detention without charge. The practice on the ground of the colonial authorities was to use methods of intimidation, harassment and victimisation, and where these failed the objective, to use fabrication.

---

[26] www.bbc.co.uk/history/worldwars/wwtwo/colonies_colonials_01.shtm
HC Deb 01 June 1956 vol 553 cc656-80; HC Deb 01 August 1958 vol 592 cc1815-58, HC Deb 04 June 1957 vol 571 cm1087.

Personal Story of Sylvester M. Chisembele

Following this period in custody at a meeting held in Chinsali, Northern Province, with Simon Kapwepwe and Kenneth Kaunda, Chisembele brought up for discussion a plan he had prepared for a campaign to be known as Cha Cha Cha. He presented the plan to them, but initially both Kaunda and Kapwepwe were dubious, not wanting to undertake such a campaign which they feared would bring violent repercussions. However, they did eventually agree and it was implemented. Freedom fighter Nephas Tembo in his book "There Goes a Fool" published in 1984 describes the period of the Cha Cha Cha campaign:

Over seventy people lost their lives in this noble cause, the fiercest fighting having taken place in Luapula and Northern Provinces under the able leadership of Sylvester Chisembele and Andrew Mutemba.

He further wrote that Luapula and Northern Provinces were the two foremost fighters in this campaign. Nephas Tembo a son of the Eastern Province had no bias in asserting this claim. In fact, Luapula and Northern Provinces were the leading provinces in the UNIP freedom struggle for independence.

So too with the coordinated burning of colonial identity cards known as 'ifitupa' which were considered to be 'symbols of slavery', this was instigated by Chisembele and, in fact, Luapula Province was the only province where this campaign was completely successfully carried out. This non-compliance operation also resulted in yet another term of imprisonment for Chisembele in Milima Prison, Kasama, Northern Province. Ms Agnes Mumba gave me an evocative description of the opening day of this undertaking telling me that when the identity card burning took place, she with other children was coming home from school when the Mobile Special Unit (a wing of the police used to combat disturbances and in operations to arrest freedom fighters) raced around them, the children scattered into the bush where they spent the night. In the morning when they returned to their homes the talk was of Sylvester Chisembele and his colleagues who had fronted the burning in the Luapula capital, Fort Rosebery (Mansa) being arrested and dragged away to prison, among them her uncle, freedom fighter, Francis Mubanga.

Ms Agnes Mumba, who for a long time has been a member of the St Ignatius Church Choir in Lusaka, speaking on Yatsani Radio shortly after the death of Sylvester Mwamba Chisembele, spoke of the time when as a young girl she belonged to the Butungwa Choir (Freedom Choir) which was composed of youths who sang 'freedom songs'. She said, each time Chisembele returned from prison or from a mission with his colleagues the choir would greet him with these songs. In fact, freedom songs were an important contribution to the campaign throughout the province and in some other provinces for they kept spirits and hopes high, especially when setbacks occurred.

The Butungwa Choir was based in Chitamba village in Fort Rosebery and in their repertoire they included songs addressed to Roy Welensky which warned him of the danger of stepping on the small black ants, which are very tiny, but when they bite it will really hurt you. Other songs were sung to the settlers in which they teased them that they came from a cold country and now that the freedom fighters were advancing towards independence, the settlers were feeling 'dizzy' and 'their coats were busy'. The Choir also performed a song surrounding the incident of the death of the unfortunate white man in Chinsali, referred to above, the theme of which was based on the issue of the identity cards which black people had to carry with them at all times. Bwalya Matilda Chisembele Mmembe recently asked Ms Agnes Mumba to record the freedom songs from that period which relate to these incidents, this she did and the recording is footnoted.

Personal Story of Sylvester M. Chisembele

Other anecdotes were related to me by Mutale Sunkutu and Steven Chalwe Kalande. Mutale Sunkutu, now resident on the Copperbelt and who was a boy during the struggle for independence stated that:

The police were very rough with Ba Chisembele and he was such a charismatic speaker that whenever he would call for a meeting there was always a big crowd of people where they would shout 'Kaole' as he spoke.

The nickname of 'Kaole' was given to Sylvester Chisembele at public rallies as a mark of great respect for it was the name of the great Warrior Paramount Chief of the Ushi people of Luapula Province named Kaole Milambo. However, his fellow freedom fighters fondly referred to Chisembele as 'Chimese', because of his revolutionary stance. This name 'Chimese' was the name of a famous Ushi chief who pioneered the struggle for independence before the days of ANC and UNIP. Actually, the Chisembele family who originally came from Mporokoso were of the lineage of Senior Chief Mwamba, brother of Paramount Chief Chitimukulu. Centuries ago Paramount Chief Chitimukulu together with his brother and subjects migrated from Kola in the Congo; they were the forebears of the Bemba people who are today settled in the Northern, Luapula and Copperbelt Provinces of Zambia. Sylvester Chisembele and his siblings were all born and brought up in Luapula Province.[27]

Stephen Kalande speaking about a protest rally in 1962 said that the party branch officials organised groups from different areas to congregate at the provincial party headquarters in Kabuta. He went along with the people:

---

[27] Recording of Ms Agnes Mumba singing freedom songs, sound file October 2014; Ms Agnes Mumba, Mutale Sunkutu and Steven Kalande have given me permission to use the quotation and anecdotes attributed to them.

women, men and the youth, from Masaba village, which is around 15 kilometres from Fort Rosebery. Once assembled they were addressed by party officials, Alex Shapi, Evans Mulenshi and the Provincial Chairman, Sylvester Chisembele and other provincial officials. After the briefing, the youth wing was then instructed to go ahead to the Boma led by the Provincial Youth Chairman, Mwape. On the way they passed the property of a white man, who was also a reservist in the police service and, therefore, considered an adversary; he had barricaded himself with his family inside his house. His garden was not respected and it was spoiled as they trampled through it. When they reached the Mansa Bridge crossing the Mansa River they were stopped by a police blockade who interrogated them as to their purpose. The Provincial Youth Chairman, Mwape, was the first person to be picked up and thrown into a jeep. The group which consisted young men and women continued pushing their way through to the Boma; the main body of people led by the freedom fighters, the elders, men and women, followed behind.

The youth group was the first to reach the Boma and there they sat quietly. A senior white police officer came out and asked what they wanted there, and when told *"we want independence"*, he replied *"independence is not here so can you move away"*. The youths continued to sit tacitly, the police officer then pulled out his baton and struck one youth, sitting in the front, across the thighs, this caused the breakout of a commotion. This policeman ran back into the building. The youth had stones in their pockets which they then started throwing; by this time the main body of people had reached them swelling the crowd and at this point the police ran back inside the building and from the windows started to shoot teargas into the crowd. The UNIP cadres began drawing water from Mansa River which was just a few metres away to extinguish the teargas, and people tore pockets from their clothes which they soaked and put over their faces to counteract the effects. When police intensified the teargas, people scampered away in all directions. Teargas was commonly used by police on assembled crowds. A report came in of a man who was building in Senama village who defied a police order to go home and was shot in the leg, but on this occasion, Kalande said, no one was killed by the police to his knowledge.

The disturbances went on for the rest of the week. On the second day the Mobile Police Units arrived. When they reached Masaba village, following usual methods, they searched every house for weapons and even the village chickens were confiscated. Kalande said that he was playing football with his friends but on seeing the police arrive they started running with the villagers in different directions and people slept in the bush. Before the Mobile Police Units arrived, the Masaba Bridge over Mansa River which was built with concrete was destroyed by UNIP cadres, broken up by heavy stones used as hammers, and trees were spread across roads as barricades, but despite these actions, the Mobile Police Units managed to get through to their village. The Masaba Bridge was also used by trucks transporting manganese from a mining concern operating in the area.

Kalande said that his father, James Kalande, was the UNIP Branch Chairman for Kaseba village, and that during one campaign he was sentenced to a month in prison for the burning of identity cards and, he said, that during the struggle many people were imprisoned.

During this particular mass protest, which is typical of the period, one group which had come from Muloka Village in Masaba area joined up with others along the route, the procession successfully manoeuvred a way around a police blockade that met them at Mansa River, and they got through to the rally which when well underway was broken up by police actions, and their use of teargas causing people to disperse running away back to their villages. When those

Zambia – The Freedom Struggle and the Aftermath

from Muloka Village passed over the Chofoshi River Bridge at the Catholic Kabunda Mission and were safely across, freedom fighters burnt down the bridge to prevent the police following them and indiscriminately arresting people during the night; night and dawn arrests were a common police tactic. This wooden bridge at Chofoshi River was reconstructed within days by local people and the Catholic priests because it crossed the river linking the Kabunda Girls School on one side and on the other side the boys school and the living quarters of the priests.

During these years, a usual method was for Mobile Police Units to cross Lake Bangweulu during the night allowing them to make dawn raids into villages and in particular on the settlements in and around Luapula's provincial capital, Fort Rosebery. As the freedom struggle intensified this was met with many arrests, imprisonments and deaths in Luapula, as well as in Northern and Copperbelt Provinces.

The use of the element of surprise was also used by the freedom fighters, for example, a newspaper of the day *Northern News* published a headline report on 20 August 1961 stating that under intimidation and threat of death, Africans in Fort Rosebery, Luapula had been forced to go on strike by UNIP agitators led by a hard-core UNIP man who was going around the province *"from hut to hut, village to village"* intimidating and threatening death. The report stated that the entire staff of the Mansa Hotel had been forced to come out on strike during a function at the hotel, which at the time was full of Rhodesia Royal Air Force personnel, police and government officers, because a waiter had been beaten up and the staff threatened.

Such reports do not stand up to scrutiny for it beggars belief that security officials and police stood by, without intervention, while a waiter was beaten up and the hotel staff forced to walk out; actions such as these would have surely caused a commotion. Far truer to accept the fact that this operation was carried out with the same meticulous, well-planned attention given to all direct actions, regardless of the degree of importance, for which Chisembele was esteemed; timed to cause the greatest embarrassment and to disparage the occupying power.[28] Many Africans employed in the civil service, including the prisons and administrative offices, as well as private concerns were surreptitious members or supporters of UNIP. The majority of people in the territory wanted an end to foreign occupation, and even if there was need to convince, there was little or no need to coerce people into taking part in the freedom fight, rather the difficulty, sometimes, was for leaders to control and reject extreme ideas, if and when put forward by individuals impatient for change.

The superior organisation and effectiveness of the Luapula leadership was the reason that in the elections under the controversial Iain Macleod 15,15,15 Constitution, the President of UNIP Kenneth Kaunda was chosen in the UNIP National Council to stand in Luapula Constituency which was absolutely safe, and Chisembele was asked to be his Election Agent. Chisembele advised Kaunda to go elsewhere to campaign for UNIP candidates as he was able to handle the campaign in Luapula, which he did with the expected excellent result.

In 1962 a serious difference of opinion developed in political ideology between the Luapula leadership and the Northern Province leadership. The leaders in Luapula were politically mature and far-sighted. Signs were emerging of a watering down of the democratic principles that UNIP initially stood for and had held sacrosanct. This came to a head at the UNIP Magoye Conference. The Luapula Province delegation, all of whom had been democratically elected at all local levels, stood alone and stubbornly, fiercely opposed the

---

[28] "Africans 'Strike' After Death Threats in Luapula Province" *Northern News* (Ndola) 20.08.61.

proposed implementation of a so-called 'democratic centralism' which meant in effect the introduction of Regions with leaders at provincial and district levels henceforth appointed only by the party leader, Kenneth Kaunda. The list of his appointees would then be rubber stamped by the Central Committee in the National Council, which itself would comprise selected leaders and to ensure that any troublesome challenge from within the conference was thwarted, a system of veto would be put in place. The other delegates massed against them but the Luapula delegation fought hard to prevent this motion being adopted by the conference, but no other province supported their stand or could see the danger that such a system would bring. The Luapula delegation alone realised that it would lead the way to dictatorship.[29]

When the delegates dispersed from this UNIP Magoye Conference the tyres on Chisembele's vehicle were slashed and he narrowly escaped death when the vehicle overturned on the Pedicle Road which links the Zambian Copperbelt to Luapula Province passing through the Democratic Republic of the Congo territory. Junior leaders from Northern Province were suspected to have carried out this attack. This was one of several assassination attempts which he survived both pre- and post-independence.

The stance that Luapula Province took at the Magoye Conference made Chisembele enemies within the Northern Province leadership, and later after independence had been achieved was the basis on which Kaunda, now the President of Zambia, branded Chisembele within the security service as 'subversive and dangerous'. The whole province was considered too militant and President Kaunda held hatred towards Chisembele and a distrust of the province from that

---

[29] Zambia, National Assembly Daily Parliamentary Debates, First Session of the Seventh National Assembly 4.12.91, column 109, excerpt, scan.

time on. His views were cemented on being told by British officials before the gaining of independence that the greatest danger to his future government would be Luapula Province.

1963 – 1964
In spite of the differences that had emerged at the Magoye Conference, the Luapula leadership remained committed to the party UNIP. The Luapula leadership agreed that unity was of paramount importance to the freedom fight. At the Magoye Conference the Luapula delegation had been isolated and all other provinces unified in the acceptance of a system that they, the Luapula delegation, knew would inevitably result in one-man rule, but they had made known their strong opposition, and now, as democrats, they had no choice but to accept the majority decision that the conference had adopted.

The goal was total independence from colonial rule and nothing could be allowed to detract from this. Minds were concentrated on the freedom struggle for which Chisembele, Kaunda, Kapwepwe, Kamanga and the other national leaders planned a strategy to obtain, based on a logical acceptance by the British Government of the justice and right of a people to self-rule. They were prepared to use civil disobedience alongside logic to force the colonial authority to negotiate an end to foreign domination. If this had failed and the British Government had not eventually given way, then the record of this brief personalised history might have been very different.
The goal, at whatever the cost, was independence, self-rule and an end to the virtual slavery of the indigenous people, who could not even move around within their own country unless they held a permit to do so. For instance, they could not enter into the main part of a white-owned store or butchery, but would have to go around to the side to be served through a hatch in the wall. And for this injustice and indignity the people were, even in poverty, charged a body

tax which, in effect, meant that they were paying for their own subjugation.

The leadership within Luapula was so dynamic and efficient that Chisembele was not confined to organising in that province only. He organised and campaigned in the Copperbelt and, when called upon to do so, in other areas.

During the struggle for independence several groups of political leaders were able to travel outside Zambia (then Northern Rhodesia) with the aim of consultation and first-hand information from countries with similar histories. Chisembele with fellow freedom fighters had meetings with African leaders seeking and successful in attaining independence, including Ghanaian and Tanzanian leaders, Dr. Kwame Nkrumah and Dr. Julius Nyerere, he spent some periods of time in Ghana and Tanzania as well as in China, passing through Russia and The German Democratic Republic prior to Zambia's independence.[30]

The *Guardian* newspaper disclosed in 2013 that the British Government under directives from the Colonial Secretary, Iain Macleod, had in 1961 ordered that records of certain activities of the British Government in colonial countries which were about to gain independence must be destroyed, so that no material which related to the questionable activities of the police, military personnel, public servants or police informers should fall into the hands of incoming indigenous governments. This massive task involved bonfires built behind diplomatic missions and a scramble by staff officers of European descent only to meet the deadline and send to London certificates to confirm that the orders were fulfilled. Just prior to the independence of Zambia, an additional directive was given to destroy *"all papers which are likely to be interpreted, either reasonably or by malice, as indicating racial*

---

[30] "Chisembele, China 1962" composite photographs; "Chisembele Visiting Chiefs on Campaign".

prejudice or religious bias on the part of Her Majesty's government".[31]

On 24 October 1964 independence was finally achieved, but at a very high cost in lives and individual personal sacrifice. Wrangling ensued right up to moments before the hoisting of the Zambian flag. The mineral rights of the country were held by the British South Africa Company [BSAC]; without the rights to the mineral resources of the land, the leadership knew that Zambia would be crippled right from the start. The indigenous leaders offered the BSAC two million pounds as a token settlement to induce the company to relinquish the mineral rights that they held. The British Government had handed over the ownership of the then Northern Rhodesia mineral resources to the BSAC and both had enormously profited from this course. But now on the eve of independence the British Government refused to take responsibility or assist in any meaningful way to redress this outrageous situation, whereby the political power to govern would be in the hands of the indigenous Africans, but the wealth of the country, the mineral rights and resources, would remain in the hands of the foreign British South Africa Company.

No resolution was made and just 11 hours before the hoisting of the flag an ultimatum was given to the BSAC that unless they surrendered all the mineral rights they held against a payment of two million British pounds [£] from the Zambian Government-to-be plus another payment of £2 million which the British Government had now been forced to offer, then on the actual day of independence due within hours the Zambian Government would take back all these rights through a referendum to amend the Constitution with

---

[31] The *Guardian* Newspaper, 29.11.2013 "Revealed: the bonfire of papers at the end of Empire".

not one penny of compensation to the British South Africa Company.

Three hours before the flag of an independent Zambia was hoisted, the British South Africa Company capitulated and surrendered the mineral rights.[32]

This forced concentration on the issue of the mineral rights was paramount in the period leading up to Independence Day, and took away the opportunity for the leadership within the country to hold a pre-conference to study in-depth the Constitution that the British Government had prepared and put in place for Zambia. Kenneth Kaunda had had private talks with the outgoing Governor and British officials. The people Kenneth Kaunda chose to accompany him in these talks included only those whom he considered amenable with his agenda, so that when the question of presidential power was incorporated into the new Constitution he was more than happy to endorse the absolute power for the Office of the President that the British Government inserted into the Constitution which they prepared for Zambia.[33]

So, no conference was held at national level to give a chance for the leadership to draw up their own Constitution, which should have been the obvious course, and instead Kenneth Kaunda happily accepted the Constitution drawn up by the British Government that gave him total power and control over the country.

Immediately after independence President Kaunda announced his Cabinet. He did not include the Luapula leadership. This was a blow, but not a shock. Chisembele who was expected to be part of the Cabinet by both leaders within and without Luapula Province was not included. The initial post to which he was appointed was that of

---

[32] Chisembele, "Constitution Contribution for Public Awareness", 2005, pt 2 p 16.
[33] "Zambia, National Assembly Parliamentary Debates, Fifth Session of the Seventh National Assembly", 07.05.96, column 127, excerpt, scan.

Parliamentary Secretary in the Ministry for Agriculture.[34] President Kaunda had appointed into ministerial positions in his Government some ex-freedom fighter leaders from other provinces and other individuals who had not actively participated at all in the struggle, some had knowledge of or had been part of the civil service.

In the first Cabinet of sixteen, representing the eight provinces of Zambia, five of its members were from Northern Province. There was a natural affinity between Northern and Luapula Provinces, both being Bemba-speaking areas. As a matter of course, mutual meetings were held of leaders from both provinces and on the whole an amicable relationship existed between them. But nevertheless within Luapula people were greatly disappointed at the exclusion of Luapula Province in the Cabinet, given their unequalled contribution to the achievement of independence, and also the scarcity of Luapulans holding appointments within the new Government at both political and civil service level.

Meetings of Luapula leaders across the province were held, and it was agreed that their objective had been freedom from foreign rule and this they had now achieved. They had already experienced at the Magoye Conference the lack of understanding from other provinces of the danger of 'democratic centralism' and had come to the conclusion and acceptance that others had not yet realised the problems that this system would entail. However, the Luapula leaders agreed that more important than individual posts was the task before them, that of the building of a Nation, and for this to happen, above all else, peace and unity was essential.

Chisembele was in private life a quiet, self-effacing man and he held no personal political ambition apart from an intense desire for freedom which, he said, in itself would be meaningless without development and if it were necessary for

---

[34] "Republic of Zambia, Government Gazette", 28.06.1966, scan.

Luapula to take a back seat, then this would be just another sacrifice towards the building of a just and fair nation without tribal or provincial affiliation. The greatest danger to Zambia would be splits along provincial lines. Not all the grassroots leaders agreed with this view, but the consensus was that Luapula would set an example and not challenge the status quo.[35]

Right from the beginning of independence Kaunda had decided to keep Luapula Province at a distance, as far as he was able. In spite of words to the contrary, he believed the advice given him by the outgoing Governor of Northern Rhodesia that Luapula Province would be a danger to his Government. This presumption had been reinforced in the thinking of President Kaunda by the behaviour of the Luapula delegation at the Magoye Conference when they had challenged his call for 'democratic centralism'. He knew that Luapula would not be acquiescent to all his pronouncements and decisions which might lead to a challenge to his position. In fact, there was no power-hungry leader in Luapula Province, the only danger he faced from that province was its understanding of the implications of One Man Rule and its total rejection of such a system.

A giant, daunting task awaited the new Government, but belief was there in spite of the availability of just a few technocrats, doctors, graduates that existed or remained in the country. To overcome this particular obstacle the Government embarked on a programme of recruitment of qualified personnel from overseas to come and work in Zambia on contract basis.

The significance of the obtainment of independence was felt countrywide, even in rural areas where communications and infrastructure were almost absent and where the few

---

[35] Zambia, National Assembly Daily Parliamentary Debates, First Session of the Third National Assembly 30.1.74, column 689, excerpt, scan.

schools and clinics which did exist were established by the churches, in the main the Catholic Church. In fact as late as 1962, for example, along the banks of Lake Mweru in Nchelenge, Luapula Province, three Sisters of the Dutch Order of the Sisters of Charity were given 10 virgin acres of land by the colonial government on which they were given permission to build a hospital. They were also given a grant which ran out when they were only half-way into the construction. They were refused further funding from the authorities and so in an uncompleted building these three dedicated Sisters started treating patients at the beginning of 1963. They had no doctor and were only assisted by young Africans, two boys and four girls. The area they had to cover was extensive and in one month alone, they treated almost 4,000 patients who, with difficulty, came from miles around.

The colonial rulers and exploiters of the wealth of the country had done little or nothing for the indigenous owners of the land, but now independence was achieved and all these obstacles and wrongs would, hopefully, be past history.

PART TWO

The Kaunda Era
1965 – 1991

Chapter 3
1965 – 1969

1965 – 1967

The resources of the country ensured that the Government was well in funds and it embarked on a massive programme of expansion in schools, roads, medical facilities, agriculture, in fact all the human occupations needed for the development so badly lacking in the country. The existing infrastructure was minimal, and in the main, concentrated on road and rail for access to the Copperbelt mines, and the settler farms most of which were sprinkled along the line of rail. Countrywide there were a few clinics and schools which were mostly provided by the Catholic Church who had, in fact, built the first schools and clinics that existed in the country. The contribution the Catholic Church had made in this respect was invaluable and recognised.

During these very early years belief in the leadership and beneficial changes to come existed in the country; by nature Zambians are a peaceful, patient people. An extensive development programme was embarked upon and the famous declaration of President Kaunda that included the words *'an egg a day, a pair of shoes and clothes without patches for every Zambian'* was good; his intentions well-meant and well-received.

Chisembele and all the elected and appointed politicians were tirelessly traversing the country, assessing the needs and listening to the aspirations of the people. In spite of the difficulties and the enormous task of Nation building, the mood of the country was, for the most part, happy with hopes high and expectations great.

These early days were full of promise, but unfortunately corruption had already raised its head. President Kaunda knew the value of the 'divide and rule' principle and this tactic he incorporated early in his regime whilst, at the same time, paying token tribute to tribal balancing. His strength came not just from the people he kept closest to him, but mainly from the absolute power the British-conceived Constitution had given him.

Chisembele was sent abroad on several occasions to various countries and then in September 1967 to the United Nations where he remained until the end of December. During his time in New York, he was hospitalised because of severe headaches resulting from the vicious beatings he had undergone during the struggle. He saw a specialist and underwent extensive tests, but no cure was possible and the only available treatment was by medication.

1968 – 1969
Under the Government recruitment programme for skilled labour in all fields, which they had no option but to source from overseas, I was recruited in London by the British Crown Agents to work for the Government of Zambia. I arrived in Lusaka in February 1968. The contract was for two and a half years with an optional renewal clause.[36]

My posting was as a stenographer in the typing pool of the Ministry of Co-operatives, Youth & Social Development. In May 1968, the Parliamentary Secretary, Sylvester Chisembele, who had been on tour, returned to the Ministry, and I was informed by the Permanent Secretary, Crispin Nyalugwe, that I would from then on be working with him as his secretary, as

---

[36] Background of move to Zambia: see Appendix B.

well as in the same capacity for Princess Nganga Nakatindi, the daughter of Paramount Chief Yeta III of Barotseland, who was the other Parliamentary Secretary in the Ministry. I had been told by other secretarial staff, all of whom came from the UK, that Chisembele was a quiet, courteous gentleman, and indeed he was. Although it did not come up in conversation at some point I learnt that he was married. Brief marital history of Sylvester Chisembele and Paulina Milambo:

Subsequent to leaving the Lubushi Seminary in the Northern Province in 1948 where he had been a student for six years, Chisembele joined politics and began establishing groups of political activists all around his own area and he then spread out to cover the entire province. People accepted his message and call for Africans to control their own lands and future and the need to actively fight for total independence from Britain, the colonial rulers. He was well received, but in many areas the Chiefs and headmen were reluctant to allow their wives and daughters to attend his meetings telling him that as an unmarried man it was not seemly for him to address their womenfolk. This was a hindrance to the campaign and after consultation with his colleagues he made the decision to take a wife, but because this was to be a political expediency he resolved not to marry a young girl, but rather a woman who had already been married so that he would not spoil a young girl's life with a marriage not properly based, and one which was not to be sanctioned by the Catholic Church. This decision was met with regret within his family and was against the wishes of his parents.

Senior Chief Chamalawa Milambo had a talented, beautiful daughter, Paulina, who had been previously married and had three children, she was politically aware and a member of one of the groups involved in organising women to join the struggle for independence. They agreed to stay together in a customary marriage. She was not altogether committed to the

Personal Story of Sylvester M. Chisembele

marriage especially during Sylvester's bouts of incarceration. The traditional marriage finally ended at the close of 1967 when on returning from the United States on Christmas Eve, he was called to a family elders meeting regarding the social habits of his wife during his absence.[37]

At the beginning of the New Year, it became obvious that their time together had come to an end. On separating, Paulina initially took all her children with her, but some months later four children born during her marriage to Chisembele were returned to live with their father, they were Mwale Finbar (boy) born in 1959 and three girls Bwalya Matilda; Mary Chewe; Christina Chishimba, born in 1961, 1964 and 1965 respectively. Later, Paulina remarried and had another family.

I started working for Sylvester Chisembele at the end of May 1968. There was a continuous stream of visitors to his office, many from the Copperbelt and his home province of Luapula. I spent some time typing reports and correspondence for some of these visitors. I fiercely believed in human rights and universal equality and it became apparent that we held similar views. Chisembele and I developed a close relationship over the coming months; he was at that time already separated from his wife, Paulina Milambo. I learnt later that he was the son of a prominent Catholic Christian in Mansa, Michael Filalo Chisembele.[38]

In January 1969, President Kaunda reshuffled the Cabinet. Under the changes, from the Ministry of Co-operatives, Youth & Social Development, Dingiswayo Banda was moved to the Copperbelt as Minister of Western Province and Chisembele as the Minister of State. As assigned secretarial staff Mrs Joe

---

[37] Letter from John Muchengwa, circa 1967, scan.
[38] Michael Filalo Chisembele, diary, 1917 - 1945 original in Bemba, scan (with English translation).

Porter and I were transferred at the same time and we were housed in a government hostel in Ndola. (At that time the Copperbelt was called "Western Province", later in the year it was renamed "Copperbelt Province" and Barotseland was renamed "Western Province").

Chisembele moved into a ministerial house where he had staying with him John Muchengwa, son of Sylvester Muchengwa a prominent freedom fighter and coordinator within the church at Lubwe Mission, Samfya. John Muchengwa was waiting for the finalisation of his travel documents in order to take up a scholarship awarded to him at the Karl Marx University, German Democratic Republic.

On 13 February 1969, Chisembele told me that he had been informed by the Permanent Secretary for Western Province (Copperbelt), E.B. Mbozi, that he had been instructed to transfer me to Chipata in the Eastern Province, no reason was given and no consultation with the minister had taken place, which would have been normal practice.

Chisembele told me that he was flying to Lusaka to see the Secretary General, John Mwanakatwe, to find out what it was all about. During the meeting with Mwanakatwe, Chisembele was informed that the instruction to transfer Miss Sophena Baptiste to Chipata had come from President Kaunda, and he advised him to book an appointment with the President if he wanted further information. Mwanakatwe also said that he had informed the President in advance of their meeting and the President was willing to meet him on the issue. Chisembele was given an appointment with the President for the following day, 14 February.

During the course of the meeting, the President spoke of his initial shock at information which had reached him to the effect that Chisembele was involved in an assignation with a woman, which, the President said he could not believe knowing the character of Sylvester. After explanation and discussion, the President said that now he understood the position he was relieved. But, he said, a bad picture had been painted of the association and that there was unrest in the Copperbelt, where racial tensions were still not settled and so, he said, he did not want the association between Chisembele and Miss Baptiste to aggravate and inflame the present situation. He then asked Chisembele to discuss the matter with me and that we should consider making an immediate announcement of an engagement. Chisembele explained that whilst it was true that we had formed a close friendship which extended beyond our professional relationship, we were still far from such a commitment. President Kaunda said that even if we considered this to be a premature action, an engagement was not a marriage and it was not irrevocable and when the situation was calm surrounding the association then it could be broken, if we so wished. In the meantime, the President said that now that he understood the true circumstances, the transfer of Miss Baptiste to Chipata would be cancelled.

A few days later, I was informed by the Permanent Secretary for Western Province (Copperbelt) that I should leave for Chipata, but in view of the discussion between the President and Chisembele, which he had relayed to me, I did not make the move to Chipata in spite of pressure to do so. I did not give reason as I thought I should not make the issue public.

On 17 February 1969 Chisembele flew to Lusaka to meet again with President Kaunda, as arranged, and to inform him that we would do as he asked and announce an engagement, but Chisembele requested that we be allowed some days to inform our parents. The President welcomed the decision and said that he would control the press and would issue a press statement at the appropriate time.[39]

---

[39] Chisembele, "Statement of the Circumstances Leading to the Engagement", 20.03.69, scan.

Zambia – The Freedom Struggle and the Aftermath

On 26 February, Chisembele flew to Lusaka to see John Mwanakatwe about the official warnings of disciplinary action that I continued to receive because of my failure to transfer to Chipata. Mwanakatwe during the course of their discussion assured Chisembele that everything was in order and then said that it was best for Miss Baptiste to take up employment in the private sector which he would arrange and asked that he, Chisembele, consult me on this issue.

I could not understand how my association with Chisembele which might or might not be permanent could be of any possible interest to the Government. Although there were underlying tensions between black Zambians and the white population on the Copperbelt, there was nothing overt. I was aware that at that time there was no leader married to or openly associated with a so-called 'white', but even so I was uneasy and bemused at the involvement of even the Head of State in what seemed to me to be a small private affair of the heart.

Chisembele left for Mansa for a political meeting on 27 February 1969 and on that day I was told by the Permanent Secretary, Mbozi, that I should report to a Mr Payne of the Rhodesian Selection Trust, a mining group of companies [RST Group] in Ndola. I had nothing in writing and so I did not comply, deciding that I would discuss with Chisembele first. When he returned the following day, he said that he had received the same message regarding the RST Group whilst he was in Mansa from the Secretary General, and he asked me to go there just for discussion. This I did, but during the meeting I found that the conditions of employment with the RST Group were far inferior to those of my Government contract.

I reported the gist of the meeting to Chisembele and had a full discussion with him. I even prophetically told him that I was afraid that if I broke my contract with the Government, I could even be deported, unless I had something in writing.

Personal Story of Sylvester M. Chisembele

Chisembele accepted that my concerns were valid and so he went to Lusaka for further discussion with Mwanakatwe, the Secretary General. Mwanakatwe's reaction was that of anger, he was furious that I should have had the temerity to question their integrity. As there was no understanding from Mwanakatwe, Chisembele went on to State House and was given an appointment for the same evening with the President whose reaction was very different. President Kaunda assured Chisembele that my fears were unfounded and that I should only be assured that the matter was in his hands and it was after all just a temporary arrangement and I could rejoin Government service with its superior conditions once the political situation in the Copperbelt had normalised.

Chisembele telephoned me and informed me of his meeting with President Kaunda and of the President's absolute assurance that everything was in order. I had already agreed to the announcement of an 'engagement' and so I now reluctantly agreed to accept the secretarial position which Mwanakatwe had arranged for me at the RST Group. My overriding thought was that I was an insignificant cog in the political wheel, and after all who was I to question the words of a man of the importance and integrity that I believed President Kaunda to be; and I did not know then the stature of the leadership of Chisembele. Chisembele had told me nothing of his individual part in the struggle for independence and beyond, this only became apparent to me after the deportation ordeal when leaders coming down from Luapula and his colleagues within the Copperbelt, and from other provinces enlightened me.

On the following day 5 March, still against my better judgement, I reported for duty to Payne of the RST Group.

I, therefore, had accepted both the announcement of an 'engagement' and the change of employment. Chisembele informed President Kaunda of our consent to his proposal and also that we would make an official engagement announcement on 8 March 1969.

On 7 March 1969, President Kaunda instructed Chisembele to go immediately to Mansa, Luapula Province as there was a crisis developing with the Watchtower Sect and UNIP. Chisembele reminded the President that the engagement party had been arranged for 8 March and in reply the President said that he should leave after the party.[40] On 9 March Chisembele was unwell and so he left for Mansa early the following day Monday, 10 March.

In the afternoon of that same day, 10 March, I was working in my new office in the RST Group when a man came in and ordered me to go with him; I was arrested, terrorised, held in Bwana Mukubwa Prison and later declared a prohibited immigrant, ironically the same prison in which Chisembele was held by the British colonial authorities during the struggle for independence.

After being picked up in the RST offices, I was driven out of Ndola and around for some hours. I was afraid because the men in the car refused to show me any identification and my questions for explanation went unanswered. I was squashed in the back of the vehicle with men either side of me. Eventually we arrived at Bwana Mukubwa Prison after what I later discovered to be a circuitous route.

On being taken into the prison, and my handbag and contents removed from me, I asked the admitting prison officer to let me contact Chisembele, and on being refused, the British High Commission [BHC] and I then asked, to the amusement of the prison officials, to let me contact State House or John Mwanakatwe the Secretary General. All my requests were ignored. I spent the night on the floor of a

---

[40] "Minister engaged" *Times of Zambia* (Ndola) 10.03.69; News "Summary Dressings:" ZANA (Lusaka) 11.3.69; Passport, Sophena Baptiste, scans.

Personal Story of Sylvester M. Chisembele

communal cell, fearful and scared. There were many women prisoners in the cell and it was unnerving to be stared at by so many strange women prisoners and be unable to speak with them because of the language barrier.

In the very early hours of the morning the same group of four men who had arrested me in Ndola came and I was again taken by car at first back towards Ndola, and told that I was free and they only needed to see my passport before taking me back to collect my car from the RST Group building where it was still parked. My passport was actually in Chisembele's ministerial house, but the man who appeared to be in charge would not believe it, finally in spite of his anger, I was taken to the house, but it was just a ruse for when I got the passport it was taken and I was put back in the vehicle on another traumatic drive, this time towards Lusaka.

I was in complete ignorance of what was going on, it was just an exercise in terror. On reaching Lusaka, we first went to various police stations and then followed a police Land Rover to a house set in fenced grounds. The man who seemed to be in charge had a discussion with the men in the Land Rover and the group went into the house. They came out and we resumed the journey. I was told that I was being taken to a country north of Malawi and the journey would take four days, and from there I would make my way back to England.

Very early at 5 am we eventually ended up at the Lusaka International Airport where I was taken through a back entrance into a room where one of the men holding me handed my passport to an official. This man hesitated when on checking the passport he saw that I held a work-permit; he left the room and then came back and said I would be deported. After some time I was handed my passport, taken to the departure lounge and later manhandled halfway across the tarmac and then allowed to continue alone to board the British Airways aeroplane. Suddenly, another man came running up behind me, he dragged me back. Struggling, I shouted my name to passengers crossing the tarmac asking someone to inform the British Government that I was being abducted. I was pulled through the airport and pushed back into a car with two other men and a driver. Once in the car I was told that it was all a mistake and they said that I would be allowed to contact the British High Commission, all previous requests had been ignored. I was convinced that this was yet another ruse, and that I would be killed, with the Zambian Government cleared of responsibility by my apparent boarding of a British Airways aeroplane with my name clearly printed on the passenger list. However, I was wrong.

I was taken first to the Ministry of Home Affairs and after further trauma issued with a 14 day temporary permit. The security and immigration men from Ndola then came and I was taken on to another building where I was informed that I would be deported if I did not leave Zambia voluntarily within 48 hours. Eventually I was allowed to telephone the British High Commission.

I was collected by car sent by the British High Commission and taken to their building where the staff treated me well. From there I rang several people requesting help in contacting Chisembele and then I rang State House and left a message for President Kaunda. Later I received a message from State House telling me that the President said that I should stay as I was and not worry; everything would be all right.

I stayed the night in an official's home. I think it was the High Commissioner's or his Deputy's house. He and his wife were hospitable to me. At dinner uniformed servants wearing red fez-type hats and white gloves stood behind the table around the walls. They served us in complete anonymous silence. There was no way I could ignore the service that they gave me, knowing full well that my *"thank-you's"* marked me out as protocol ignorant, for memories of my father are always strong in my head:

Personal Story of Sylvester M. Chisembele

Before the Second World War, my father as a young man had come from India on merchant ships trading between India and the London docks. After meeting and marrying my mother in London, he no longer travelled the seas and among other occupations, he became Court interpreter for Indian seamen caught out in misdemeanours. He also worked as a doorman in full colonial style regalia with an elaborate turban on his head, in the Veeraswamy Restaurant in Piccadilly, London, trained to dart forward to open vehicle doors for arriving and departing diners, who would sometimes press a coin into his hand. My father also had part-time employment in the Alexander Korda films which featured the Indian child actor Sabu, in which my father appeared together with us children in bit parts. Sabu's elder brother was our nominal 'uncle'.

All the Indians around us were politically minded and at one time there had been a walkout on the set, organised by my mother, because the lunches being given to the extras were found to have been prepared using pork fat. Being mainly Muslims pork fat was, of course, prohibited. The outcome was that those unable to accept the set lunches were given an allowance to provide their own food.

Towards the end of the Second World War my father, Yusuf Mohammed Ali, who had been enlisted at the start of the war and who was at the end of the war serving with the British Air Forces of Occupation in Germany, Belgium and France,[41] *was found lying collapsed on a street in Paris by US Army MPs travelling in a military jeep. Doctors thought he was near death and so the RAF flew my mother to Paris, she returned on Christmas Eve 1946 leaving him apparently improved. My mother told me that he said that Sophie stood by his bed and told him not to leave us. My father lingered on and was brought back to England where he died in the RAF Halton Military Hospital on the 12th of May 1947. He was*

---

[41] "1945 Xmas Card from L.A. Y.M. Ali", scan.

Zambia – The Freedom Struggle and the Aftermath

buried in the Woking Muslim Military Cemetery, [42] *established by the War Office during the First World War, set close to the Sha Jahan Mosque, the first Mosque to be built in Britain. This Burial Ground was small and unique set in a wooded area in Horsell Common and held the bodies of just 27 servicemen of the thousands of Indians who lost their lives during the First and the Second World Wars. Over three and a half million Indians fought and died alongside the British in those wars. As a family we made regular visits to the cemetery, going first to the Mosque to pay our respects and where the key was kept. In 1968 the graves were vandalised and when my mother made one of her regular visits to the cemetery and saw the destruction, she immediately took up the matter with the War Graves Commission. In fact the insecurity and lack of a caretaker for this Muslim Military Burial Ground had been the subject of a complaint raised by the Head of the Sha Jahan Mosque during the First World War. On the 19th of February 1969 the War Graves Commission arranged exhumation and re-burial of all the bodies in a section of the Commonwealth War Graves Cemetery in Brookwood, Woking. The land selection was made so that the Muslim graves faced the East. The original Burial Ground has now been restored as a Peace Garden. Dr. Zafar Iqbal spent some years on ensuring that this Muslim Burial Ground was preserved in order to now respect, acknowledge and honour the men buried there whose lives were lost in the service of others.* [43]

---

[42] "Muslim War Graves, Shah Jahan Mosque"
[43] "Brookwood Military Grave of Yusuf M. Ali", photographs.
Opening of Peace Garden, 12.11.2015 scans; Sophena Chisembele, speech.
http://www.exploringsurreyspast.org.uk/themes/places/surrey/woking/woking muslim burial ground/; http://www.964eagle.co.uk/news/local-news/1791694/prince-edward-unveils-new-woking-peace-garden/
http://www.bl.uk/learning/images/asiansinbritain/largl24395.htm

Personal Story of Sylvester M. Chisembele

On their marriage in the late 1920s my mother, Ethel Emma Ali nee Wallace, was disowned by her family. She told us that she had made, what I think was the only attempt, to reconcile with her family through her sister when their first child, my brother Peter, was born in 1930. But her sister's response was to tell her that she could visit, but she must not bring her husband nor would she allow half-caste children into her home. My mother was a woman of spirit and loyalty and could never even contemplate such conditions. I think my father would have been proud of her greatness, left a war widow of 37 years of age with four school-going children, totally alone, holding together their family, with sacrifice and courage, working as a full-time cook in Woolworths in Kensington High Street, London and later in the staff canteen of Hammersmith Hospital. Eventually their two sons, Peter and Edward would both became successful businessmen; their elder daughter, Sheila, would become Senior History Lecturer at Victoria University, Wellington, New Zealand and a writer; and their other daughter, Sophena, through the incredible threads of history would one day stand beside her husband, Sylvester Mwamba Chisembele, hosting the Prime Minister of India, Indira Gandhi when she made a State Visit to Zambia in 1976.

On 15 October 1976, Prime Minister Gandhi came to the Eastern Province for an official visit and we escorted her on an evening game viewing and a stay-over in the Mfuwe Presidential Lodge in the Luangwa National Game Park. She was, of course, the daughter of Pandit Jawaharlal Nehru, the political heir of Mahatma Gandhi, and made her visit to Zambia during the time of Sylvester's posting as Cabinet Minister for Eastern Province.

My father and the Indian diaspora were, naturally, passionately concerned with the right of Indian independence and with the India Round Table Conferences held in the early 1930s. Just months before the 1931 conference, reports of Gandhi, who was not just the political leader, but considered a

Zambia – The Freedom Struggle and the Aftermath

holy man, being called by Winston Churchill 'a seditious half naked fakir', was an insult which had angered Indians everywhere. My father feigned illness in order to attend, with hundreds of his compatriots, the arrival of Mahatma Gandhi to London for this second India Round Table Conference in 1931 in order to negotiate an end to British occupation and to demand total independence for the continent of India. A photograph in an evening newspaper identified my father among the crowd surrounding Mahatma Gandhi and he was sacked from his job in the Veeraswamy Restaurant as a result. After her short stay at the Luangwa National Game Park, Prime Minister Indira Gandhi sent us a fine filigree silver bowl to commemorate her visit.[44]

My birth certificate has my father's occupation recorded as 'Pedlar' and indeed at the time of my birth that is what he was in those dreadfully hard days of the Depression. After losing his job at the Veeraswamy Restaurant in 1931, my parents went through a very difficult time, unemployment was rife and my father could not find full-time work to support his family. They were living in 27 Phillip Street, and later moved to 42 Christian Street, off the Commercial Road. My mother found part-time employment working in a Synagogue which was in the same street, i.e. Christian Street, London E.1. She worked there cleaning and preparing the Synagogue for Services. The family along with many others in that period lived on credit provided by Jewish shops nearby.

My father to supplement their income used to go around the public houses and to Petticoat Lane market with a tray of small items and multi-coloured beans. He would tell fortunes and sell these beans, telling people that they were 'lucky snake eggs'. My mother told us that he would say that he was surprised that English people believed in his 'lucky snake eggs'! My father could be accused of being disingenuous, but

---

[44] "Prime Minister of India, Indira Gandhi - Card 1976", October 1976.

times were desperately hard and who is to say that the amusement, the light relief and perhaps the little hope that he brought into the lives of people in those difficult days were not as valuable as or of even of more worth than the pennies he received with his 'lucky snake eggs'. In the evenings he would take his tray around the public houses selling cigarettes, matches and other small items. He smoked Woodbine cigarettes, but he did not drink alcohol. I was born in St George-in-the-East Hospital on the 28th of February 1936 and on that very day my father got a regular job, calling me his 'lucky bonnia' as a result.

We used to receive exotic gifts from Indian seamen on shore-leave from the merchant ships. One unforgettable incident occurred when I was sitting in the backyard, aged around two or three, eating a banana. On the tin roof of a shed sat a small monkey which had been a gift from one of the seamen. It jumped down and bit me on the knee. My mother was so furious, shouting at my father that his friends must not bring any more wild animals into her house. We lost our monkey because of this incident. My parents were people of intelligence and integrity and held in respect within their community.

The following morning, an immigration official came to the British High Commission and told me that my work permit had been revoked, and he handed me a document declaring that I was a Prohibited Immigrant and must leave the country within 24 hours. Later, the British High Commission staff took me into an office where I was interviewed. The room was almost bare; a table with a telephone and some chairs were virtually the only furniture. I guessed the interview was being electronically recorded. During the course of the interview I was told that I could be provided lawyers to pursue a case for compensation against the Government of Zambia for wrongful arrest and imprisonment. I was guarded in my report to them, not wanting in any way to be used to the detriment of a newly independent country; my views on equality and the right of a people to self-government were strong and above all I did not want to harm Chisembele. I was thankful for the offer of legal assistance to bring a case against the Zambian Government, but I refused it. I spoke nothing of the reasons or circumstances surrounding the 'engagement'. And, in fact, I have never spoken of the details surrounding the background to this 1969 deportation issue to anyone that is until after the death of my husband in 2006.

Later that day, Chisembele came to the High Commission and I left with him. John Muchengwa had been in the ministerial house when I was driven back there by immigration officials, after being held in the prison, on the pretext that they wanted to see my passport. I had had words with John Muchengwa who came out of the house with me when I got my passport and he had tried initially to speak with the men, but then he was told to *"keep quiet"*. When he saw them take my passport and, after first agreeing that he could come with me to collect my car, then refuse him when he tried to get into their vehicle but just immediately drive off, he knew that something was very wrong. When I had been driven away, he rushed to send a telegram to Mansa to inform Chisembele that I had been picked up by immigration men. He also went to police headquarters and arranged with them to send an immediate priority police message which would reach Chisembele quickly. On receiving the message, Chisembele instantly left Mansa travelling back to Ndola and then on to Lusaka.

After locating my whereabouts, he came to the British High Commission to collect me, and from there we went to the Ministry of Home Affairs, Immigration Department, where suddenly no one knew anything. We also saw the Permanent Secretary, Crispin Nyalugwe, who now was very different from the way he had been when I saw him the previous day.

Personal Story of Sylvester M. Chisembele

(The above is a much shortened résumé of this incident; a fuller account is contained in a brief Statement of Arrest which I wrote, even though this statement has omissions, as it was written within three days of the ordeal, when I was still in a distressed condition).

On leaving the Ministry of Home Affairs, we drove back to Ndola and then returned to Lusaka where we spent several days in a government hostel. Hectic days with many people and groups coming and going and Chisembele called to State House for meetings with the President. The Statement of Arrest, which I had written,[45] together with his covering letter,[46] dated 13 and 19 March 1969 respectively, Chisembele took to President Kaunda. At the meeting they had the President asked that my statement not be released, promising that everything would be quickly sorted out and our names exonerated. When we again returned to Ndola I moved out of the hostel and for protection into the ministerial house with Chisembele because I was shaken and nervous and I had received no assurance, verbal or written, directly from the Government of a cancellation of the Deportation Order against me.

Rumours were rife and through the media the Government continued to issue defamatory statements about me via the *Zambia Daily Mail* and *Times of Zambia* newspapers.[47] The most prevalent rumour was that Miss Baptiste was a British spy and Chisembele had compromised the Government by his association with her. This rumour initiated from Northern Province political leaders. At that time the people of Luapula Province were considered by Northern Province to be their natural allies, both provinces being Bemba-speaking tribal areas. They did not appreciate the fact that the reason Luapula had allowed Northern Province leaders to assume

---

[45] Statement of Arrest Sophena Baptiste, 13.03.69.
[46] Chisembele letter to President Kaunda, 19.03.69, scan.
[47] "Minister's fiancée told to leave" *Times of Zambia* (Ndola), 12.03.69; "Reprieve for Minister's fiancée" *Times of Zambia* (Ndola) 14.03.69.

representative positions at national level for Luapula as well as Northern Province was because Chisembele and the Luapula leadership were setting an example of unity and peaceful progress towards a just and fair nation, without tribal or provincial affiliation. However, this attitude had been deliberately misinterpreted by the Northern Province leadership who privately considered it to be a weakness to be exploited.

There was also an incident during this 1969 deportation issue when Chisembele during a meeting with President Kaunda in State House told the President in the presence of the Minister for Home Affairs, Grey Zulu, that *"I care nothing for life, if you want to shoot me, do so"*. Later, President Kaunda used this incident to back up his assertion of the madness of Sylvester Chisembele. We were told years later by a senior official in the security service, named Nyirenda, that this was written on the secret dossier on Sylvester Chisembele kept by the security service. There was nothing mad in or about Sylvester Chisembele. He was a man of total honesty, fearless with such a deep belief in God that went beyond even my, his wife of forty years, understanding.

During the following weeks, in spite of the promise that the matter would quickly be sorted out, the situation remained unresolved; continuous defamatory statements and letters were still being issued against me.[48]

A delegation of Northern Province leaders went to all the districts in Luapula Province evincing false sympathy at what had befallen their leader, they also sent a delegation to the parents, Michael and Salome Chisembele, to convince them that they must make a public announcement of their rejection of the so-called 'British spy fiancée' who was destroying their son's reputation. The project was a dismal failure, it served to anger the UNIP leadership in Luapula and in the Copperbelt

---

[48] Folder, "1969 Issue".

and Michael and Salome Chisembele had welcomed the news of the engagement, wanting their son to establish a marriage within the Catholic Church.[49]

In the meantime, in Ndola, leaders were coming down from Luapula Province to repudiate the implications surrounding the derogatory publicity; it was clearly understood that the issue of the deportation was in itself immaterial, Miss Baptiste had just been used as a convenient pawn; the target was the Luapula leadership. Delegations were coming from within the Copperbelt and other areas. Leaders from other provinces were calling and visiting with sympathy and well-wishes. Reuben Kamanga who had been Zambia's first Vice-President threw a party of support and celebration for the engagement; Dingiswayo Banda, Cabinet Minister for the Western Province (Copperbelt), who was on a trip to the UK, contacted my mother to assure her of support within Zambia for the marriage and to wish her well. Several parties were arranged for us in Lusaka by provincial leaders among them Nephas Tembo, the lawyer Daniel Lisulo, and others with the exception of Northern Province, although some leaders from that province were supportive.

Mwanakatwe, the Secretary General, in an attempt to wash his hands, during a meeting with Chisembele told him that the plot was not aimed at him, but at the President. He said that the President had played no part in it and he had been out of the country during that day. The political situation was hot especially in Luapula and on the Copperbelt.

A few months earlier a gross insult had been levelled on the people of Luapula Province by political and government leaders from the Northern Province, following the appointment of a Luapulan, Aran Mulwe, to the post of Youth Regional Secretary in Ndola. The Northern Province leaders

---

[49] Michael F Chisembele letters to Chisembele, circa 1969, 15/2/70 and 25.5.70, scans.

had tried to incite people in Western Province (Copperbelt) to demonstrate against the appointment of Mulwe saying that he had come from the province of the batubulu and because the people were 'batubulu' the people of the Northern Province were their ordained rulers. This word 'batubulu' means 'foolish fishermen'.

This insult had caused great anger and resentment in Luapula Province, in the Copperbelt and among Luapulans elsewhere. And so following this incident and the current attempt still in progress to discredit the leadership of Chisembele, a series of intensive meetings began of Luapula grassroots leaders and Members of Parliament; it was resolved that Luapula Province would not allow the continuation of the status quo as far as representation of the province was concerned. To this end a strategic plan was discussed and as an initial step the Members of Parliament emanating from Luapula delivered a diplomatic letter to President Kaunda on 21 April 1969 to inform the President of their astonishment and rejection of the 'batubulu' slur and to express their determination to correct the existing state of affairs as far as political representation was concerned; they also expressed their allegiance to the Head of State. The hope was that President Kaunda would appreciate and support their loyalty and stand.[50] However, even after receiving this letter from Luapula's Members of Parliament, which was a statement of their support and expressing aspirations for peaceful, justifiable actions to correct the political imbalance in appointments, President Kaunda showed no understanding or perception of the deteriorating relationship between the leadership of Northern and Luapula Provinces.

Political pressure had become intense in Luapula Province and on 22 April 1969 President Kaunda held a meeting in State House, which lasted for almost three hours, with leaders

---

[50] "Excerpt Luapula MPs letter to President Kaunda, 21.4.69", scan.

from Luapula. At the end of that meeting he asked Chisembele for a written report on our personal present position, again with assurances that everything would soon be straightened out.

On 29 April Chisembele wrote to the President outlining our present personal position, as instructed. [51] Weeks continued to pass with no correction being made. Chisembele saw President Kaunda several times. President Kaunda continuing to maintain that the mistaken action to deport Miss Baptiste had been caused by an administrative error and that the matter would very soon be put right. But other Cabinet Ministers and provincial leaders were saying that the Vice-President, Simon Kapwepwe, had instigated the plot, aiming to take complete control of the Bemba-speaking areas which would include Northern, Luapula and Western (Copperbelt) Provinces, and this power play would only be successful if Sylvester Chisembele could first be discredited and brought down. Luapula and the Copperbelt were both being controlled by Luapulans at grassroots level, although this prominence was not reflected as far as political appointments were concerned. However, Chisembele believed that the plot instigators were not confined to Simon Kapwepwe and the Northern Province leadership, but included President Kaunda who had orchestrated events. President Kaunda was a master in the practice of the 'divide and rule' policy used by colonial governments and ruthless politicians. The Northern Province leadership played into his hands by their arrogant selfishness and greed for political positions and power to the exclusion of Luapulans.

Simon Kapwepwe had taken over the post of Vice-President from Reuben Kamanga in 1967. He had at that time been given the full support of the Luapula leadership in the hope and belief that as the personal friend of President

---

[51] "Chisembele letter to President Kaunda, 29.04.69", scan.

Kaunda he could influence the President to agree to changes in the British instigated Zambian Constitution which invested all power in the Head of State. Initially, other provincial delegations had not accepted the Luapula delegates' assertion that a so-called 'democratic centralism' was the path to dictatorship. They came to realise this after independence and this belated realization was the basis on which the Committee of 14 (also called 7 Committee) was formed later in the year of 1969. Simon Kapwepwe, however, after obtaining the post of Vice-President found and stated that the position held no power and the family ties between them held no sway (*when Kenneth Kaunda's parents came to Northern Province from Nyasaland they had been welcomed by the parents of Simon Kapwepwe and the two men had been friends from boyhood*).

On 15 May 1969 President Kaunda spoke by telephone to Chisembele again assuring him that he was handling our personal situation. On 20 May 1969 Chisembele saw the President again who this time asked him to see various people and the President through his secretary arranged the appointments.[52] By this time I was becoming disillusioned, but still clinging to a belief in the integrity of the words of President Kaunda. In the meantime, I booked a flight to London for 4 June 1969 in order to see my mother, who was extremely concerned for my safety.

I was unwell and on 30 May 1969 Reuben Kamanga accompanied by his wife Edna Kamanga and several government ministers called to see me. Lewis Changufu, a Northern Province Cabinet Minister, also came saying that he would arrange for a doctor to attend me. These dignitaries had accompanied President Kaunda to a function in Ndola. The next day when the President and his entourage were to return to Lusaka, Chisembele had a brief discussion with him

---

[52] Statement of Chisembele, 20-21.05.69, scan.

at Ndola airport and a meeting was arranged for the following day.

On 2 June 1969 Chisembele attended the meeting in State House. The Secretary General, Mwanakatwe and the Minister of Home Affairs, Grey Zulu were also called by the President to attend the meeting. During the course of this meeting President Kaunda gave Chisembele one thousand five hundred Kwacha [K] in cash to take to me and among other kindly words said that he was *"eager to meet"* me. Chisembele brought the money to me, I instantly pointed out that there was no covering letter or Government document to indicate that the money properly belonged to me and so I said *"this money will be returned tomorrow"*. Chisembele said that he was embarrassed to have brought the money to me and that he was of the same mind, but as the President had sent the money to me through him, he had to bring it for me to make my own decision.

Totally disillusioned now, the following morning 3 June 1969, I decided to photograph the money,[53] alongside the day's newspaper and my airline ticket with the hazy thought that the two documents would somehow prove the cash came within that period. With the constant 'run-around' that we had been given and the promise after promise never kept, I thought that this is just another set-up. Chisembele then left for Lusaka taking the money back to State House together with a letter, as diplomatic as I could make it given the circumstances, to President Kaunda.[54]

On arrival at State House, Chisembele had a meeting with President Kaunda who told him that he understood my reasons for returning the money and gave again positive assurance that he was going to take action to clear our names.

---

[53] "President Kaunda's Money", 3.06.69, photograph.
[54] S. Baptiste letter to President Kaunda, 3.06.69, scan.

Zambia – The Freedom Struggle and the Aftermath

The President replied to my letter,[55] and Chisembele brought this to me when he returned to Ndola very late in the evening.

I was due to leave for London the next day, 4 June 1969, but yet another defamatory statement appeared in the morning press. [56] We were extremely upset, and so I immediately cancelled my flight. Chisembele called a press conference for the following day to announce his resignation from the Government and he telephoned State House to leave a message for the President of his immediate resignation.[57] At 11 pm President Kaunda telephoned Chisembele to say that he could not accept his resignation and to tell him to do nothing until he had seen him, and he asked that we both attend a meeting with him the following day.

The next day, 5 June 1969, we left in the morning for Lusaka. On 3 June 1969 when Chisembele had returned the fifteen hundred kwacha which I had declined to accept, he was pressed by the President to accept five hundred kwacha to cover his own travel expenses for a visit to the UK to meet and explain the situation to my family, this money Chisembele also returned to President Kaunda.[58] Chisembele had first a private meeting with the President and then I was called in. The President told me that there had been a breakdown in communications. He told me that he would issue a statement to rectify my position and that I could rest assured that all my issues would be dealt with. He asked me to assure my parents that my future in Zambia was bright. I asked how such a situation could have developed when I was only following his wishes as relayed to me through

---

[55] President K.D. Kaunda letter to S. Baptiste, 3.06.69, scan.
[56] "Miss Sophena can stay on" *Times of Zambia* (Ndola) 4.06.69, scan.
[57] Sophena Baptiste, diary excerpt, 4.6.69, "We were both very upset. I was booked to leave for London but after another defamatory statement in the press, I cancelled the flight and Sylvester announced his resignation. KK telephoned at 11pm saying he wanted to see us both tomorrow at 2 pm".
[58] Chisembele letter to President Kaunda 5.06.69, scan.

Chisembele, and all I was trying to do was to prevent a political situation developing in the Copperbelt, which I had been told was the reason for the premature 'engagement' announcement. I repeated that Chisembele and I had not reached a stage of commitment and, I said that my mother and family in the UK had known nothing of my friendship with Chisembele until I had informed them of my 'engagement' to Chisembele, about whom my family had been totally in ignorance. I said that they would be very worried as my prohibited immigrant status had been broadcast on the BBC World service and covered in the media. The President reiterated that I was welcome in Zambia and that everything would be put right very soon.

President Kaunda said that he understood from Sylvester that I had cancelled my flight to London. He said I should only make my visit and reassure my parents and then when I came back to Zambia I could rejoin Government employment if I so wished. I told him the statement I had written on my arrest, together with a covering letter dated 4 June 1969, I was intending to send to the British Crown Agents as the Zambian Government had seen fit to inform them of my 'dismissal' from Government service. The President asked me not to send the documents. He said that I could rest assured that he was going to correct the wrong impression given about Chisembele and me, and that everything would be sorted out by the time I returned to Zambia.[59] The President asked us to attend another meeting arranged in Cabinet Office and read through a statement of correction which had been prepared for him to issue, and to adjust it if we felt it necessary. I came away believing that this would now be the case, but disappointed in the President.

---

[59] Statement of Chisembele 17.06.69, scan; S. Baptiste letter to The Crown Agents, 4.6.69, scan.

Zambia – The Freedom Struggle and the Aftermath

We went on to Cabinet Office to the arranged meeting with the Secretary General and the Minister of Home Affairs and were shown the prepared statement of correction, it was not adequate, it was ambiguous and held no tinge of regret, we adjusted it and we were assured that the amended statement would be covered in all media which had carried the earlier defamatory reports. The following day on 6 June 1969 a short statement was issued from State House to say that I had broken no laws in Zambia.[60] It was not the full statement which had been agreed at the meeting in the Cabinet Office the previous day and it was not attributed to President Kaunda himself as he had told us it would be.[61]

On 7 June 1969, Reuben Kamanga organised a farewell dinner at his residence at which other colleagues emanating from various provinces, who were in the main Lusaka-based ministers, attended. The next day I left Zambia and returned to London.[62]

I was shaken by the whole affair and I was not sure that I would have the courage to return to Zambia, but in any case I knew that I would not work again for the Government and so during my absence in England the financial issue was settled on my behalf by Chisembele. The question of the money owed to me had become immaterial; however, it was sorted out and all monies outstanding and due to me were paid.[63]

June 1969 – England
I remained in the UK with my family. Many friends who had seen or been told of reports in the newspapers of my

---

[60] "Sophena's name cleared" *Times of Zambia* (Ndola) 6.06.69, scan.
[61] Ibid. Fn.59 Statement of Chisembele, 17.06.69.
[62] "LONDON Fly-away Sophena" Zambia News (Ndola) 8.06.69, scan.
[63] Chisembele letter to Secretary General, 18.06.69; Secretary General letter to Chisembele, 24.6.69; Permanent Secretary, Establishments letters to S. Baptiste, 23.6.69 scans.

'deportation' joined with my family in urging me to remain in the UK. Dr. Douglas Latto* also spoke to me over the telephone and told me that he had heard on the BBC of my 'deportation' and added his voice to those advising me to remain in the UK.

However, Chisembele and I kept in constant contact by telephone and mainly by letter. I was unwell and two weeks after my return to the UK I was referred by my GP to Hammersmith Hospital where I was advised that I should go in for an exploratory operation for an undiagnosed problem.

In Zambia, a National Referendum was carried out in June. The purpose of this referendum was to consider a proposed amendment to the Constitution of Zambia to remove the referendum clause.[64] If accepted, this would allow future amendments to particular clauses to be made in the National Assembly provided a two-thirds majority of the Members of Parliament was obtained. This would remove the present need to hold public countrywide referendums which were a costly, complex exercise given the size of the country and the difficulty involved for people to make long trips to centres to register their views.

The Government stance was that in place of the existing referendum clause, power would be placed in the National Assembly which as an elected representative body would give Members of Parliament the authority to exercise the wishes of the people in their constituencies. This made pragmatic sense and subsequent to the National Referendum the Constitution was amended to this effect. This was the first referendum held in Zambia since independence had been achieved.

However, President Kaunda had his own agenda and in fact his underlying objective was to legislate by manipulation the establishment of a One Party State, this later in 1973 he would

---

* See Appendix B.
[64] President Kaunda, letter to Central Committee and Ministers, 18.06.69, scan.

do using his authority to appoint people of his own choice into positions of executive power.

Chisembele arranged a flight to London in order to visit my family. Before leaving, as a result of a decision taken at one of the series of meetings held by Luapula leaders and to start the process of total self-representation for Luapula Province, a letter was written to President Kaunda by Luapula Members of Parliament with suggested names of candidates for the forthcoming by-elections. John Mwanakatwe from Northern Province was not eliminated by the Luapula leadership from the selection at that stage.[65]

Chisembele arrived in the UK on 3 July. I went to meet him at Gatwick airport, but did not do so because I collapsed in the arrivals hall and was taken by ambulance direct to Redhill Hospital in Surrey, where I underwent an emergency operation for a life-threatening haemorrhage.[66] After some weeks I was released, and Chisembele delayed his return to Zambia until 1 August.

August 1969

The situation in Zambia particularly as far as Luapula and the Copperbelt were concerned was tense. A UNIP National Council at Mulungushi Rock was scheduled for later in the month and the Northern Province leadership had instigated an all-out campaign to win over control of the Bemba speaking population, which would have given them control over Northern, Luapula and Western (Copperbelt) Provinces. The absence of Chisembele for the preceding month was seen to be advantageous to this end. Appointed leadership posts in the Copperbelt below that of the Cabinet Minister and

---

[65] Luapula MPs' letter to President Kaunda, 3.7.69, scan.
[66] *Times of Zambia* (Ndola), 15.08.69, scan.

Personal Story of Sylvester M. Chisembele

Minister of State were mostly held by people emanating from Northern Province.[67]

However, leaders were waiting for the return of Chisembele and within days, on the 9th of August, a comprehensive meeting of Luapula leaders was held in Ndola to which all Regional Officials; all District Governors; all leading figures from Copperbelt and Lusaka who originated from Luapula Province attended. The meeting started at 5 pm and continued until 7am the following day.[68] The main issue for the delegates was the fact that in the national interest the Northern Province leadership had been allowed to put their people in positions of representation in as far as Luapula Province, Western Province (Copperbelt) as well as Northern Province were concerned. It was resolved at that meeting that from this time on no longer would this state of affairs be allowed to continue, Luapula would fight for justice and equality and assert her own interests with representatives selected from within the province. The leaders regretted the fact that UNIP had strayed from the democratic ideals of the early struggle period concentrating instead on the myth of the propaganda of the day that One Great Leader had brought Zambia to independence and that impregnable leader alone was capable of making decisions for the fate of the country, in other words cementing the ground for a system of One Man Rule.

The week before this meeting was held, on 3 August, President Kaunda accompanied by Northern Province leaders had gone to Luapula Province to address the Luapula leadership at a conference in Mansa, Chisembele, who had arrived back in Zambia two days prior, was not called by the President to attend this meeting. On the platform President Kaunda sat flanked by the Vice-President, Simon Kapwepwe,

---

[67] UNIP Mufulira Representatives letter to SM Chisembele, 26.6.69, scan.
[68] Chisembele letters to S. Baptiste, 1.08.69; 2.08.69; and 10.08.69, scans.

and other leaders, mainly of Northern Province origin, and at one point during the proceedings the 'deportation' issue involving Sylvester Chisembele came up. The dignitaries, speaker after speaker, tried to rally the delegates with words which in effect were to the detriment of the leadership of Sylvester Chisembele. Eventually President Kaunda took the podium and continued along the same line. The reaction of the participants was hostile even to the President. Delegates stood up and challenged the attacks on Chisembele saying that even during the struggle for independence Chisembele had never sought leadership or tried to influence anyone for his personal gain. People cheered when their spokesmen affirmed the total faith and support the people of the province had in Chisembele's leadership,[69] which went back to the early days of the struggle when Chisembele as well as national leaders in Lusaka had been in active, constant contact with the Colonial Office in Whitehall sending petitions demanding independence and he had, moreover, undergone imprisonment, beatings and assassination attempts and people were well aware of the risks and personal sacrifices he had accepted, as well as did other Luapulans, for the common good to bring freedom and self-rule.

I quote below an excerpt from a letter written to me by Chisembele on 16 August 1969 concerning this meeting:

... you are now widely acceptable by all the people as my wife (to be), particularly in Luapula where they were telling the President and those other friends* who went to receive him in Mansa, when my issue was raised at the Conference, that those people have been using the marriage of our leader as a means to destroy him, let us tell you openly that marriage has been welcome here in the province, and we wish and pray that

---

[69] Ibid. Fn. 7, Chiwama, history note, April 2011, scan.

our leader will have peace at home we are not children to be asked to destroy our leaders ... for what ? because of marriage? what about whites who are accessible to secret documents where our leader has no access, because we are hated as Luapula and because we are not wanted to have our own leadership that is why they are using all these stupid tactics to destroy our leaders. We are declaring, they said, categorically that he who touches on our leader's marriage touches on Luapula as a whole. It is not only that, even many people in Lusaka and Copperbelt are widely and openly saying Sylvester is now having a stable marriage ...

* friends = Northern Province leaders accompanying the President

Seeing the way the meeting was going President Kaunda changed course and started speaking well of Chisembele and of the Luapula leadership telling the conference members that he knew how the people of Luapula always spoke straight and for this reason, he said, he liked coming to Luapula because he knew that if the Government was going wrong the people of Luapula would tell him the truth and put him right. President Kaunda referred to the nickname given to Sylvester Chisembele during the struggle for independence saying he knew that the people of Luapula had a great respect and confidence in 'Kaole'. President Kaunda was shaken at the hostility of the delegates at the meeting. President Kaunda frequently visited Luapula. He used to tell the people that he had been advised by the last Senior Provincial Colonial Commissioner, E.C. Thomson to be careful with Luapula because it could destroy your Government. President Kaunda said that his response was *'No, I know that Luapula Province is full of wisdom and that is where I learn and get knowledge of how to lead this country'.*

Such statements of President Kaunda were at odds with his actions; he distrusted the Luapula leadership, and as a result Luapula and its leaders were kept at arm's length, and the relationship was strained.

Zambia – The Freedom Struggle and the Aftermath

In 1961 when the President of UNIP Kenneth Kaunda, returned from London after holding Constitutional talks with British Members of Parliament and officials, he announced at a rally in Chilenje that the British Government had rejected the demand for 'Independence Now' for Northern Rhodesia. He went on to say that the British Government had stated the country was not yet ready. He said they told him that if the country was as organised as Luapula Province they could give us independence and if Luapula Province wanted independence, she could be given it straight away.[70] After independence, President Kaunda let it be known in Luapula Province that during discussions with the British, just prior to independence, he had been warned by them to keep Sylvester Chisembele out of his Government as far as it was expedient. He said this advice was never accepted by him; but his actions, however, refuted his words.

During the month, August 1969, many meetings were held in Ndola by Chisembele and, in turn, the leaders who attended these meetings held independent meetings to disseminate information and decisions to grassroots leaders in their areas, i.e. Copperbelt, Lusaka and Luapula. Leaders from Northern Province were also very active trying to cement their position of dominance and it was a widely held view that Vice-President Kapwepwe, was actively preparing the ground for a future bid to take over the presidency of the Republic.

Chisembele and his Luapula colleagues held meetings with top leaders from other provinces who feared the possibility of Kapwepwe taking sole power, concerned that he was capable of enforcing an even more repressive dictatorship. Also, the consensus was that Kapwepwe if he became President could not be trusted to change the Zambian Constitution insofar as to devolve the absolute power the present Constitution gave

---

[70] Chisembele letter to Vice-President., 29.10.03, p.6.

to the Head of State; the changing of the Constitution was now an important objective of these provincial leaders.

However, Kapwepwe and his followers were confident that they had the ammunition that would give them control of the three provinces, Northern, Luapula and Western (Copperbelt), which would ensure him sufficient numerical support when it became possible to challenge for the presidency, and with a snapping of his fingers, Kapwepwe infamously told his followers that: *"Chisembele is a mosquito - I can squash him like that"*.

The scheduled UNIP National Council was duly held in August 1969 at Mulungushi Rock. It was a crucial conference which ended in disarray.

Shortly after this turbulent UNIP National Council, Kapwepwe announced his resignation as Vice-President; he rightly said that the position of Vice-President held no power, stating also that ever since Mulungushi in 1967 some of his colleagues had not recognised him as a popularly elected Vice-President. President Kaunda followed this statement of Kapwepwe by dissolving the entire Central Committee under the emergency power granted him in 1961.[71] Simon Kapwepwe later withdrew his resignation when asked to do so by President Kaunda and agreed to complete his term of office.

President Kaunda then announced the setting up of a committee called the Chuula Commission to review the UNIP Constitution.

In the meantime, I was still in England and I received a telephone call from Chisembele in the latter half of August 1969 telling me that President Kaunda had appointed him Cabinet Minister for Barotseland now renamed Western Province. I also received contact from Dingiswayo Banda, the Cabinet Minister for the renamed Copperbelt Province,

---

[71] Chisembele, letters to S. Baptiste, 13-14.08.69 and 25.8.69, scans.

who was to be absent for some considerable time in the UK where he was undergoing eye surgery. He assured me that all was going well in Zambia and that things were quiet and calm and that I should not be afraid to return.[72]

In spite of all the assurances I was receiving I still agonised about going back to Zambia. I was afraid and uneasy ... it was against the advice of my family and friends, everyone close to me urged me to remain in the UK, but I did not want to be used as a means of destroying the reputation of Chisembele and give credence to the rumours that he had allowed himself to be duped by a British spy and so, with trepidation, after an absence of three months, I went back on 7 September 1969.

We transferred to Western Province on 22 September. The house we moved into was the former residence of the British Resident Commissioner, Gervas Clay.[73] The province was an African National Congress stronghold and adherent to customary rule. Hostilities between the supporters of UNIP and those of the ANC were rife. UNIP supporters, who were heavily outnumbered, were unable to move freely. Attacks on UNIP supporters were frequent and UNIP members moved with fear, especially in the evenings. Previous administrations had failed to make any headway in the province and there was particular tension between the Office of the Cabinet Minister and the Kuta of the Litunga, HRH Godwin Mbikusita Lewanika II.

---

[72] Dingiswayo Banda letter to Chisembele, August 1969, scan.
[73] Sophena Baptiste, letter to family, 24.11.69, scan; I was young and sufficiently naive to be a little astonished by the fact that in the Government Residency in which we now lived, I was sleeping on a bed which had engraved on the headboard a British Royal Coat of Arms. I was informed by the head house servant who had served in the house for years going back to Colonial times when the house was the Residency of the British Resident Commissioner, that the bedroom and certain other furniture in the house (the dining room chairs carried the same insignia) had been especially brought in from the UK for the visit made by Queen Elizabeth the Queen Mother in 1960.

Personal Story of Sylvester M. Chisembele

In December, John Mwanakatwe was appointed temporary Cabinet Minister for Luapula Province. This was of little concern. The able Luapula leadership in the province and elsewhere was firm; determined to change the status of Luapula Province, no longer prepared to accept the domination of Northern Province as far as political and government posts were concerned.

Initially, the political problems in Western Province (Barotseland) were intense. There was so much conflict and instability. In the 1968 General Elections, the UNIP ruling party lost the entire Western Province to the opposition. Not even a single parliamentary seat was won by UNIP. UNIP Ministers, e.g. Messrs Arthur Wina, Munukayumbwa Sipalo and Nalilungwe all lost to the opposition. President Kaunda reshuffled the provincial leadership there and sent in Humphrey Mulemba as Provincial Minister and appointed District Governors to try to win the province back to the ruling party, but they failed lamentably and Mulemba was flown back to Lusaka because he became ill.

Western Province bordered Angola and in that country a freedom war was raging bringing many problems across the border into Zambia. Guerrilla groups of three liberation movements: the Popular Movement for the Liberation of Angola; the National Front for the Liberation of Angola; and the National Union for the Total Independence of Angola, ["MPLA", "FNLA" and "UNITA" respectively] were in an all-out struggle for freedom from Portugal, the coloniser. This conflict was not confined within Angolan borders, Portuguese soldiers regularly made invasions into Zambian territory maiming and killing villagers on both sides of the border. Shortly after we arrived in the province there was one sad incident of a white Portuguese woman who was brought in by Angolan freedom fighters. She had been captured and had spent months with them living in the bush and trekking with them to various bush camps. She was in the late stages of pregnancy and was handed over to the Zambian authorities and brought to Mongu where she was immediately admitted to hospital, and although I do not know the later details, she was, undoubtedly, repatriated.

This was the situation existing at the time of the transfer. Chisembele was called upon to attend crisis meeting after meeting. It was necessary for him to rush from place to place in order to control flashpoints of unrest. His personal health was affected in that the headaches he had suffered since the beatings he underwent from the colonial authorities during the freedom struggle became more frequent. No sooner was one area quietened than trouble would erupt somewhere else in the province.[74]

On the national level, by December 1969 the organisation which Chisembele and leaders from other provinces had established called the Committee of 14 (also known as 7 Committee) was active throughout the country. This Committee consisted of two leaders from each of seven out of the eight provinces of Zambia, the exception was Northern Province. Among the members were, Reuben C. Kamanga, Dingiswayo Banda, Ackson Soko, Henry Shamabanse, Humphrey Mulemba, Jethro Mutti, Amock Phiri, as well as Sylvester Chisembele and others.[75] [76]

Luapula's interest and reason for taking a prominent part in the Committee of 14 was clearly defined; it served her purpose of involvement, in that it provided a platform for emphasising the need to change the Constitution clause placing power in the hands of one individual and also to secure support for her objective of democracy at all levels which entailed direct representation in Government, not by

---

[74] Excerpts S. Baptiste family letters, June and July 1970, scans.
[75] "Interview with Yatsani Radio" sound file, 22.11.05 (please note that Chisembele was already very ill when this interview took place. His normal voice and fluency are absent and he died some few weeks later).
[76] Chisembele "Agenda Jottings", 1969.

proxy. Later for the first time Luapula was to be represented in the National Assembly by people from Luapula, i.e. in the 1973 General Elections when Luapula successfully fielded candidates selected within Luapula by its own leadership to the cost of the so-called 'quasi-official' candidates approved and placed by President Kaunda.

The Committee of 14 leaders were not meeting in secret. Their purpose was to democratise the party and bring about real unity, equality and democratic development and to achieve this, one objective was to change the Zambian Constitution. President Kaunda agreed to receive the Committee of 14 leaders and a meeting was held at State House at which they presented their views and suggestions. During the meeting they tried to convince the President of the need to change the Constitution, especially the need to devolve the absolute power held by the Head of State under the present Constitution, and they aired issues of concern at both the national and provincial level. The President listened to their views intimating that he would consider and respond in due course; but President Kaunda was, in fact, furious and he later called the Committee of 14 leaders representing six of the seven provinces separately to threaten and dissuade them from continuing their association with the Committee. The only province whose leaders he did not call or attempt to influence was Luapula Province, this would in any case have been futile and there were no 'skeletons in the cupboard' to use as leverage.

However, after taking up the post of Cabinet Minister for Western Province (Barotseland), a visit was made by Dr. Simon Mwewa, a Luapulan, who came to Mongu to see Chisembele with an offer of Buffalo Threads Transport Co. which, he said, could be 'given' to Chisembele and which would ensure his financial future and that of his family. Dr. Mwewa came merely as an emissary from President Kaunda. Buffalo Threads was a long established transport company which was taken over by Government and was now operating as a parastatal company.[77]   Chisembele thanked Dr. Mwewa for his visit but refused the offer telling him that he did not think it right for leaders to seek to enrich themselves instead of concentrating their efforts for the good of the people who put them in power.[78]

The sphere of influence of the Committee of 14 was not confined to Zambians within the country, several diplomats and students attending universities abroad were also involved. For example, John Muchengwa who was now studying in Karl Marx University, Leipzig was busy with other students organising support for the Committee of 14 within their community in Germany and to this end he was used to receive information to disseminate sometimes via Zambian diplomats passing through the German Democratic Republic. In a letter he wrote to Chisembele on 27 November 1969 he made reference to the word 'arabs', used idiomatically as a loose translation of the Bemba word 'abalungwana' which means 'slave traders'. This word he used as a consequence of the insult levelled towards Luapulans by Northern Province leaders ('batubulu' see above, page 79). The other word used by John Muchengwa in his letter 'Mandefu' which means 'bearded one' was a nickname in use for Simon Kapwepwe.[79] This letter was an affirmation of support among his fellow students not emanating from Northern Province for the Committee of 14 and its objectives.

---

[77] Comment: Dr. Mwewa was a parastatal chief as Managing Director of the National Building Society previously known as First Permanent Building Society; he originated from Chief Milambo's area in Mansa. ("Parastatal" State owned and run company in Zambia usually taken over from a private concern).
[78] Valentine Kayope, "Eulogy for Chisembele", 9.2.06, scan.
[79] John Muchengwa letter to Chisembele, 27.11.69, scan

Chapter 4
1970 – 1972

1970

An excellent working relationship was being established between The Litunga, HRH Mbikusita Lewanika II; his Kuta; the Ngambela Suu; and the Cabinet Minister, Sylvester Chisembele, and through this cooperation the political situation began to change. The Litunga was the most important person in the province and Chisembele found him to be a very understanding personality.

On 22 January 1970, Chisembele and I were quietly married in St Ignatius Church in Lusaka. The officiating priest was Fr. Max Prokoph S.J.

On 21 February, the Kuomboka Ceremony was held. This traditional ceremony is held yearly marking the day when the flooding of the plain due to the rising water of the Upper Zambezi River requires the Litunga to move from Lealui to Limulunga, the wet season capital. The Litunga's famous barge called the Nalikwanda is followed by the barge of the Moyo (wife of the Litunga) and a procession of other vessels bringing the people to dry land. The boats lead a dance in the water, play around; pulling alongside and around each other, but never overtake or draw level with the Litunga's barge, with the exception of the boat designated for Government dignitaries whose boat might drew near but respectfully never beyond the Nalikwanda. As the President's representative, Chisembele travelled with the Litunga.

Personal Story of Sylvester M. Chisembele

There was strict segregation as far as women and men were concerned. I started this traditional journey in the boat with Government officials, but when at one point we drew alongside the Litunga's barge, he came out on deck and putting out his hand, not as I thought to shake hands with me, but to escort me across into the Nalikwanda. This was a mark of respect to Chisembele, for the Litunga allowed me to travel with them for much of the journey. I was told that I was the only woman ever allowed to travel with the Litunga during this ceremony. I was very conscious of the honour but as with extraordinary moments in life, it was too much, too overwhelming to take in at the time, only in recollection did I understand the real value of the privilege.

However, I learnt recently that I was not in fact the first woman to board the Nalikwanda: during a visit made by The Queen Mother to Barotseland in 1960 she had been received on board by the late Litunga Sir Mwanawina Lewanika III.

The Nalikwanda was propelled forward by two lines of ceremonially dressed oarsmen and in the centre of the barge there was a covered hut-type structure and within the Litunga HRH Mbikusita Lewanika II sat on his throne, Chisembele was seated alongside him and I sat on the floor with the Ngambela and other Indunas; there was a cauldron of burning charcoal in the centre. Drummers were pounding away; the heat, the smoke fumes, the strange drink that was served from a communal huge pot of a white thick potent liquid and passed around in a big wooden cup, together with the swaying of the boat moving at times through thick rushes, caused me to feel nauseous, making the trip a mixed blessing; but above it all I was in awe. This ceremony is elaborate and goes on for hours in stages. At a later stage, I joined the Moyo and her attendant women.[80]

---

[80] "Queen Mother boarding the Nalikwanda", May 1960, photograph courtesy of Robin B. Clay; Sophena Chisembele, letter to family, 9.03.70, scan.

Zambia – The Freedom Struggle and the Aftermath

President Kaunda did not attend this Kuomboka Ceremony, he did, however, make a visit to Mongu some days later on 2 March. There was the usual modest assembly to receive him at the airport, mainly government officials, District Governors, civil servants, schoolchildren, missionaries and UNIP supporters and, of course, Chisembele and me. The Litunga, HRH Mbikusita Lewanika II and the Moyo came to the Residency to greet the President, along with other local dignitaries.

However, enormous progress was being made in Barotseland. The political situation was changing. Tensions in public areas had diminished to such an extent that national leaders in Lusaka found it hard to believe.

In August, President Kaunda made another visit to the province.[81] Previous visits had been largely boycotted by the people and the Litunga had not accepted to be in the welcoming party at the airport. However, on the day of this visit a huge crowd of people came to the airport and the Litunga, HRH Mbikusita Lewanika II, together with Ngambela Suu and his Kuta, were present to receive President Kaunda on a platform erected for the occasion. President Kaunda and his entourage were surprised at the size and tone of the reception. To the bafflement of those present, he used his speech from the podium to make an attack on the Litunga. There was disappointment and bewilderment throughout. What was intended to be reconciliation between the Royal establishment and President Kaunda with its resulting cooperation had been put back a step.

The District Governors based throughout the province had, as was usual, been appointed by President Kaunda, their initial behaviour towards Chisembele had been polite but distant. Cooperation between the Cabinet Minister's Office

---

[81] Sophena Chisembele, letter to family, 13.08.70, scan; "President Kaunda visit to Mongu". Zambia Information Services, photograph.

and the District Governors was not as it should have been. As time went on and the positive influence of the approach of Chisembele became so evident, a change set in resulting in the Minister of State, Fines Liboma, and the District Governors, after a provincial meeting, confessing to Chisembele that there was a hidden agenda and that President Kaunda had instructed the District Governors to make their reports directly to him, largely bypassing the Office of the Cabinet Minister. Once this was out in the open, the resulting cooperation between the Offices saw a rapid change in the whole province with eventually all ANC Members of Parliament crossing the floor to UNIP.[82] The Minister of State, Fines Liboma, a son of Barotseland as indeed were most of the other political appointees, was particularly keen to see Western Province developments on a par with that of other provinces.

In spite of the progress being made, there was still at grassroots level distrust to be overcome, but with the co-operation now existing between the Kuta of the Litunga and the Cabinet Minister's Office, progress was continuous. The Paramount Chief of the Barotse, Litunga Mbikusita Lewanika II, the most influential man in the province, held Chisembele in such esteem that when his son was dying of cancer, he came to the residence to ask Chisembele to pray for his son. Later he also wrote to my mother in England sending her his iconic 'fly-whisk', made from ivory, elephant hair and wood. This respect was mirrored in the political sphere and a great factor in the peace now existing in the province.[83]

The fact that President Kaunda had instructed his appointed officials in Western Province to bypass the Office of

---

[82] Sikota Wina telegram to Chisembele, 17.08.70, scan; Secretary, Credit Organisation of Zambia letter to Chisembele, 7.04.70, scan; Jonas Mwambwe letter to Chisembele, 12.08.70 with reply 19.08.70, scan.
[83] "The Litunga – Petitions Court – 1970" Zambia Information Services, photograph; "Mrs E Ali – Home Chiswick, London", photograph.

the Cabinet Minister came as no surprise to Chisembele. I learnt that this enmity and distrust went way back to before the obtainment of independence when at the Magoye Conference, as previously mentioned, the Luapula delegation had fiercely rejected 'democratic centralism'. Since that time Chisembele continued to insist that the most basic economic and political problems in Zambia lay in the Zambian Constitution drawn up and imposed on Zambia by the British Government and adopted in the last hours before the raising of the flag of an independent Zambia.[84] This Constitution gave all the executive power to the President of the Republic leaving other leaders, elected or appointees, with no power to correct or make meaningful changes unless with the permission and approval of the President. President Kaunda the recipient of this power had no intention of relinquishing any part of it. For his stance and the contrary views of Chisembele, President Kaunda hated him – hatred that never diminished.

President Kaunda tolerated Chisembele in Government only because of grassroots pressure and the need which surfaced now and then to calm a brewing situation somewhere in the country, for Chisembele had a unique ability to calm and resolve ugly situations. For example, in 1966 there was a long-standing conflict in North Western Province threatening to ignite into a conflagration. Because of the seriousness and urgency of the problem, which was between the tribes of the Lundas led by W. Nkanza and the Lovales led by S.C. Mbilishi, both government ministers, President Kaunda sent Chisembele by government aeroplane to resolve the issue. Chisembele spent two days in controversial meetings which if not properly handled would result in bloodshed as tension and tempers were very high from both tribes. The situation was brought under control,

---

[84] Chisembele, "Constitution Contribution for Public Awareness", 2005, pt 2 p 17.

peace restored and the problems were resolved by negotiation calmly monitored. It was agreed that the name of the District had to be changed from "Balovale" to that of the river which divided the district and so the name of the District and Boma was changed to "Zambezi".

On 21 June 1970 a meeting was held in Clement Mwananshiku's home in Lusaka of all the Regional Officials from Luapula Province [85] and to follow this, arrangements had been made for Chisembele to make a tour of Luapula Province in July. The tour was several times postponed, twice he left Mongu to start the tour only to reach Mansa and be instantly recalled by President Kaunda. Eventually, the President instructed him to cancel the tour.[86]

The local Government Elections which took place in August 1970 were a tremendous success in the Western Province (Barotseland) a surprise and delight particularly to politicians emanating from that province. This achievement brought Chisembele a telegram from Cabinet Minister Sikota Wina, which read: *"This is to congratulate you on behalf of the party and the President in connection with the recent results of the local Govt. Elections. Your job has not been an easy one but it is significant that we have started to make tremendous progress …."*[87] In Luapula too all 93 candidates, selected by the Luapula leadership, all under the UNIP ticket, were successful.[88]

President Kaunda in a surprise move banned the Committee of 14 which had been established the previous year. Some leaders and less influential adherents he sacked, but the organisation had already become effective and far reaching. The objective of the Committee of 14 was equality particularly at provincial level, and the serious consideration

---

[85] Chisembele excerpt of letter to Sophena Chisembele, 21.06.70, scan.
[86] Ibid. Fn.74 Excerpts from family letters June and July 1970, scan.
[87] Sikota Wina, telegram to Chisembele, 4.09.70, scan.
[88] Ibid. Fn.82 Jonas Mwambwe letter to Chisembele, 12.08.70 with reply 19.08.70, scan.

of the establishment of a democratically elected council of two leaders from each province to lead the country by consensus with the President as Head of State, Chairman and spokesman, possibly elected on a revolving basis, but with a fixed term of office. If this had been achieved, it would have meant the curtailing of the absolute power residing in President Kaunda.

It was campaigned for and believed that if citizens were able to voice their preferences through the referendum held the previous year and now through the Chuula Commission announced that same year, this would give a chance for changes to be made in the existing Constitution of Zambia and the UNIP Constitution respectively, which would enable a peaceful transition of power from One Man to a democratically elected body of provincial representatives elected by and within the individual provinces.

The initial Chuula Commission findings, when made public did, in fact, support the establishment of a Central Committee of 16 members to represent the 8 provinces in Zambia, these 16 members were to be elected 2 from each province and elected within each province. However, this particular Chuula Commission recommendation went against the plans of President Kaunda and so he then called the Chairman of the Commission and put forward to the Chuula Commission his own proposed amendments, which included the establishment of an enlarged Central Committee of 28 members, not elected by and within each of the 8 provinces, but appointed and elected by the National Council. Furthermore, President Kaunda proposed that there be a Political Bureau of 7 which, as Head of State, he would lead and appoint a Vice-President; plus as Secretary General he would again appoint a Deputy, and finally, as Head of State, he would appoint the other 4 members.[89] In other words, all the members of the Political Bureau of 7 which would be the

---

[89] Chisembele, "Points to Remember", 21.09.70, scan.

overriding body would be appointed by President Kaunda. President Kaunda's address to a Seminar held in Mulungushi Hall, Lusaka on the 6th of October 1970 reads: [90]

> *The Secretary General, in his capacity as head of the Party, should appoint one Deputy Secretary General. As Head of State he appoints one Vice-President. Further I propose that he should appoint 4 others to form a Political Bureau of 7.*
>
> *He is the Chairman of both the Political Bureau and the Central Committee. He is also Head of State and Chairman of the Cabinet which is on the Government side.*

President Kaunda's proposals did not meet the aspirations or the expressed views of the populace. Some Cabinet Ministers and government officials, who had no political base within the country, gave unreserved backing to President Kaunda, but those who were courageous and nationalist mounted a campaign to counteract the imposition of an amended Chuula Commission Report which was scheduled to be presented to the UNIP National Council in November.

In October 1970, by a series of reshuffles and appointments, President Kaunda was manipulating the leadership within the country by moving and appointing people to make certain that his decisions would stand.[91] The imposition of a Political Bureau of 7 and the declaration of a One Party State being his prime objectives, which would ensure his perpetual position as Head of State. Chisembele had already started to organise Luapula and Copperbelt Provinces to reject both the amended Chuula Commission Report and the establishment of a Political Bureau of 7 whose members would be appointed in toto by President Kaunda, and any attempt, known to be waiting in the wings, to impose a legislated declaration of a

---

[90] President Kaunda's Address at Mulungushi Hall, 6.10.70, scan.
[91] Chisembele letter to Stalin Kaushi, 7.10.70 and reply October 1970, scan.

One Party State.[92] The belief held for so long by the Luapula leadership that the danger in 'democratic centralism' was that it equated to one-man rule was now spreading out and leaders in other provinces made known their shared disquiet at the turn of events.

The UNIP National Council had been called for November 1970 and this among other matters would consider the findings of the Chuula Commission. The three day National Council was opened by President Kaunda on 7 November and an amended Chuula Commission Report was accepted, but this did not include the attempted imposition of a Political Bureau of 7. The Central Committee Members were to be increased to 25 with 4 nominated members. The party's Central Committee Members would not be elected by the individual provinces which would have ensured a democratic process of provincial representation, but would be elected by the delegates at the National Council. Once this amended Chuula Commission Report had been accepted by the National Council, the onus through collective responsibility was then on leaders holding Government and party posts to explain the decisions taken at the National Council to the populace.[93]

In early November 1970, Simon Kapwepwe announced his resignation from the post he held of Vice-President. President Kaunda appointed Mainza Chona in his stead and Simon Kapwepwe was then appointed Minister for Provincial & Local Government. In this post Kapwepwe was in a far better position to attempt to stem the organisation and influence achieved by the Luapula leadership, and also to re-establish the influence lost by his own section of the Northern Province leadership. Chisembele's posting to Western Province (Barotseland) was not affected by the changes.

---

[92] Chisembele letter and attachments to Peter Chanshi, 8.10.70, scan.
[93] Chisembele, "Speech at Blue Gums Rally", 15.11.70, scan.

Personal Story of Sylvester M. Chisembele

Meanwhile, Portugal had intensified its provocations and incursions into Zambia, setting up military camps near the border with Western Province. The Portuguese were violating Zambian airspace and during incursions into Zambian territory were kidnapping and attacking people causing death or severe injuries to villagers living along the border. People were in such fear that they were sleeping in the bush afraid to remain in their homes during night times. On 12 November 1970 a serious bombing incident occurred in Shangombo District necessitating Chisembele to make an immediate report to State House, which he did.[94]

A few days after returning to Mongu he received a letter of reprimand from President Kaunda accusing him of attending a meeting of the banned Committee of 14 at the home of Dingiswayo Banda and ordering him to pay the full cost of flying from Mongu to Lusaka and back.[95] In fact Chisembele had not attended any meeting; the security report to State House was wrong. Chisembele replied to President Kaunda and flatly refuted the accusation. He wrote *"it must be exactly proved that I attended such a meeting"*.[96] His letter was firmly couched and nothing further was heard from President Kaunda on this particular issue. The cost of the return aeroplane journey was not levied and likewise not referred to again.

1971

At the beginning of the year in January 1971, Justin Chimba, Minister of Commerce & Industry, was suspended for corruption and tribalism, and this was followed in February by changes in leadership positions; among them former Vice-President Reuben Kamanga, who had been a member of the

---
[94] Chisembele letter to President Kaunda, 13.11.70, scan.
[95] President Kaunda letter to Chisembele, 17.11.70, scan.
[96] Unfortunately, I cannot locate a copy of this letter but it will be on government files. The quotation, however, is accurate.

banned Committee of 14, who was moved from his post of Minister for Foreign Affairs to Minister of Rural Development. A few days before these actions, another member of the banned Committee of 14, Henry Shamabanse, Minister for North Western Province, was suspended under a charge of corruption and so too was Munukayumbwa Sipalo under the same charge.

In the meantime, while on a visit to Lusaka we were invited to lunch with Aaron Milner, a coloured Zambian, who had been appointed Cabinet Minister/Secretary General. Aaron Milner's overwhelming allegiance was always with President Kaunda for as he stated in an article he wrote for *The Post* newspaper, he had in the early days been sitting with a group of others listening to Kenneth Kaunda at a public meeting and Kenneth Kaunda had noticed him and called him forward at the end of the meeting and brought him into a leadership position. Aaron Milner had always been a friend and he expressed a great respect for Chisembele. During the lunch he informed us that he had had all records relating to the issue of my arrest and deportation removed from government records and destroyed. He said that he had done this in our interests. I thought it was probably to the contrary, but I thanked him nonetheless.

The Kuomboka Ceremony was held in March 1971 and the Minister for Provincial & Local Government, Simon Kapwepwe, and other government ministers came from Lusaka to attend the ceremony. Again for this most exciting ceremony HRH the Litunga allowed me to board and travel part way with him, Chisembele and ex-Vice-President Simon Kapwepwe on the Nalikwanda[97]. A few weeks later on Sunday 18 April, President Kaunda announced the suspension from office of Sylvester Chisembele. Chisembele

---

[97] "Kuomboka The Litunga, Chisembele and Kapwepwe" Zambia Information Services, photograph; Sophena Chisembele letter to Family, 19.03.71, scan.

was not informed directly by the President of this action and he was given no reason. His replacement arrived on the same day as the radio and press announcements, with no other communication. On going to his office in the morning, Chisembele found security police guarding the entrance and he was informed that he could not be allowed to enter the building.

This action to suspend Chisembele caused shock. A few days later on 21 April President Kaunda announced the suspension of various leaders from other provinces.[98] The following day the same newspaper the *Zambia Daily Mail* printed the caption "LUAPULA SALUTES KK MOVES", the Government managed to get three appointed individuals within Luapula to support President Kaunda's action to suspend Chisembele. This was a sham. People in the province and the leaders were furious. Some weeks later in June other ministers were fired, namely, Dingiswayo Banda and Nephas Tembo. Justin Chimba was also fired but in his case mainly because he was part of an organisation within UNIP campaigning for leadership change from Kenneth Kaunda to Simon Kapwepwe.

Chisembele was not allowed contact with any of his officials in Western Province (Barotseland). When venturing out of the house, we were followed by security officers everywhere we went. The Litunga, Mbikusita Lewanika 11, the Ngambela, other traditional leaders, missionaries as well as local UNIP officials came to express complete shock and disappointment with the news.[99] The traditional leaders and local politicians expressed the feeling that the reason behind

---

[98] *The Zambia Daily Mail*, Zambia 21.04.71, excerpt "KK announced suspension from UNIP of leaders from various parts of the country in the second crackdown this week on indiscipline in the Nation. The latest move follows the suspension of Mr Sylvester Chisembele, the Cabinet Minister for Western Province, announced by the President on Sunday".
[99] Sophena Chisembele letter to family, 23.04.71, scan.

the suspension was Chisembele's work for their province; this was not the reason however. The Litunga, Mbikusita Lewanika 11, also wrote to my mother in England to express his disappointment at the action taken and assuring her of his respect and friendship for Chisembele and her daughter.[100]

On our return to Lusaka, Sylvester and I were housed in the home of his brother Dominic Chisembele. Sylvester held meetings in Dominic's house with political leaders and, in particular, Members of Parliament from Luapula Province. These meetings sometimes started with the singing of songs from the time of the struggle for independence. Later it emerged that these discussions were being reported back to President Kaunda, who was particularly angered at the singing of political songs from the freedom struggle period.

In the period after suspension from office, we were openly tailed wherever we went. All salary payments were stopped, including the housing and parliamentary allowances to which Chisembele was still entitled. All attempts made by Chisembele to regularise the situation were met with promise after promise which were never kept.[101] It took six months before an entitled payment was made.

In the meantime leaders from Copperbelt and Luapula Provinces, were urging Chisembele to allow them to instigate a campaign against the action taken by President Kaunda. The wish was to retaliate and plan a way forward, but Chisembele always a cool head called for calm. He did not consider a post in the Government to be an all-important issue; rather he believed the fight for democratic elections at local, provincial and national level to ensure true representation of the populace to be of paramount importance, and now being

---

[100] Mrs E Ali family letter to Sophena Chisembele, 30.07.71, excerpt "…also if Sylvester sees the Litunga will he tell him that I will answer his last letter which I received last April as soon as I am better", scan.
[101] Cabinet Office letter to Sylvester Chisembele, 7.7.71, scan.

out of the Government he was free to work to this end as an ordinary Member of Parliament.

In August 1971, Simon Kapwepwe resigned his post of Minister of Provincial & Local Government and the following day announced that he was in fact the leader of the United Progressive Party [UPP]. This party was not officially known, though its existence was widely rumoured; it was initially an underground movement established by mainly Northern Province leaders inside UNIP. Within days Kapwepwe announced that his new party UPP would form an alliance with the ANC, African National Congress, led by Harry Mwaanga Nkumbula. Two months after this announcement was made, President Kaunda ordered the arrest and detention of several UPP leaders but, at this time, he did not detain Kapwepwe, this would happen later.

Reuben Kamanga who was then the Minister of Rural Development advised Chisembele to purchase a farm which would solve our housing problem and at the same time establish a sound financial future. Chisembele had a house in Lusaka which was being purchased on mortgage. He had as well as other government ministers been allowed loans to purchase houses shortly after independence when these leaders were moving from their provincial homes to take up national duties in Lusaka. However, as we had not been based in Lusaka but stationed in other provinces, this house was leased out so that the rental fees would cover the mortgage repayments, and for this reason we were living in the house of Dominic Chisembele and his family.

Reuben Kamanga suggested that the best way for us was to bid for a property in Chisamba which was relatively close to Lusaka and where several leaders had already purchased properties. Several farms in the area had been lying vacant for some considerable time because the previous white occupiers had left Zambia to resettle elsewhere, particularly in South Africa which was still in the hands of a white minority government. The Agricultural Finance Company [AFC], a government parastatal, had issued a list of vacant properties around the country which were being offered for sale by tender.

Chisembele pointed out to Kamanga that he did not have funds for such a venture but Kamanga advised him that once a bid was accepted on a property it was always possible to apply for a farm mortgage which would be available unreservedly from the AFC.

In the event, later on in October 1971 on tendering for a property in Chisamba for a second time, as the initial tenders received by the AFC from several interested parties were all considered too low, we were successful in our bid. We originally named the property Yusuf Farm but later changed the name to Filalo Farm when we were informed by the Registry that too many properties carried the name of "Yusuf". We moved onto the farm even though there was no water, no electricity and only a partially built skeleton of a house. But after initially agreeing to grant a Capital loan which would cover the property mortgage, machinery and the normal seasonal farming loans for a programme which an AFC representative had helped to draw up for us, the AFC in January 1972 inexplicably withdrew their offer of a Capital loan and we were asked to vacate the farm forthwith. After a very unsettling period, fighting to keep the property for which we had already outlaid what for us was a considerable sum, we were eventually granted a real estate loan in October 1972.

Chisembele embarked on an extensive programme of building and development. The buildings and houses for the labourers were erected physically by Chisembele together with farm workers and contracted artisans in order to minimise the costs. All the buildings were erected with bricks which were made on the farm and the window frames and doors were made from wood cut from trees which we felled on the farm.[102]

Previously, in September 1971 Dominic Chisembele and Frank Chitambala, a politician and appointed UNIP Member of Central Committee, who together had taken over the Baluba Transport Company, which was not actually a transport company but operated a stone quarry in Luanshya, Copperbelt Province, approached Sylvester with the proposition that he should take on the function of transporter for the quarry as they were expecting to be fully occupied with the running of the quarry itself. Sylvester initially refused outright as the idea was wholly impracticable financially, especially given that we had plans to go into commercial farming if our tender to the AFC was accepted, and which would involve heavy financial commitments. Their reaction was to assure Sylvester that their project would be viable and not a difficult operation for him to supervise, moreover they already had in place the financial backing he would need which would be arranged by an American company called TAW International Leasing. TAW International was said to be not merely a business concerned with making profit, but rather an organisation of black Americans wishing to take part and facilitate the development of Africa as a continent. After considerable discussion and several meetings, Sylvester agreed to the proposal.

In October 1971, TAW International Leasing Company purchased two Mercedes Benz tipper trucks which were supplied to Sylvester Chisembele on a lease/purchase agreement. The trucks worked at the Baluba quarry until May 1972, when they were removed by an agent of TAW, called Trio Construction Limited. The reason for the removal by TAW was that we were behind in our lease/purchase payments and this was purely due to the fact that Baluba

---

[102] Folder "Filalo Farm" correspondence, photographs and scans.

Transport Company never paid their bills. TAW then informed Chisembele that on his behalf they had found work for the trucks through their agent, Trio Construction Limited, and so the trucks were put to work for them on an agreed fee. However, Trio Construction Limited also never paid their bills. As a result, we were placed in the ignominious position of failing to meet our debt to TAW whilst at the same time the trucks were actually working for the Agent of TAW. We had no choice but to obtain a loan from Grindlays Bank International (Zambia) Limited in order to regularise the position with TAW.[103] Other work was found for the trucks, but it was intermittent and not viable.

Efforts were made to recover the debts incurred to Chisembele, but all failed. Neither Trio Construction Limited, Baluba Transport Company, nor TAW themselves honoured their commitment. [104] Eventually, in January 1974 TAW repossessed the trucks and sold them. It was a sorry episode in our lives and took us years before we finally paid off completely the debt and interest incurred to TAW and to the bank through this venture.[105]

1972

There was political unrest which was not confined to one province but was particularly prevalent in the Copperbelt and northern part of Zambia. Alex Shapi was a Luapulan, a fellow freedom fighter who had worked with Chisembele during the struggle for independence, he was based in the Copperbelt but he was out of step with the mood in Luapula and the Copperbelt and he was not fully committed to the aspirations of those struggling to achieve a true political democracy. His allegiance was with President Kaunda who had appointed

---
[103] "Chisembele Statement of Events 1971 to 1975", 19.7.75, scan.
[104] Governor of Bank of Zambia, B.R. Kuwani, letter to President Kaunda, 3.10.75, scan.
[105] Grindlays Bank Int (Zambia) Ltd. letter to SM Chisembele, 5.02.73.scan.

him Cabinet Minister for Copperbelt Province where the political situation was not under control. On 23 January 1972 a report appeared in the *Sunday Times* which stated:

> *President Kaunda returned to Lusaka yesterday after a marathon 4 hour Copperbelt Provincial Political Committee meeting in Kitwe ... sources close to the committee state the committee was to have discussed the current political situation on the Copperbelt which Cabinet Minister Alex Shapi has described as "unhealthy".*

In February 1972, a few days after President Kaunda returned from this series of meetings in the Copperbelt, he detained the leader of the UPP, Simon Kapwepwe, accusing him of involvement with white supremacists. A number of his fellow members of the UPP were also detained. Following these arrests the party, United Progressive Party, was banned.

During the same week, we received a visit to the farm by Shadreck Soko, Minister of State, Freedom House (UNIP), who informed Chisembele that President Kaunda had announced the lifting of the suspension from Chisembele and had appointed him Senior Minister of State in the Office of the President. Shadreck Soko brought with him a confirmatory letter and some files. We had not heard of this appointment and Soko expressed surprise that Chisembele was unaware of the development.

Nothing had been heard directly from President Kaunda since the suspension from office in April 1971 and no reason for it had ever been given. Chisembele, therefore, explained to Soko that in the circumstances there was no way he could accept the post because by doing so it would indicate that his acceptance of a junior ministerial position, in effect, meant that he had also accepted a reprimand proving guilt for an undisclosed crime and this he could not do.[106]

This announcement of President Kaunda caused confusion within the leadership of Luapula, Copperbelt as well as other provinces, especially as the press and Zambia National Broadcasting Corporation [ZNBC] TV had also carried erroneous reports that Chisembele had been present and with others was sworn in at a ceremony held by President Kaunda in State House. There was a photograph in the press purporting to show the swearing in; in the case of Chisembele this had not happened for he was not there.

During the same month of February, President Kaunda announced the appointment of a Constitution Review Commission, to be headed by Mainza Chona and known as the Chona Commission, the purpose of which was to bring in a One Party State. It had been known by the former members of the banned Committee of 14 for some time that President Kaunda wanted to change the Constitution in order to bring about his wish for a One Party State and they had campaigned vigorously against it during the 1969 Referendum and the following Chuula Commission.

Over the next few months, Shadreck Soko continued to bring official files and letters to the farm addressed to Chisembele as 'Minister of State' even though the true position and reasons for Chisembele's rejection of this appointment were explained to him. The documents that Soko brought were never accepted and were returned with him. However, Soko, who originated from the Eastern Province and was a friend as well as a colleague, continued to bring official documents to the farm and tried his best to convince Chisembele to accept the position, assuring him that it would be only for a short time and then the President

---

[106] Ibid. Fn.70, Chisembele, letter to Vice-President, 29.10.03, p 7; Cabinet Office, letter to Chisembele, 7.02.72, scan.

would reappoint him to the Cabinet. This phantom post continued to exist at a public level, even though Chisembele never accepted the post or the ministerial emoluments which, unaccepted, were soon stopped by the Ministry of Finance.

In the recurring repeat of history, efforts to have the press and Government rectify the erroneous statements and published reports of his acceptance of the Minister of State position were met with unfulfilled promises that a correction would be issued.

Regardless, the consolidation of Luapula and Copperbelt continued with the leaders emanating from Luapula Province committed to ensure that the province would be represented by popularly elected Luapulans and the Copperbelt properly representative of the peoples residing there.

Chapter 5
1973 – 1977

1973

The Chona Commission had presented its report and recommendations to the President in October 1972 and a few months later, in February 1973, President Kaunda announced the establishment of a One Party State. Sylvester Chisembele and other national leaders had fought hard to prevent the imposition of a One Party State and campaigned against it in the UNIP National Council and outside of it. This had been successfully blocked at the time of the 1969 National Referendum. However, their objections were not successful in 1973 when a One Party State was declared under Constitution changes, brought about regardless of any opposition. This declaration of a One Party State did not have the full support of UNIP leaders and grassroots members of the party in spite of government statements to the contrary.

In the following General Elections of 1973, the first under the One Party State system, with the slogan 'Participatory Democracy' unlike the presidency more than one candidate was allowed to contest a parliamentary seat provided it was under the UNIP ticket. In the Chembe constituency, represented and held since independence by Sylvester Chisembele, his ex-wife, Ba Mayo Paulina Milambo was engineered by President Kaunda to stand against him. Paulina Milambo was of the chieftainship lineage and she became the preferred 'quasi-official' UNIP candidate for Chembe constituency and, alongside all the candidates selected as 'quasi-official' by President Kaunda, was provided with all physical needs, transport, money making it possible to give out supposedly disallowed gifts for voters, et cetera, in order to mount an extensive campaign which was often bitter and harassing.

In the Parliamentary Elections for 1973 Chisembele demonstrated his superior organisational skill throughout Luapula Province where President Kaunda lined up his chosen candidates; for example: in Chembe: Paulina Milambo; in Mansa Central: Wilson Chakulya, Minister of Labour & Social Services who was also a son-in-law of President Kaunda who stood against Stalin Kaushi; in Bahati: a lawyer, Chikako Kamalondo, who stood against Valentine W.C. Kayope. President Kaunda had in situ a Central Committee Member, Mbilishi; a Cabinet Minister and a District Political Secretary full time at Provincial level in Mansa; and at District level a District Governor, Michael Kangombe; Regional Secretary; Womens Secretary; and Youth Regional Secretary in charge of the party. Notwithstanding, Chisembele took direct control of the party at grassroots level so that President Kaunda's opposing functionaries became irrelevant.

All President Kaunda's chosen candidates in Luapula were defeated. Only the candidates selected and approved by the Luapula leaders themselves went through the elections successfully and as a direct result President Kaunda refused to appoint anyone from Luapula into his Government even Clement Mwananshiku who was returned unopposed and, therefore, not a candidate previously rejected by President Kaunda.

Luapula Province had from the earliest days of the struggle for independence been a united political entity and since the attainment of home rule UNIP was the only functioning party in Luapula, and all Members of Parliament were UNIP. This did not change until the fall of Kaunda and the formation of the Movement for Multiparty Democracy [MMD] which took power in Zambia in 1991.[107]

1974 – 1975
Things were moving well both politically and on the farm. Being out of Cabinet gave Chisembele the freedom to organise and direct the political fight for true representation particularly of Luapula Province and the Copperbelt. The leaders at grassroots level were active, motivated and unity of purpose was being maintained, however, harassment continued. On the farm we were doing well. Arable farming was proving not to be viable, and so we had embarked on poultry broiler production which was very promising.

At the beginning of the year, Dominic Chisembele came to the farm and told Sylvester that President Kaunda wanted to bring him back into the Cabinet. I sat in the room with them and immediately pointed out that to do so would jeopardise the progress we were making on the farm which was assisting us to pay off the debts incurred by and through our involvement with the Baluba Transport Company, as well as farm commitments. My words were not well received by Dominic who counteracted with the statement that Sylvester was first a politician and had a duty towards the country which I could not know about or appreciate.

Sylvester had, of course, known and understood all these arguments. He told Dominic during the meeting that he could not go back into the Government especially as we had debts to pay off and in any case there was a Leadership Code

---

[107] Zambia, National Assembly Parliamentary Daily Debates, First Session of the Third National Assembly 30.1.74, column 692, excerpt, scan; Valentine Kayope, "History note", 18.9.10, scan.

which at Cabinet level would mean that he would be prohibited from business activities. He said his priority would have to be to regularise his financial position before any other consideration.

Some weeks later Dominic made another trip to the farm. This time he said President Kaunda wanted to see Sylvester and an appointment had been made for him. He said a car from State House would be sent to collect him.

Privately, after Dominic had left, I asked my husband not to go back into government, but to continue as he was, a serving Member of Parliament. I pointed out that the farming progress we were making would be put in jeopardy and I had no faith that our workers would be as strict as we were as far as vaccination and feeding of the broiler birds especially the day-old chicks, which needed checking throughout the night. Our brooder heating system was basic; we used imbabulas (charcoal open burners, made using cut in half petrol drums with holes made all around the sides) which needed fresh charcoal at intervals, night and day, as the temperature had to be controlled. Our farming methods were unsophisticated but effective. We were beginning to take a hold on the debts incurred by the unsuccessful transport venture as well as meeting our farm commitments and we were still trying to recover the money due to us from Baluba Transport Company, and Trio Construction Limited.

It was against this background that I urged my husband not to rejoin the Government for I was doubtful that we could continue growth without a physical presence on the farm. I also pointed out that whereas now when he was attending Parliament or making trips to the Copperbelt, Lusaka and Luapula Provinces for various political meetings, I was always at the farm to supervise and make sure things were running smoothly; but if he rejoined the Government I would, of course, move away with him and we would have to supervise the farm from a distance which might not be as effective.

However, Sylvester attended the meeting with President Kaunda. He pointed out during their meeting the obstacles which would prohibit him from rejoining the Government. President Kaunda said the important thing was for Sylvester to continue in government leadership and as far as the leadership code and the financial situation were concerned he, President Kaunda, would get these matters looked into but in no way could they be allowed to prevent Sylvester's appointment as Cabinet Minister for Eastern Province which was the post he wanted Sylvester to accept in the national interest.

Sylvester had pointed out that under the rules now in place for ministerial appointments, he could not rejoin the Government because he owned a farming property making him active in business. President Kaunda said this could be overcome and was no obstacle. Sylvester also informed the President that on a personal level he wanted to delay a return to government because his wife had used her savings in the UK to guarantee a bank loan and with the progress being made on the farm, the goal of clearing this particular debt would be achieved in the relatively near future. President Kaunda immediately offered and arranged an advance of five thousand kwacha to clear the lien Grindlays Bank had placed on my savings account in England, and this was done in due course. President Kaunda said that he would arrange for a document to be drawn up on Sylvester's business position which would enable him to legalize the appointment.[108]

President Kaunda had used the familiar language which would certainly appeal to Sylvester of 'duty' and

---

[108] Ibid. Fn.105 Grindlays Bank Int (Zambia) Ltd. letter to Chisembele, 5.02.73, scan; Ibid. Fn.104 Governor of Bank of Zambia, B.R. Kuwani, letter to President Kaunda, 3.10.75, scan.

Personal Story of Sylvester M. Chisembele

'commitment' and he appeared to acknowledge the need for greater democracy in as far as the leadership of UNIP was concerned. Sylvester on explaining this to me told me that, in truth, the independence struggle would not be over until Zambia was free economically as well as politically and he felt an obligation to the country. Sylvester had also been receiving calls from senior leaders and from Luapula and Copperbelt Provinces, in particular, who had been informed by Dominic of the issue, urging him to accept the position, believing that having a voice in Cabinet would assist in the ongoing struggle for real political democracy.

Under pressure from both sides, Sylvester accepted the post and so we moved to the Eastern Province, again into a ministerial house with a rich colonial history. The internal political situation in this province was noticeably quieter than that in the Western Province (Barotseland), but still there was a considerable amount of organisation to handle.

An initial tour was arranged which covered all the Bomas, government institutions and visits of respect on all Chiefs throughout the province. [109] Eastern Province shared international borders with Malawi, and, as in the case of Western Province, also with a colonized territory of Portugal. Portuguese East Africa was officially referred to as the Mozambique Province of Portugal. Mozambique was to obtain independence this year and Portugal had caused many problems along the border resulting from the bitter freedom war between the Portuguese and the Mozambique Liberation Front [FRELIMO]. There were constant border skirmishes, incursions and violations by Portuguese soldiers on Zambian territory.

---

[109] "Chisembele, in Eastern Province". Zambia Information Services, composite photographs.

1976

Chisembele was working hard. The Leadership Code did not in theory allow leaders to run a business while holding office. However, President Kaunda had used his power to 'exempt' certain key leaders who had reasons which could be considered justifiable and others from this regulation. He, therefore, exempted Sylvester from the Leadership Code. [110] The Government then implemented a proviso so that he worked without salary although allowances were to be paid.[111] This stipulation was enforced as far as Sylvester was concerned, but we knew, however, that there was a question mark as to whether it was applied in all cases. The recommendation contained in the report of B.R. Kuwani, Governor of the Bank of Zambia, to President Kaunda that Chisembele should, under the exemption, continue to receive a salary was implemented for just a few initial months and from then on he worked with no salary. [112]

Whilst the exemption from the Leadership Code meant that Chisembele worked without a salary, it did enable us to continue to receive seasonal and development loans for the farm. We were told by the Zambia State Insurance Company that we were an exception in that we had paid on time the due half of a development loan we had received and that they were happy to continue to assist us with further advances. However, I was very much concerned with thefts on the farm and especially worrying to me was the bird vaccination programme which because of our absence from the farm, I

---

[110] President Kaunda, "Exemption letter", 3.3.76, scan; UNIP Secretary General, "Exemption letter" 12.3.76, scan.
[111] Comment: - allowance claims for travel and tours, internal and external, were allowed but even at the time of leaving government service in 1983 the government never fully honoured this commitment in as far as Chisembele was concerned. He left office with nothing and outstanding allowance claims remained unpaid.
[112] Ibid. Fn.104 Governor of Bank of Zambia, B.R. Kuwani, letter to President Kaunda, 3.10.75, scan.

feared, might not be enforced rigorously leaving our birds vulnerable to Newcastle Disease which was a recurring threat to the poultry industry in Zambia.

1977
Chisembele was making many trips by air and by road to Lusaka to attend Cabinet meetings, Parliament, official functions and so on, and we were fortunate in that we had an excellent government driver, Amos Katontoka, a man originating from Mansa who knew the Chisembele family and who became a friend both during and after Chisembele's political career. We were never involved in an accident whilst he was driving, but when circumstances dictated the use of drivers from the government pool, it was not the same story. On the way to Lusaka to attend a meeting using a pool driver, we had an accident when the vehicle overturned three times, the driver ran away but apart from a few bruises, we both walked away shaken but relatively unharmed.[113]

In spite of the difficulties and the long journey by road, which was only slightly more than the approximately 400 miles between Mongu and Lusaka, we were continuing to make progress on the farm and we decided to expand our bird population.[114]

The Eastern Province was home to the Luangwa National Game Park, where President Kaunda had a private lodge which was used for the holding of important talks which, because of South Africa's covert aggression and the sensitive nature of Zambia's border areas, would be announced at the last minute. For example, on 22 February Chisembele was called to Lusaka and left by road, on reaching Lusaka he was

---

[113] Sophena Chisembele, letter to my mother, 13.12.76, scan.
[114] Sophena Chisembele, letter to my brother-in-law, John Ahern, (New Zealand), 22.1.77, scan.

informed that President Kaunda would hold one day's talks with the President of Mozambique, Samora Machel, on 24 February. He left the following day to return to Chipata by road reaching home at 1 a.m. for a few hours rest and by 8 a.m. he was at the airport in Mfuwe to receive the two Presidents. This sort of pressure was commonplace.

Elsewhere, in the Copperbelt Province, an unhealthy political situation had developed. Presidential and Parliamentary Elections were due to be held the following year. Simon Kapwepwe, whom it was announced had been 'forgiven' by President Kaunda for his attempt in 1971 to oppose him, had rejoined UNIP. He was, however, reorganising his base, particularly in the Northern Province and in the Copperbelt. He had previously campaigned together with Harry Nkumbula against the One Party State which when declared by President Kaunda had prevented them from challenging President Kaunda for the presidency and their individual party members from contesting the General Elections under their party banners. The unsuccessful campaigns against the One Party State, had carried a potent message resounding with many people who hated the imposition of a One Party State, but in spite of the welcome involvement of Kapwepwe, popular in Northern Province and with some emanating from that province in the Copperbelt, he was considered by many to be a tribalist and a fanatic. Moreover, as far as Luapula Province was concerned he had never regained his status within Luapula or the Copperbelt since the 'batubulu' incident in 1969 and the attempt to discredit Sylvester Chisembele in order to take control of the Bemba-speaking peoples of Copperbelt, Luapula as well as Northern Provinces.

The harsh approach being used on the Copperbelt by government officials, including the Cabinet Minister and Member of Central Committee, to control the political unrest was doing nothing to improve the situation which was deteriorating by the day. Presidential and Parliamentary Elections were not due until December the following year, but the situation in the Copperbelt did not augur well for a peaceful transition of the intervening period.

On 19 April 1977 Chisembele left for a tour of Luapula which was to last for a week and on this occasion I accompanied him. The situation was reasonably calm, but reports from grassroots leaders were of representatives of Northern Province again campaigning support for Kapwepwe. We returned to Lusaka on 24 April and the following day Sylvester was informed by President Kaunda that he would be transferred to Copperbelt Province in the position of Cabinet Minister and that Shadreck Soko was now appointed Copperbelt UNIP Member of the Central Committee [MCC].

I had a pre-booked visit arranged to the UK to coincide with a visit of my sister to UK from New Zealand and so I left on 29 April. I was not able to accompany Chisembele on his farewell tour of Eastern Province or assist in the move to Ndola, Copperbelt Province.

In June, Sylvester joined me in London for a short private visit to see my family and whilst there we went to see an ENT specialist, Mr Peter McKelvie, who confirmed what we thought that there was a total loss of hearing in his right ear where the eardrum had been shattered, this occurred during the ferocious beating he had endured during an assassination attempt in 1958. Mr McKelvie said the hearing in the left ear was diminished and the loss of hearing in this ear would be progressive with, unfortunately, no solution.

We returned together to Zambia in July and I moved into the Government residence in Ndola; again into a house with history for it was here that Patrice Lumumba the first elected Prime Minister of the Democratic Republic of the Congo was said to have sheltered incognito when trying to evade the eventual horrors of his capture and murder in 1961 by Mobuto and the Belgian Government with the assistance of the USA and British Governments. It was the conflict which developed in the Democratic Republic of the Congo which resulted later in 1961 in the plane crash in Ndola which took the life of the UN Secretary General, Dag Hammarskjold, a hero of integrity and decency.

Although this new posting of Chisembele to the Copperbelt was for us more demanding politically than Eastern Province had been, I was personally pleased with the transfer for it was much closer to our farm and meant it was possible to visit there more often.

There was much to do in the Copperbelt which was and is heavily populated and diverse with its copper mines and industries and, on the social side, it was a major attraction for foreign Heads of State and dignitaries to visit. Sylvester was again in very severe headaches; there was also the pressure of the political situation in the Copperbelt, not the least of which was the campaigns, often underground, at night time and violent, by the supporters of Simon Kapwepwe and Harry Nkumbula and by the retaliation in kind by angry UNIP supporters.

It was a very difficult period and required diplomacy as well as firmness in applying a restraining hand to hold in check the political situation in as far as the Government, the party and the opposition in the province were concerned. Apart from the control exercised by provincial Cabinet Ministers and party MCCs there was the ever present security service which was under the direct control of State House and whose unknown, faceless operators kept under surveillance not only the activities of dissident group leaders, but also on government officials, including provincial Cabinet Ministers and Members of Central Committee, especially those of whom President Kaunda held suspicions.

Chisembele was not immune from this surveillance, particularly so because he had never been a supporter of the

One Party State system, but he believed a change would not come about by the thinking or the methods used by many of Kapwepwe's group and others advocating change by forceful intimidation. His overriding concern was that Zambia should work towards changing the Zambian Constitution in peace without bloodshed. He and others rightfully believed that this British drawn-up document was the cause of the economic and political problems in Zambia, giving as it did absolute dictatorial power to the President right from the start of independence. Chisembele held fast to the belief that until the majority of the population understood this, meaningful, peaceful, lasting democratic change would not come about.

President Kaunda was making frequent visits to the Copperbelt sometimes for tours lasting days and other short but numerous visits, usually to address public rallies. But any hope that President Kaunda may have had that Kapwepwe would now support him was short-lived. Kapwepwe and Harry Nkumbula, who had also been 'forgiven' by President Kaunda and joined UNIP, were busy organising a base from within UNIP to support a challenge both would make to Kaunda's sole candidacy at the forthcoming UNIP National Council; to enable one or both of them to stand in the Presidential Election due the following year, in the same manner that Members of Parliament could be challenged by others on the same ticket in the same constituency provided they were card-carrying members of UNIP.

There were many rumours circulating along the line of rail in the country. Underground, leaders from Northern Province were insinuating that Chisembele was organising for a Luapula take-over and that his private visit in June to the UK was for the soliciting of funds towards this purpose. This further scurrilous campaign was aimed at discrediting Chisembele and thereby uniting the Bemba-speaking provinces under the banner of Kapwepwe which would give him the grassroots strength needed to take over the presidency of the Republic from Kaunda. Given Chisembele's strong spiritual background and contribution not only to independence but also in furthering peaceful development in the country, e.g. in conflict resolution issues in Zambezi District in North Western Province; in Western Province (Barotseland) and in other instances, at no time did or would Chisembele entertain any idea of illegal ousting of a legitimate government.

When we had returned from the UK in July, Sylvester's suitcase went missing at the Lusaka International Airport. As was usual practice, we had been received by officials and taken through the airport via the VIP lounge, which meant passport and luggage clearance was done by them through their direct procedure. Two days later the suitcase was returned to him intact but the signs were that the contents had been rifled through. Earlier in the year in April Sylvester had attended a Cabinet meeting where he had given a talk in support of allowing capitalists to start up industries in Zambia, this was well received. Afterwards the Minister of Legal Affairs and Attorney-General, Mainza Chona, gave him a lift and made a comment which I quote from my diary of 5 April 1977:

SMC (Sylvester Mwamba Chisembele) to Cabinet (Cabinet meeting in State House). He gave a very good speech in support of allowing capitalists to start up industries here. Very good speech well received. Chona gave him a lift in his car afterwards and told him that he, Chona, told people in his Province (Southern Province) that 'you think Mr Chisembele is a nice quiet man but he is a dangerous man'!! Why tell SMC this?

Another disturbing incident occurred when some leaders on the Copperbelt came to Chisembele's office bringing with them some documents and a letter from two prisoners stating that they had been approached while in prison and asked to say that Mr Chisembele had attempted to hire them with a plan to assassinate President Kaunda. A meeting of leaders was held and in view of the serious implications, Daniel Lisulo, a lawyer born in Western Province (Barotseland) who was a nominated Member of Parliament and the following year appointed by President Kaunda as Prime Minister, said the document and a sworn statement from the two prisoners should be kept in his law office for security and this suggestion was agreed. Some years on when attempting to retrieve the documents, we were told that they were somehow lost along the way.

Chapter 6
1978 – 1979

1978

On 22 January, a day after a seminar held over several days in State House, President Kaunda came to Kitwe to start a tour of the Copperbelt, this was a continuance of the frequent visits and tours which the President was making to the Copperbelt.[115] At the end of May, the President arrived in Kitwe, where he was received by Chisembele and other government officials, in order to open the Agricultural Show on 2 June. After the Show was officially opened, one of the President's entourage, Ananias Chongo MCC (a Luapulan) told Sylvester, and I quote from my diary:

> SMC told by Chongo that H.E (President Kaunda) has indicated that SMC is classified person and will never be allowed to become an MCC. I was furious and did a bit of shouting – (why) should SMC build up H.E when he is a confirmed enemy.

I knew the accusation I made was wrong; it was a childish, foolish reaction. Chisembele did not 'build-up' Kaunda, he worked towards change but wanted peaceful change which

---
[115] "President Kaunda and others – Copperbelt Rally" Zambia Information Services, photograph.

he believed would come about when the Zambian Constitution which he called 'rotten' would be re-written and the total power given to an individual removed. But he was always adamant that the peace of Zambia was paramount, quoting the Bemba proverb 'apalelwa insofu chani cifutauka' which means 'when the elephant fight, it is the grass that suffers'. Too many countries in Africa have gone the route of coups d'état resulting in untold misery, starvation and death to the weakest and most vulnerable in their populations and this Chisembele was not alone in believing had to be avoided in Zambia.

However, some weeks later Sylvester was called to a meeting in State House and President Kaunda informed him that he knew the call from Luapula Province was that Chisembele should be appointed a Member of UNIP Central Committee (MCC). President Kaunda said he had heard the call and it was his intention that this would happen at the National Council at Mulungushi Rock, which was to take place in September.

In the meantime we made a private trip to the UK to visit family returning on 26 August in time for the Leaders' Seminar and National Council Conference due to take place at Mulungushi Rock, Kabwe on 7 September 1978. An attempt was made at the National Council by Harry Nkumbula and Simon Kapwepwe to challenge President Kaunda for the presidency this time on the UNIP ticket, but this attempt also failed as both men were prevented and disqualified by the manipulations of President Kaunda. Kapwepwe and Nkumbula later challenged in the High Court the election of Kaunda, who stood as the sole candidate, but their action was unsuccessful.

Some few days into the conference, on 10 September a bombing incident occurred in the Copperbelt and Sylvester immediately left the conference to return to Ndola to investigate the circumstances, returning in the early hours of

11 September. On this day, 11 September 1978 President Kaunda appeared on ZNBC TV to announce the names of Members of the new Central Committee, Chisembele was not included. I was shocked. I quote from my diary:

> *I am very shocked, but I should not be (because) the man is bad and we can only expect bad actions from him. Promises, promises, promises but he never honours the things he says.*

For the next few days in spite of the lessons of history, I continued to be shocked at President Kaunda's duplicity. I was bitter, particularly as I considered that progress on the farm was being held back by our absence working for the Government. As a Lusaka-based MCC we could have moved back to the farm, and even though Sylvester would continue to work with no salary, at least we would be present on the farm.

The day after the announcements were made, Fr Jan Wessels, M.Afr. came to visit and we discussed many things. His visit uplifted my spirit. Sylvester, who was still away, rang and spoke with Fr. Wessels who was always a source of comfort and strength to me. The following day I left Ndola for the farm where Sylvester had gone after the conference. We discussed the issue and it was decided that he would stand for parliamentary re-election, which he would not have done if he had been selected to stand as a Member of the Central Committee.

The 1978 General Elections were held in December. Several Cabinet Ministers and Members of Parliament lost their seats during these elections, some controversially. From the Luapula Province Valentine Kayope and Peter Chanshi had both been vetoed by the UNIP Central Committee in January 1978 and thus prevented from standing. On 9 October 1978 a report was carried in the *Times of Zambia* that Valentine Kayope former Bahati, Luapula, MP, had been involved in an assassination plot against President Kaunda, this was a baseless, fabricated claim. Valentine Kayope was not allowed to stand as a parliamentary candidate in any later Parliamentary Election during the reign of Kenneth Kaunda.

For these 1978 Parliamentary Elections Chisembele was opposed by two others; he was only able to spend three days on campaign in his constituency, when he was suddenly taken ill and brought back to the farm on 18 November. It was a very worrying time, his face was swollen, he had diarrhoea and he was so weak he could hardly stand. I insisted we go to the University Teaching Hospital, [UTH] in Lusaka. When we saw a doctor, he was admitted to the hospital straight away with suspected food poisoning.[116] The doctor told me that Sylvester had enteritis and a swollen liver. Dominic Chisembele sent messages to Mansa through the Zambia Flying Doctor Service to request a delay in the scheduled meetings, at which all candidates vying for the parliamentary seat would be presented at public gatherings, but the District Governor replied to the effect that the meetings could not be postponed.

Chisembele remained in the hospital for over a week and came home still weak but out of danger. He was not able to return to Mansa for the campaign which went ahead, his campaign virtually at an end before it began, although his long-time election agent, Noah Type, did his best to campaign for Chisembele under the restrictions imposed upon him. Chisembele returned to Mansa on 10 December 1978 to be present at the announcement of the election result due to be made on the 12 December 1978. In spite of his absence from the campaign, he was still returned Member of Parliament for Chembe constituency, the seat which he had held since

---

[116] Sophena Chisembele, excerpt of letter to Mrs E. Ali, 6.12.78, scan; D.M. Chisembele, telegram to Mansa District Governor, 21.11.78, scan; Kayope, letter to Chisembele, 30.11.78, scan.; Stalin Kaushi, excerpt of letter to Chisembele, 30.11.78, scan.

independence. His colleagues would say of him *"Chisembele doesn't need to campaign, people will always elect him"*.

After the elections, President Kaunda announced his new Cabinet but he did not include Chisembele, a decision that was welcomed by me, but which confused others, especially Dominic Chisembele who came to the farm to express his views. Dominic and his friend and companion Frank Chitambala had a close connection with President Kaunda and he was not at ease with Sylvester's total freedom of thought and independent nature which were reflected in his politics. Dominic too had been a seminarian but although he had participated in the struggle for independence he was not a politician in that he was never a Member of Parliament or held a political office, although he was a Mayor in the Copperbelt in the early days. He held a directorship in the Bank of Zambia.

This action of exclusion by President Kaunda was to me just a continuation of his usual policy of keeping Sylvester at arm's length until a difficult situation developed that he could not handle and needed the political skills of Chisembele, then he would call him to State House and use the persuasive argument of 'the National interest' and 'the need to prevent bloodshed' to talk him back into the Government. I had also indirectly been indiscreet, a note in my diary for 7 October 1978 reads:

I saw Reuben Kamanga in town and said I do not want to work in Government. SMC told me I was wrong to make any such comment.

As was his way, Sylvester never reproached me or mentioned the incident again.

Personal Story of Sylvester M. Chisembele

1979

In January, we moved from the Government house in Ndola back to Chisamba. During our absence from the farm the rate of thieving had steadily increased affecting the chicken sales so much that I started to fear and hate the going backwards and forwards between ministerial houses and the farm with usually only bad reports to hear and, to me, unbelievable stories of how 2000 birds at one time had died from flooding and of birds at point of sale that would suddenly, mysteriously die. To me, it was really imperative for us to return permanently to the farm and concentrate on recovering the ground that had been lost both financially and in development.

We began to stabilize albeit slowly. We started to rebuild on the farm and make plans to put our development programme back on track, and a few months later a chance came to re-establish our presence in a very pertinent way - in that we staked out the house of market-ready birds and on the night when the thieves came we surprised them, firing a shotgun into the air, causing the group of thieves to scatter with us giving chase. My weapon was a broom. The episode had all the elements of a farce, but it was successful and we had peace for quite a while afterwards.[117]

We were selling live and processed birds to the marketeers and to hotels in Lusaka, such as the Intercontinental Hotel and the longstanding Ridgeway Hotel as well as the Cold Storage Board of Zambia.

A word on our farming programme ... all the broiler houses were made on and from materials mainly available from the farm itself. We had started retaining the major part of our maize crop to use for chicken feed. A grinder and diesel engine were purchased to grind our own produced maize which was then used with bought-in broiler feed

---

[117] Sophena Chisembele, letter to my brother (E. Alison), 5.7.79, scan.

concentrate, vitamins, minerals, etc., to produce our chicken feed. One year we produced so much maize that one of the buildings used for storage was over-stacked, resulting one early morning in a rumbling, strange noise which on investigation proved to be the collapse of the maize storage building.

This programme of producing our own maize was so successful that the profit margin increased quickly allowing us to expand until we were bringing in a new intake of 4,000 birds every week, meaning that at any one time we were holding a stock of 36.000 birds. In fact at one time we were the largest indigenous producers of broilers in the country. Our birds were even being supplied to State House through the Cold Storage Board of Zambia who was the purchaser of the main part of our production.

Our broiler houses were made on the farm with pole and dagga (a type of wall made from mud, clay and perhaps a little cement). The farm covered three and a half thousand acres mostly virgin land covered in trees. The poles were cut from the trees and the dagga made from mud and clay; the flooring too was made from mixing sand and/or clay found on the farm and mixed with cement. The only bought-in materials were cement, iron sheeting and small hardware incidentals such as nails and screws; these items were used for concrete flooring and roofing, not only for farm buildings and workers' houses but also for our house in which we lived even though it had only been partially built and which we completed over the years. Bricks for building workers' houses too had all been made on the farm, again only the cement and roofing were purchased. Window frames and doors for the houses were made from hardwood cut from our farm trees, but the glass panes and a few metal frames were purchased.

The large open-sided structures used for the poultry houses had hessian sacking which was rolled up during the day and let down at night. During the rainy season the hessian sacking was covered with plastic sheeting; both coverings we converted from the sacks and bags in which the broiler concentrate and mealie meal had been purchased. The bags of roller mealie meal were issued monthly to our staff, there being no nearby shops, and in fact we opened a small grocery shop on the farm which supplied essentials to our staff and nearby villages.

The poultry houses whilst looking primitive were admirably suited to our local climatic conditions. The birds thrived and visiting vets and poultry technicians, mainly employed by the Government, expressed surprise at our batch mortality rates which were usually below one or even half a percent, telling us that we were on a par or even lower than the mortality rates achieved by farmers in Europe.

Neither of us had any farming experience, it was the common sense approach adopted by Chisembele and my lesser contribution of the reading of relevant literature that proved to be effective. This enabled us to repay half of one of the capital machinery loans from the Zambia State Insurance Company which was used to purchase the grinding plant and other items exactly on time, which had so pleased them that they were more than prepared to assist us further.[118]

---

[118] "Maize Building Collapse", photograph. Ibid. Fn.102 "Filalo Farm"; Ibid. Fn.104, Bank of Zambia Governor, letter to President Kaunda, 3.10.75, scan.

1. S.M. Chisembele
Lusaka, 1961

Below:
2. Mr and Mrs Michael Chisembele with sons, Joseph and Sylvester

3. Chisembele visiting Chiefs on campaign

PICTURED at Mbeya, Tanzania, on return from China in 1962, Cde Nyirongo (seated right) poses with (standing from left) an unidentified Tanzanian, H. Kikombe and C. Mwananshiku. Seated from left are Sylvester Chisembele, Hankey Kalanga and Isaac Masaiti.

Above: 4. Chisembele and compatriots in China 1962
Below: 5. Return from China via Tanzania 1962

6. Mrs S. Chisembele, Cabinet Minister Sylvester Chisembele Litunga, Mbikusita Lewanika II – Petitions Court, Mongu 1970

7. Sylvester Chisembele and Mrs Sophena Chisembele, - Opening of Parliament - 1975

8. Chisembele arrival Chipata, Eastern Province, 1975

9. S. Chisembele, R. Kamanga, A. Shapi, President Kaunda - Copperbelt Rally, 1978

10. Fr. Jan Wessels – farm visit, Chisamba, 1981

11. Archbishop James Spaita visit Lusaka, 2005

Chapter 7
1980 – 1983

1980

In January, I received urgent messages from my brothers calling me to return to the UK because my mother had been taken very ill to hospital. I returned immediately to London to be with her and my family, my sister too came from New Zealand and we remained with my mother until she died on the 1st April 1980. Whilst I was there I heard that Simon Kapwepwe had died. President Kaunda attending his funeral had shed tears, not an uncommon occurrence with him. During the period when Kapwepwe had tried to challenge him for the presidency, one of the salacious reports that was covered in the Government-controlled media was to the effect that pornographic material was found in his home; even those who did not support or admire Simon Kapwepwe did not believe this slur, not only was it an un-Zambian trait but unbelievable of a man of his character.

Sylvester came to London to attend the funeral of my mother and we returned to Zambia together.

We had an outbreak of Newcastle Disease on the farm and over a period of some months we fought hard to control it. The disease was spread over a wide area resulting in a critical shortage of vaccine. Daily we were collecting hundreds of dead birds from the houses. We battled on but in vain, we were not able to control the outbreak. We had footbaths containing disinfectant outside every bird house to prevent the spread of the disease, but they were ineffective. We even moved the day to week-old young chicks into a brick building well away from the main chicken houses, but all the measures we tried failed. Eventually, we were informed by veterinarians that we would have to completely stop all production, fumigate and sterilise all equipment and then wait at least a minimum of three months before attempting to restart production.

In spite of being out of the Government, harassment was a constant in our lives. In August Sylvester on his way to Parliament made a brief stopover in town, his briefcase was stolen and later returned. A letter I wrote to my brother, on the 15 September 1980, reads:

> *ps Forgot to tell you that Sylvester's briefcase was stolen in Lusaka. It was brought back to Parliament the following day by police. They said it had been recovered in Cairo Road (the main road in Lusaka) from a man who was a thief. When asked by Sylvester if the thief had been arrested they said no because it was a member of the public who took it from the thief who ran away. When asked who the member of the public was, they said they did not know. All his papers were there ... A very odd affair. He had parked and locked the car for only 10 minutes while checking for a market for our mealie meal, when he came back the briefcase was missing, the car had not been broken into. The 'thief' had keys. The car had not been parked in Cairo Road.*

In my diary I have a note: Sylvester is pretty sure that it was the Secret Service who took the briefcase. The police story is ridiculous, they told him that they saw a man walking in Cairo Road with it and they just stopped him and removed it.

Our small farm shop had proved successful but on a very modest scale and so we decided to expand this type of business in town and we rented a small shop in Cha Cha Cha Road. In the meantime, we were busy on the farm renovating, cleaning and fumigating buildings. In December, I went to the UK to purchase items for the Lusaka shop.[119]

We had recently imported a poultry processing plant in order to streamline and improve our chicken production, but in light of the Newcastle chicken disease outbreak and the closure of our unit, we did not install this equipment. However, in the circumstances, we decided that in the meantime we would grind our own maize production, purchase additional maize from NAMBOARD, a parastatal sole official dealer of maize purchased and sold at Government-controlled prices, and then after grinding with an appropriate plate, bag and sell as mealie meal, which is a maize meal ground to a certain fineness and which is the staple food in Zambia; we had been doing this on a very small scale in our farm grocery shop to supplement the mealie meal supplied to our workers and to sell to the villagers around us during the season when their own crops were exhausted.

The shop we rented in Lusaka was eventually opened in April. The sales proved disappointing in that we only managed to cover overheads, but it was not a profit-making concern. The monies due to us from the transport venture which we had, in hope, earmarked to clear commitments were not forthcoming and, in fact, were never paid. In order to clear these, other outstanding debts and to restart our poultry project, this year we took out a second mortgage on our house in Lusaka which was rented out on a lease.

---

[119] Sophena Chisembele, excerpt from a letter to my sister (Dr. Sheila Ahern), 3.11.80 "Business-wise we are doing very little, but we have rented a shop in Lusaka and when a trading licence is granted we shall sell jewellery and groceries, So I shall go to UK to select some stuff for the shop which is called Ethel Ali City Shop. I bet you are wondering at the combination of groceries and earrings! But here that would not be an improbable combination. The farm is more or less at a standstill. We are getting chicken houses reconstructed and chickens will again be kept but in a smaller unit."

Personal Story of Sylvester M. Chisembele

1982

I was feeling very unwell. My sister with her husband and family were in the UK on an extended stay. Both she and her husband, who was a teacher and lecturer in physics, had taken a sabbatical. She had previously written a thesis on the English 16th century printer and publisher, William Harrison, for her M.A. and was now furthering her research in the UK for a Ph.D.

At her insistence, I left for the UK in March 1982 to join them for a short holiday and in order to get a medical check-up. In the event, I remained with them in the UK for almost a year. I was diagnosed with angina and underwent a series of tests in Charing Cross Hospital where I was told that an ECG had indicated some heart irregularities which required further treatment.

During this time, I accompanied my sister to Cambridge University where she was in consultation with a professor. This was a particularly poignant period because as children during the Second World War we had been evacuated first to Brighton and then to Royston, Cambridgeshire and one of the few memories I have of my father is that of a rare leave when he had taken the family on a row boat along the River Cam. Cambridge was the place my mother took us to for family days out during the several years we lived in "The Old Bank House", Royston with six other evacuee families, each allocated a single room with a communal kitchen and bathroom.

Before I left for this trip to the UK, we had resumed our chicken production, initially on a smaller scale and we changed our intake schedule to monthly instead of weekly. Cold Storage Board of Zambia were no longer purchasing birds as a new parastatal had taken over, called the Poultry

Zambia – The Freedom Struggle and the Aftermath

Development Company of Zambia, with whom we had negotiated a contract to supply. This was going well.[120]

It was my custom on a trip to the UK or to New Zealand for that matter to finance my living expenses by working as a temporary stenographer, usually through the Brook Street Secretarial Bureau and during this extended visit to the UK one of my assignments was with Toughs Insurance Company in Chiswick, West London. I had the relative luxury of using an electric typewriter which took away the heavy pressure needed on the keys of the manual machines to which I was used. In August, for the first and only time in my life I surprisingly developed a real pain in my wrist preventing use, this was diagnosed as repetitive strain injury. Some days later I received a letter from Sylvester telling me of a serious car accident he had when passing through the Pedicle Road, Zaire (Democratic Republic of the Congo) on his way back from Luapula Province. The road was not tarmac, but dirt and some sharp, unnoticeable debris strewn beneath the surface of the road had caused the accident. He was returning from a constituency tour and meetings with political colleagues in the province, which had been held in Mansa. Among other injuries, he had hurt his wrist and hand. The accident had occurred the same day I had developed the problem with my wrist; this was a strange coincidence the like of which seemed to permeate our lives. He wrote in a letter I received from him dated 28 August 1982:

> *I was not surprised to read that you developed pains around your wrist, hand, then the arm the same night after my accident, because it was just unbelievable how I could work otherwise ... The doctor gave me straight away five days to be in bed resting. I have never rested even a single day since ... I*

---

[120] Chisembele and Mwale Chisembele letters to Sophena Chisembele, 28.5.82 and 19.6.82, scans.

am sorry darling for all the pain you underwent but to be open to you as you know if my health would have been so bad to stop me even a day's work, it would have been a disaster to chickens. However, things and the situation is coming down as we are linking our chain ... My wrist is a thing which gives me pain ... There will be a Luapula Provincial Conference on 14th September 1982 ... held in Kawambwa ...

Chisembele was due to attend a Commonwealth Parliamentary Conference in the Bahamas and it was arranged for me to join him from London. The wives of several other delegates from various Commonwealth countries also accompanied their husbands to this particular conference and a separate programme of events had been arranged for us. Sylvester duly passed through the UK and spent some few days with my family. We went on together to the conference held in the Paradise Island Hotel from the 10th to the 24th October 1982. We returned via London and stayed together with my sister's family for a further two weeks after which Sylvester returned to Zambia. I remained in London as I still had appointments to attend at Charing Cross Hospital. On his return to Lusaka, at the airport he had been received, as usual practice, by officials through the VIP lounge, but again it was a familiar story of his suitcases missing. Some days later the suitcases were found in the airport and when collected were seemingly undisturbed.

1983
Since May 1982, I had been receiving treatment and undergoing various tests at Charing Cross Hospital which continued until the beginning of February 1983. But finally, I returned to Zambia on the 23rd of February 1983. The farm was extremely active as Sylvester during my absence had increased the chicken population. Shortly after I arrived back

onto the farm it was invaded by a herd of elephant. The elephants had come via a nearby village where, unfortunately, they had caused some damage and they had made our farm their home. The Wildlife Authority apparently had been tracking this herd for months and their game rangers came with the hope of chasing the herd away, but they failed to frighten them off and had to kill one beast. The elephants came back and it was a sad thing that they had to kill again before the herd eventually moved away.[121]

In May, Sylvester decided not to renew the expired lease on our house in Buckley Township, Lusaka. The house had been leased to Motor Holdings Limited part of the Lonrho group of companies, for several years. His decision was made because I had been diagnosed with coronary heart disease and Sylvester wanted me to have an easier time and be nearer medical assistance. An ability to stay in town would provide this, if needed. We were traveling most Sundays from Chisamba to Lusaka in order to attend St Ignatius Church, a distance of slightly more than 50 miles. By taking back the house, we could remain on the farm throughout the week and spend the weekend in Lusaka and when Parliament was sitting we could reverse the arrangement and spend the weekends at the farm.

In June, Sylvester was contacted by Lonrho and asked to come and see the Managing Director. We thought it was probably to do with the house because they had not been happy with our decision to repossess the property on the lease expiry date. However, Sylvester went to the appointment on 29 June. I quote from my diary:

SMC to Lonrho. Nothing to do with the house. M.D. offered to help SMC in any way at all. Wants to go into some business with SMC. Wonderful opportunity or danger?

---

[121] Sophena Chisembele, letters to Dr. Sheila Ahern, 20.3.83 and 11.4.83, scans.

Personal Story of Sylvester M. Chisembele

Among other inducements, Sylvester was told that our son Mwale could be sent overseas for further schooling. Sylvester was sure that this was a political ploy, he told me he had been surprised by the content of the meeting but had been non-committal. He said that he would not be taking up any such offer.

In October, there was another outbreak of Newcastle Disease in the country, we carried out the same precautions as we had previously but could not prevent the disease from spreading into our farm. Again there was a shortage of vaccine in the country and we attempted to import vaccine and other chicken formulas, but we could not get the necessary import licence, the import of these items apparently and weirdly, it seemed to me, was restricted to poultry breeders. We appealed the refusal decision but without success. However, the losses were not on the same scale as the previous outbreak.

Sylvester had not been brought into the Government by President Kaunda during the 1978-1983 parliamentary term, but prior to the lodging of nomination papers for the 1983 General Elections, President Kaunda called him to a meeting in State House. The President told him that he knew how difficult it had been for Sylvester to supervise his farming activities in Chisamba when he had appointed him Cabinet Minister for Copperbelt Province and, he said, that in the forthcoming elections, he wanted him not to stand for re-election because it was his intention to nominate him and then appoint him Cabinet Minister for Central Province. President Kaunda told Sylvester that as he would be based in Kabwe, he would be very close to Chisamba and well able to run the farm.

However, Sylvester thanked the President but declined the suggestion explaining that he was not willing to become a nominated Member of Parliament because as a leader and democrat he believed that he should only represent the people of his constituency provided they elected him.

During the election period, Chisembele was in Mansa. Sylvester was well received as he always was whenever he visited his constituency and we had no cause to doubt the result, but when the counting of votes was taking place, after several delays, both he and his election agent, Noah Type, were not allowed to be present.[122] This was not the usual practice and it was a shock result to hear that Chisembele had lost his seat. There was disbelief and a commotion. Several other former sitting Members of Parliament from various provinces also lost their seats; a pattern was emerging of people who had not pleased President Kaunda losing their seats.

Sylvester was urged by political leaders within and without Luapula Province to challenge the election result, as others were intent on doing. When he returned to the farm, where I was staying as I always did during his absences, I had had sufficient days for the shock to settle and I told him I thought it was time for him to retire from politics and concentrate on our personal life.

My family held Sylvester in high esteem and had always been supportive, especially so my sister who even covered my travel expenses on visits I made to New Zealand. My brother had for some time been advising Sylvester to retire from politics and concentrate on personal business. I am not in a position to judge myself, but I was thought culpable within the Zambian family and political circles for Sylvester's refusal to challenge the robbed election of 1983.

---

[122] Comment: I have no note on the reason in my diary, but from memory the reason was that counting had been delayed several times and candidates were told to leave and return later, but when Mr Chisembele and Mr Noah Type did return at the given time they were told counting had already begun and they could not be allowed to enter.

Personal Story of Sylvester M. Chisembele

My most pressing reason was that there had been yet another serious attempt on his life during the campaign, from which he had had a narrow escape. We did not have a suitable vehicle to use for canvassing and so shortly before the campaign began, in September 1983, we had purchased a sturdy second-hand Renault 4 from Fr. Jan Wessels, M.Afr. for this purpose. [123] Fr. Wessels was a special, longstanding family friend and on several occasions stayed with us. [124] His ties with the Chisembele family went back a long way to the time when he a White Father (now called Missionaries of Africa) was stationed in Mansa, he had known and regularly visited with Michael Filalo Chisembele. Fr. Wessels had been transferred from Mansa in 1983 and was now stationed in Ndola, Copperbelt Province.

As was common practice during an election campaign the vehicle was parked at night in the Mansa Police compound. On this particular morning, Sylvester had collected the car and started to drive back to Chisamba for a short break during the campaign and on travelling through the Pedicle Road the car went off the road and overturned causing him injury. The police from Mansa collected the car and after it had been examined Sylvester was told that the cause of the accident was that the steering column was broken and had been tied up with string. There was no way that this vehicle had been purchased in that condition, the only possible explanation was that it had been tampered with whilst in the Mansa Police compound. When informed, Fr. Wessels was shocked and dismayed assuring us that the vehicle was in good condition when handed over to Sylvester, not that we needed such an assurance, we never for a moment thought otherwise.

---

[123] Fr. Jan Wessels, M.Afr. excerpt letter to Chisembele, 27.10.83, scan.
[124] Fr Jan Wessels, composite photographs.

Zambia – The Freedom Struggle and the Aftermath

Whilst still stationed in Mansa in 1981 Fr. Wessels had been threatened with deportation; this issue, unasked, Chisembele took up with the Minister of Home Affairs who expressed ignorance of the matter. The threat eventually faded away. Fr. Wessels died in Holland in 1989.[125]

The car accident was serious and the car was a write-off. This was not the first or last attempt on Sylvester's life, but it was the second serious car accident during this election campaign and in considering this together with his severe headaches and the need to rebuild the farm, it is true that I urged him to retire from politics and concentrate on us.

I felt that he had done enough as far as the country was concerned and that it was time to put family first, but even more important was the health issue, the headaches he suffered from were terrible and debilitating. I complained to him as I had more than once that he allowed President Kaunda to 'use' him when a situation developed and then push him aside when he felt things were quiet enough. I knew in my heart that this was not true. As previously stated Sylvester was a true nationalist, wanting Zambia to develop in peace and firmly believing that the end of President Kaunda's dictatorship would be brought about through a groundswell of public rejection which would also bring the Constitution issue to the fore. However, in the event he agreed that the time to retire had come while he was still young and fit enough to build a solid foundation for our future.

Meanwhile, the poor economic performance in the country saw President Kaunda accepting and introducing the International Monetary Fund [IMF] economic restructuring programme for Zambia. However, once the implications of

---

[125] "Fr. Jan Wessels with Chisembele", photographs and correspondence, February 1981, scans.

this programme filtered down to the general population it was not a welcome development.

Within a few months, the effects of this programme were biting into the daily lives of people everywhere ... the towns, the villages, in fact, in every part of the country.

PART THREE

Life and Events after Retirement
1984 – 2009

Chapter 8

Some words on the youth and character of Sylvester Mwamba Chisembele

At this point, I will attempt to describe something of the youth and character of Sylvester Chisembele. At birth he was given the names Sylvester Chisunkanya Chinyamano Chisembele; but on reaching maturity he would not use his real, traditional names (amashina ya pamutoto) because they carried extraordinarily powerful meanings: Chisunkanya meaning 'revolunionist' and Chinyamano meaning 'full of new ideas and of wisdom'. He said that he did not want the influential hold such names placed on him and so he adopted the name Mwamba in their stead

He had a charisma difficult to explain. He was self-effacing, so quiet and unassuming that he sometimes gave the impression that he had not taken on the implications of this or that issue with his low-key reception of difficult news, but usually problems would be solved or the impact lessened and hostilities between people would ease or even disappear. No matter how insignificant a person he would listen without impatience until they were through, even to the irritation of others who might also be attending any meeting, personal or political.

Sylvester was the third surviving son of Michael and Salome Chisembele, born and brought up in Fort Rosebery (Mansa). His parents were different to others living in the village for they were practising Catholic Christians. They had married in 1917 in a ceremony officiated by a Catholic priest, Fr. Rose. Several children were born to them but these children died soon after birth. People in the village would not eat food with them, believing that visiting demons were killing their children. They were an object of derision among those who had not yet accepted Christianity and a frequent taunt was *"If your God is so great, why can you not produce a child to stand"*. Their faith did not waver and eventually in 1921 Salome Chisembele gave birth to a son who did survive; he was followed by a sister and 5 brothers. All of whom grew to adulthood.

Michael Filalo Chisembele and his brother, Romano Filalo Lupambo, in the early years of the 20th century, trekked from Mporokoso, Northern Province to Fort Rosebery in Luapula Province. Romano the elder brother went ahead and Michael Chisembele followed. With time, the two brothers became the most respected leaders in the surrounding villages and with friends started building the first Catholic Church in Fort Rosebery at Esekiya's village. In 1920, they had been given permission, after much trouble from the District Officer, a Mr Stocks, to build a Church. When it was finished, the District Commissioner called them and accused them of building a school, not a Church and ordered them to stop using the building.

Michael Chisembele and Romano Lupambo then informed the priest at Lubwe Mission, in Samfya who took up the matter with the District Commissioner and eventually after a meeting held between the District Commissioner, Fr. H.V. Fwengeni, and the District Officer, they were allowed to use the building as a Church. But after this permission was granted the District Officer then warned them that if they did not use the building for prayer every day, they would be arrested.

Subsequently the two brothers with their converts started building another church in bricks in the Chimese villages. In 1923, there was much opposition and difficulties with the colonial administrators, but undaunted they continued and later the brothers built the first Catholic school. The opposition from the administration to the building of Catholic schools continued for years, even later in 1957 the Jesuit priests were prevented by the authorities from opening a multi-racial college for boys over the age of fifteen, to be called St. Augustine's College, under a Government policy that multi-racial education should not be extended below university level.

By 1925, Romano Filalo Lupambo and his brother Michael Filalo Chisembele had organised groups of people to preach in the name of the Catholic Church in all the villages in Chimese, Mabumba, Kalaba, Chipasula and Shimumbi areas. Chiefs Chimese, Mabumba and Kalusa welcomed them wholeheartedly inviting them to preach in their areas and Chief Kandafumu and his subjects called upon them to start teaching their children. As a result of the amazing evangelical progress they made, the priest at Lubwe Mission sent Michael Chisembele to Rosa Mission to be trained as a teacher. There is more written history of this early period recorded by Michael Filalo Chisembele in his diary.

The contribution to the establishment of the Catholic Church in Mansa by Michael Filalo Chisembele and his brother Romano Filalo Lupambo was recognised and they received a Citation from the Vatican during their lifetimes. After the death of Michael Filalo Chisembele in 1973, Bishop Pailloux wrote a letter to Sylvester Chisembele in which he stated that:

> *I have no doubt that your good father has received his reward in heaven. The priests of my generation will never forget that it was he and Ba Romano Lupambo who established the*

Personal Story of Sylvester M. Chisembele

Catholic Church in Mansa, and that they did suffer in so doing. Whenever I think of them, they remind me of Paul and Timothy ...[126]

Sylvester Chisembele grew up against this Catholic background. As a boy, he had a difficult start with illness and he was different from his brothers and the children in the village, in that he was quiet, contemplative, obedient, earnest and respectful. His elder brother Joseph and Joseph's group of friends were bright, outgoing boys full of fun and mischief. When the elders would gather in an evening for a special occasion, they would do so around a big fire; the women previously would have prepared drums of munkoyo, a sweet non-alcoholic drink made from maize meal, and drums of katubi and katata alcoholic beers made with finger millet or sorghum, and/or other substances. They would also have prepared a feast, which would be eaten first by the men and then the remainder would be for the women and children. Joseph and his friends would be sent to call the surrounding villagers to come for the celebration and also sent running to buy tobacco as and when required.

It didn't take long for the elders to realise that Joseph and his group were the wrong children to send on errands. Joseph and his friends would run off, loiter some distance away larking about and then come back with the report that this village or that village could not come because they had gone to the bush for hunting or for some other believable reason. In this way, the boys ensured that the children and women who would be last to eat at their designated place would surely get some of the choice food as well. These tricks of

---

[126] Hansard HC Deb 04 June 1957 vol 571 cm1108; Ibid. Fn.38 Michael Filalo Chisembele, diary; Bishop of Mansa, René-Georges Pailloux, M.Afr. letter to Chisembele, 20.5.73, scan.

Joseph and his group became well known and for this reason Sylvester was later frequently on call and he became the boy chosen for errands; his change would always be exactly right and his messages correctly delivered.

When as a child of 12 he was selected to go to the Lubushi Seminary in Northern Province, he was put in the care of a white lady who was travelling to Kasama. His father, Michael Chisembele had made his school shorts and shirts and he was sent off with his precious bag, warned to be a good boy and not to leave the side of the white lady. At one break in the long journey, they went to the District Commissioner's home to spend the night and Sylvester was told by the driver that he and the driver would go to sleep in the native compound, which was some distance from the house. Sylvester refused, telling the driver that he had been ordered not to leave the side of the lady. After failing to persuade him, the driver reported the problem to an indoor servant. The Commissioner himself and Sylvester's travelling guardian came out, amused, and Sylvester was brought into the kitchen of the house, fed and he slept there on a blanket on the floor. When he eventually reached the Seminary, the Father Superior delighted by the story called him into his office and asked him to relate the journey. When Sylvester told him of how he spent the night, the Father Superior smiled. He had heard all this from the travelling guardian but wanted to hear it again from the boy. It was an amusing incident of a little African lad who had actually spoken to a feared District Commissioner and 'demanded' the right to sleep under the same roof!

On a later occasion when his younger brother, Dominic, had also been selected for the Seminary, they were travelling back to Kasama by bus with a fellow student, Albert. At Mbenge, the bus which had no window panes had a puncture. All the passengers and the driver left to go to a nearby village to sleep, but Sylvester convinced Dominic and Albert that they must stay with their luggage by the bus. The boys collected firewood and they made a big fire to sleep around. Some time later, one of the boys roused the others to say that he could hear lions murmuring. Then a big male lion came prowling near the fire and they could hear villagers shouting *"close your doors, lions are here"*. The boys scrambled back on the bus and spent midnight to morning banging on an empty petrol drum to keep the lions scattered away.

During their holidays, the boys had visited a lady called Sabina at Chembe pontoon. She was a coloured lady and she talked to the boys about the whites and how they subjugated coloured and black people and even though these white people had their own lands they were not satisfied, but came to other peoples' lands and took them away. The first political action that Sylvester took was on their way home he picked up a stone and threw it at a white settler's vehicle. But actions of that sort were out of character and, he soon realised, futile.

Sylvester spent six years at the Lubushi Seminary. He was obedient, truthful and very quiet in his demeanour, but he was also questioning, wanting to know why men who were all the children of God and loved by God were treated differently; why the words in the bible were different to the way people lived; why were black people not allowed into the shops; why did they have to have permits when they travelled and so on. He wanted to know what made white people better and he could not accept that he was of an inferior race, he wanted to know where in the bible or in the teachings of Jesus it was said that white people were superior.

Sylvester's days at the Seminary were in the main happy and although he had the reputation of being difficult, he was a deeply religious boy and he was well liked by the priests with the exception of his latter-day house priest (who later returned to Germany as the harsh conditions had taken a toll on his physical and mental health) who took a dislike to him, considering him to be obstinate and a disruptive influence with his questions on equality and other philosophical issues. Sylvester had an inquisitive nature, always wanting to know the reason behind actions or words. He also on one occasion was at fault for being found sitting at a piano attempting to play, this was a breach of the rules as he had not been selected or given permission to touch the piano. This minor incident was considered serious and punishable by his house priest.

When eventually after six years of study he was told in 1948 that he must leave the Seminary, he was of the mindset that he must organise people to reject what he already knew was the slavery and subjugation of the indigenous people.

He had studied and greatly benefited from the philosophy taught by the priests. He began organising and quickly rose to prominence in the political field. He was a brilliant organiser and people responded to the calm, gentle, rational way in which he talked of the right of all God's people to be equal in the eyes of men, and in particular in the eyes of the very laws imposed upon them by the occupying colonial rulers. On a public platform, he spoke with passion, logic and could rouse people to a degree where they would be prepared to accept suffering, imprisonment and worse for the belief in their Cause. He had a courage that was tested and proven beyond doubt.

Apart from beatings and imprisonment there was an occasion, not unique, when at a public meeting the Senior Security Officer, Belman, pulled a gun on him causing pandemonium and a stampede. Sylvester remained calm and unmoved; incidents like this and others gained him such a respect and reputation among the people because they saw and knew that he lived by the rational Christian beliefs which he accepted as true. He did his best to convey the need to hate the deed but not the man and to fight for independence through a logical interpretation of the very law of the colonialists themselves alongside the higher law of God and on an accepted, just, basis of equality in the eyes of God and the Law.

In spite of the ordeals and sufferings he endured, he retained all his life a sweetness of nature but this gentleness of Chisembele did not mean that he was retiring or reticent in any way, no! not at all. In 1970 whilst we were in Mongu we went to the Teachers Training College run by the Holy Cross Sisters where Sylvester addressed the students. After he had delivered his address we went for light refreshment with the Sisters, and I was told that his talk was *"the best sermon the girls had ever received"*. Long after we had left Mongu we remained in contact with the Sisters and, in particular, Sister Maurice, a dedicated and selfless person.

But when we were stationed in Eastern Province at the start of our time there, we went on a tour of all the districts. Chisembele addressed many political meetings and visited with each local District Governor and other government and party officials, various institutions including secondary schools. At one government boys secondary school (I believe it was in Lundazi or Chizongwe – we covered all the secondary schools in the province) there was an audience of 500 plus boys and when we entered onto the platform and had sung the National Anthem, noise broke out. The headmaster introduced Chisembele, but the noise only simmered down slightly. He was reading a prepared speech but, because of the noise, deviated and started telling them to behave and listen and then began talking about the sacrifices their parents had made to give them the chance of education; but the noise, veering towards derision, continued. Suddenly, shockingly he smashed his fist down on the table, shattering a glass standing alongside the water container. There was instant silence. We were all stunned. He stood there with blood dripping from his hand seemingly oblivious to the pain and with fury he started talking about the political struggle and the sacrifices, including deaths that people had endured to bring the country independence, human rights, dignity, freedom which, he said, they seem to find amusing. He continued in this vein for some time and then talked of the God given incipient greatness that lies within every human being and reminded them of the huge landmass of the country and the need and the opportunity they received as a free gift to get the skills in whatever field of learning they wished. He told them to take up the challenge to develop themselves and their country. When he had finished we left the platform, still in total silence. When we passed through the hall doors, a roar of noise broke out; but they had heard and hopefully had taken something positive from the talk. A medic had been called in who removed glass splinters from his hand and dressed it. Days later, his hand was terribly swollen and on returning to Chipata he had to receive further medical treatment.

Chisembele was patient to the extreme but when faced with blatant rudeness, intolerance or his integrity questioned he certainly would react, prior to independence and afterwards, and if he were provoked beyond endurance, he would react with ferocious, fearsome anger. He possessed a natural humility and in normal communication with people he was soft spoken and always ever respectful, but on occasions, when fighting an issue with government officials, prior and after independence, (I have an example in mind of the seizure of our farm and property after he had retired from politics, and which we knew to be politically motivated) he would patiently follow the laid-down procedure; but the odd official or individual, who did not know him and who in arrogance, mistook his humility for inferiority would treat him with contempt and disrespect - this would be to their cost, his reaction and anger would be formidable - of course, I do not mean with physical violence on a person.

Personal Story of Sylvester M. Chisembele

Whenever Chisembele addressed public or private political meetings, he would take you painstakingly through a given situation, talk of its beginning, how and why it started, where it was going, where this path would take you and where another path would lead. He would talk of aspirations, pitfalls and the consequences each option might bring; he would take you through step by step and then at the end he would say ... *"You make your decision"*. He would sweep you along, inspire you and he would always give others the chance to challenge or suggest. The final decision would usually be carried by a judgement that appealed to reason, human rights and the better side of human nature. If, however, the decision went in a way he did not think right, that decision would stand, always provided a majority vote was obtained. There would be no intimidation, coercion or threats.

Chisembele had the propensity to shy away from personal publicity. He had no qualms in taking a back seat and never sought publicity or acknowledgement for his own part in the achievement of independence. At no time did he stop his participation in the onward struggle for democracy which he believed was the only way Zambia could develop a just and fair society. He was the most effective political organiser in the country, a fact that President Kaunda even though he was his enemy, both before and after independence, freely acknowledged.[127]

At one Cabinet meeting, the question came up of giving women the right to obtain financial contribution for their children from the paternal parent, married or not. It was decided that Zambia was not yet in a position to impose such

---

[127] Ibid. Fn.6 "Zambia The Politics of Independence", David C. Mulford, (Oxford University Press, 1967), excerpt scan; ibid. Fn.78, Kayope, "Eulogy for Chisembele", 9.2.06, scan.

a ruling. Chisembele had supported the proposal and after speaking on it, several other ministers seemed ready to change their opinion. President Kaunda stood up and asked why they allowed themselves to be swayed by Comrade Sylvester. The idea was put on hold.

Sylvester also had the ability to revive flagging morale, for example: when we were stationed in Chipata we had travelled in a Land Rover over hundreds of miles and reached our farm in Chisamba very late in the night. We were five people and all very tired. When we entered the house, it was in pitch darkness. We lit candles (there was no electricity) and found the floors in the kitchen and dining room covered with thousands of red ants well on their way through the house. We were weary and dispirited, we certainly did not want to start a battle with ants at that hour, but the ants could not be ignored – they have a stinging bite.

Sylvester with candle in hand suddenly started dancing the Twist (a dance in vogue at the time) on top of the poor ants, he had us all laughing and then we set to preparing imbabulas (a type of brazier) to boil water for flushing and sweeping out the ants and putting around the affected parts of the house exterior barriers consisting of lines of mealie-meal, flour and oil. Sylvester and Amos Katontoka, our driver, diverted the course of the ants and set them off in another direction. He had the ability to draw out the best, even amusement from certain difficult situations and encourage people around him. He could revitalize, renew hope and banish disillusionment when it seemed that a particular endeavour was going nowhere. He was a man of courage notwithstanding the brutality he endured at the hands of the colonial administration. He was rarely dogmatic but on those rare occasions when he had to be, he would always explain in great detail the reason.

Naturally, Sylvester Chisembele had faults. One of which might perhaps be that he had a deference to prayer. He said several Rosaries a day and he would never leave the house without completing his morning prayers. This would make us late for functions or even for Church (when we were at the farm in Chisamba we had a 60 mile drive and from our Buckley house an 8 mile drive to St Ignatius Church in Lusaka). Many a time the family would be dressed and prepared, but we would have to wait on him until he was ready.

In private life, he would not quarrel. He would become quiet and distant withdrawing into himself. If I am to be totally truthful he was at times a difficult person to live with, but so sincere and honest that those occasional difficult times were a small price to pay for the privilege to be with someone such as he.

And perhaps another failing would be that he could do wonderful things and be successful in any enterprise that he really wanted to do, but often people around us, including family members, exploited that understanding, tolerant side of his nature to our cost and to a degree insensible to me.

Chisembele was ambitious, but this ambition was not personal but on a national level. He wanted the country to develop in peace and lives to be bettered, especially for the poor. It may be a fault that he was not prepared to claim or fight for a position in the Government for which his intellect and political stature qualified him, in spite of urgings from leaders around him, especially from Luapula Province. At independence, he accepted the junior position of Minister of State. People could not understand this, expecting that he would be appointed into the Cabinet and urged him to insist on a post of seniority for which they were prepared to demand through action. But though he was an idealist he was also realistic and he knew that President Kaunda held an

Zambia – The Freedom Struggle and the Aftermath

enmity towards him that dated back to the Magoye Conference,[128] and he believed that individual positions which were, in truth, dependent on the will of President Kaunda, held no real power for change. He was, therefore, more concerned that at the start of independence the provinces should be unified so that tribal differences should not be allowed to cause splits which would be far more dangerous to the peaceful development of the country. To be honest, I did not understand either why he would not assert himself as far as personal ambition was concerned.

Chisembele was a religious man. A committed Catholic, but though he lived by faith and belief in the Church, he did not follow without conviction.[129]

It seemed at odds that in spite of the years of affliction and the difficult experiences that he had gone through, which appeared to leave no visible sign on him except physically in the loss of his hearing and constant headaches, that there was a sweetness and innocence about Sylvester Chisembele. Sometimes he would speak of an incident using words so descriptive that it would become unbearable and you would have to turn your head away because the pathos or emotion his words engendered would become too much, and yet he would be speaking in his normal manner, unaware of the effect his words were having. He rarely talked about himself and perhaps it goes without saying that he was absolutely faithful to any commitment which he undertook with conviction.

During my life, I have seen this characteristic of sweetness and innocence in a few other people. I think I should say that I found in the most part that it was in people with a deep belief in God. I don't know whether I ought to single out individuals, but I saw it in Fr. M. Kelly SJ an inspirational

---

[128] Ibid. Fn.29 "National Assembly Debates 4.12.91".
[129] Ibid. Fn.4 "Documents Submitted to ECHR 29.4.04" - Claim Reports 1-5 p 2.

priest who served many years in Zambia; in a Church of England minister who was a patient of Dr. Gordon Latto; and in an old man who worked as an odd-job carpenter on our farm. This old man had previously worked for years in a Catholic mission but had been retired and he was no longer able to produce accurate work and would need to do again and again, but when I complained to him about the quality of his work, he would always answer me with such apologetic sweetness that I would go away feeling guilty and hating the need to criticize a man more than old enough to be my father. I wanted to remove him from the workforce because he was too old, but Sylvester would not hear of it, that was in our early farming days when we were struggling so hard to establish ourselves and meet many commitments. He was rarely inflexible, especially with me, and we could ill afford to carry people, but there was nothing I could do about it. And perhaps this could be counted as one of Sylvester's failings, but, of course, it depends on the point of view. I know that there are many good and decent people in the world and that heroism is everywhere, in the religious and in the secular, but it seems to manifest itself visibly, rarely in just a few here and there. I have met many people from all walks of life and persuasions but the people whose memories have remained and influenced me the most have usually been those who live by faith.

I will end this attempt to describe in brief a part of Sylvester Chisembele's character by saying that whenever on a public platform, forum or a private meeting he talked away from a prepared script, he was the most sincere, inspirational person I have ever heard or met.

Chapter 9
1984 – 1990

1984

Now that Chisembele was retired from active politics, we concentrated on the farm. As well as poultry we decided to continue with arable farming and expand into vegetable production. The shop we were renting in Cha Cha Cha Road, Lusaka in which we were selling groceries and inexpensive costume jewellery, was barely meeting its overheads, and so we decided that we would convert it into a restaurant, which would also be an additional outlet for our farm produce and, at the same time, would keep our restaurant production costs to a minimum.

The premises were being rented from the Zambia National Building Society [ZNBS] and although under the terms of the lease certain basic requirements fell under their responsibility, i.e. an electricity supply, water and upkeep of the building, the ZNBS did not meet its commitments or maintain the several other shop premises it leased out. There had been no water supply directly into the premises; the only water available was from a tap and sink servicing several shops situated in an alley at the back of the row of shops. The shop we occupied consisted of one very large room fronting the Cha Cha Cha Road, the walls were cracked and unpainted, the roof leaked and the electricity was supplied by just one bare overhead light bulb in the centre of the room. When we had moved into the shop in 1981 we had improved it considerably, with unmet promises from ZNBS to refund the costs involved. In fact, to convert the room into a restaurant was a substantial undertaking in that it needed to be partitioned, repainted, 3 phase electricity and water installed and an internal infrastructure put in place. Much of the interior building work and renovation we did ourselves using artisans, only bringing in Zambia Electricity Supply Co. [ZESCO] to check and approve the wiring and thereafter supply the property with the increased load required; and the local Government Water Department to approve the piping.

It took several months to complete the renovations, all of which were done after discussion and with the permission of the ZNBS who promised to meet that part of the costs incurred relating to the actual building and basic installations, e.g. the water connections, upgrading the electricity to a 3 phase commercial supply, the building materials for the interior wall partitioning and including a new roofing. In fact, ZNBS were extremely pleased to have their property restored and maintained in the way we did. However, they never paid that part of the costs incurred to which they had been committed. After finishing the extensive alterations, we installed the restaurant machinery.

The harsh measures that the IMF economic restructuring programme introduced during the past year brought an uneasy climate in the country. University students were out on the streets protesting against the measures which directly affected them and demanding the release of student leaders who had been picked-up in pre-dawn arrests. The rage of the students was such that they did not confine their anger against government institutions alone but were attacking vehicles of ordinary motorists and passers-by. Many people were injured in the fighting that ensued between police and students before the situation was brought under a shaky control.

Zambia – The Freedom Struggle and the Aftermath

1985

The conversion of the shop premises to a restaurant proved to be a right move for us. It was hard work and difficult to run because of the constant shortages and difficulties in obtaining basic foodstuffs, in particular, flour, cooking oil and soft drinks. In theory business houses such as restaurants and hotels were given set allocations, but this was never adhered to, in part because the commodities were just not available, and priority was given to hotels which catered for tourists, and partly due to corruption. We improvised, taking such measures as extending the meagre flour allowance used for buns, cakes, pies, etc., by mixing in a percentage of finely ground maize meal; using concentrated fruit squashes when Pepsi, Fanta and Coca-Cola were unavailable; when the supply of minced meat was reduced we mixed in a percentage of soya meal, experimenting until we achieved the right taste; and when the price of sauces, which were imported, became uneconomic we made our own using tomatoes, onions, etc., produced on the farm.

Through these and similar measures, we got through the constant, difficult periods of food shortages. The restaurant became so successful that it outstripped our hopes and expectations, but if we had not improvised we would not have survived. We were not concentrating on providing sit-down meals but rather along the lines of a fast-food outlet providing burgers and soft drinks and the like to the local shoppers, marketeers and traders. Later we also provided takeaway group meals for various organisations such as student groups from UNZA [University of Zambia] who were working on field projects which involved travel.

The situation in the country was tense and worsening. Now ordinary people were out on the streets of the capital demonstrating against government policies. Shops and business houses were closing and barricading their doors and windows for protection.

Personal Story of Sylvester M. Chisembele

1986

We were not social people and we did not go out in the evenings, ever, unless to an official function or on an emergency but when our daughter Christina was selected to go to the University of Zambia in 1985 we decided to celebrate this important achievement and we arranged to take the family to the Intercontinental Hotel in Lusaka on 1 March which was also the birthday of Sylvester. A table was booked in the Makumbi Room of this prestigious hotel for the early evening and a taxi was prearranged to take us to and from the hotel.

When we left the hotel to return home around 9.30 p.m. we got into the taxi and after driving less than 10 minutes a paramilitary lorry pulled alongside and shouted to the driver to stop. There were at least 10 soldiers in the back of the lorry, they and the officer in charge jumped out surrounding the vehicle. The officer in charge told the taxi driver that he was breaking the law because he had too many people in the car (we were five and the taxi was ordered for that number of people; our elder daughter Bwalya Matilda was not with us because she had entered the novitiate of the Irish Sisters of Charity from school in 1982 and was to take her final vows later in the year). The officer then walked around and ordered Sylvester out of the car; he told him to get onto the back of the lorry and ordered the taxi driver to continue the journey with the rest of us passengers.

If indeed there was fault, it would not be with the passengers but with the driver and so I immediately got out of the taxi and told the officer that if he was taking my husband away for whatever reason then they would have to take me as well. There was some shouting and threatening from the officer in charge but eventually we were both told to get back into the taxi and leave. The paramilitary vehicle continued to follow us for 3 or 4 miles and then pulled away. Incidents like this were the reason that we were always cautious as far as

Zambia – The Freedom Struggle and the Aftermath

social activities were concerned, especially those that involved driving after dark.

Early in the year President Kaunda had said that the food riots and bloody suppression experienced in Tunisia could not happen in Zambia.[130] But his complacency was shattered when the continuing erosion in the standard of living of the general population and the food shortages caused widening protests and political unrest. These disturbances and riots were beginning to become part of the landscape. Students at UNZA quickly joined by their peers had rioted in 1984 and 1985 and as the situation worsened in the country, President Kaunda intensified repressive intimidation and violent actions through the paramilitary and the security services.

This time, unlike previous rioting involving students and political cadres, ordinary Zambians were out on the streets protesting corruption and food-price hikes and facing a furious reaction from the State which saw individuals being chased indiscriminately, beaten and arrested by paramilitary police. The violence reached a level never seen before in Zambia. This time the paramilitary had descended into using their weapons and people were shot and killed. The numbers of people beaten and injured were in the hundreds.

In spite of the worsening political climate, we were doing well with our restaurant and farming activities, we still had mortgages and a backlog of farming debts which we were tackling successfully. However, my sister and her husband, John, were anxious for me to visit them in New Zealand and eventually we accepted their offer to completely finance my trip. So on 12 December 1986 I left for an extended holiday in New Zealand where I was fortunate in obtaining employment with the Alfred Marks Secretarial Bureau enabling me to accumulate sufficient funds to purchase sophisticated

---

[130] Ibid. Fn. 84 Chisembele, "Constitution Contribution for Public Awareness", 2005, pt 2 "Corruption and Moral Decay of 1980's".

restaurant machinery, albeit second-hand. This was a most successful trip because John took me to various catering machinery suppliers of both new and second-hand equipment. I managed to purchase several items which were to prove invaluable in improving both the appearance and sales in our restaurant.

During my stay in New Zealand, I received letters from Sylvester informing me of the increasing political unrest in the country.

1987

I returned to Zambia on the 6 March 1987. Sylvester was again being called by grassroots leaders to return to political organisation, but though he was always ready to advise, he remained outside the active political arena, which is what my family and I advocated; but he was his own man and made his own decisions. President Kaunda had lost respect throughout the country and the openly repressive measures he was now employing had destroyed any evidence of good faith which the people had had in him. He had successfully weeded out of the Government and Parliament the genuine leaders of the pre-independence struggle days and kept only those who were prepared to give him uncritical support, but this had backfired. He had no dissenting voices around him which might have kept him some little respect among the populace had he been prepared to listen. He had used corruption, coercion and intimidation which had permeated down through his Government administration.

The IMF measures that the President introduced in 1983 which had not been successful and had only resulted in terrible poverty and inflation, coupled with the corruption and the lifestyle of many of the Government and UNIP leaders, compounded the anger and frustration of the people. President Kaunda was forced by the internal situation to re-think and then sever relations with the IMF. President

Zambia – The Freedom Struggle and the Aftermath

Kaunda stated that the social fabric of the country was disintegrating and sowing seeds of unrest and he went on to say that this state of affairs would not be allowed to continue.

The situation was so taut in the country that opposition and voices of criticism were being silenced by the State. There was a great deal of unrest and strikes were not infrequent. President Kaunda detained Union leaders, including Frederick Chiluba and following this President Kaunda banned the May Day Parade and rally by the Zambia Congress of Trade Unions [ZCTU]. Instead, this traditional Labour Day was presided over by President Kaunda with civil servants marching under flags of the various arms of the Government passing before him.

As the political unrest began to spiral out of control in the country and even though Chisembele was not involved in active politics, we were still under surveillance. Our telephone lines would work for a few days and then for months on end would be 'out of order'. Near misses on the road continued, and there was yet another serious attempt by an unmarked lorry to run Sylvester off the road when he was driving from our home in Buckley Township, Lusaka to the restaurant.

In the meantime, an upmarket restaurant in Cairo Road called The Garden Restaurant which was under the ownership of Theo Bull and Gaudenzio Rossi, both well-known respected businessmen, was being offered for sale. The Garden Restaurant had proved to be a 'white elephant' and the owners were trying to dispose of it. It had been advertised in the press for some time and so we decided to approach Theo Bull for more information. We had meetings with Bull and Rossi. They were asking for one hundred and fifty thousand kwacha for the lease and a few items of equipment. The amount asked was large, the equivalent to ten thousand US dollars which, in effect, was just for the lease; the building belonged to the Christian Council of Zambia.

Though we had exceeded expectation in the restaurant we were running in Cha Cha Cha Road, named after my mother, Ethel Ali City Restaurant, we could not produce an amount of this magnitude.

Bull was also a partner in a company called African Properties Limited which owned a farm that bordered our Filalo Farm in Chisamba and one suggestion that he made was that we exchange the farm for The Garden Restaurant. This would have been a foolish action on our part and, of course, we did not even consider accepting such a proposal. Another suggestion favoured by Rossi was that we enter a partnership, but the terms were not favourable and so we decided against this proposal.

However, Messrs Bull and Rossi put forward another proposal that they would accept a down payment of half the asked price and we would have to pay the balance within six months. The terms were harsh in that the agreement stated that if we failed to pay the balance in full within that time, the restaurant would revert to the ownership of Messrs Bull and Rossi and we would forfeit all monies paid. This was the proposition we decided to accept as we were confident that we could meet the conditions and turn the restaurant around, and this we did. So much so that as well as paying off in full the debt to Messrs Bull and Rossi, we even won the International Award for Tourist, Hotel & Catering Industry for 1990 for The Garden Restaurant. [131]

1988

We were continuing to do well with the two restaurants we were now running and with the farm, even with the political

---

[131] The Garden Restaurant, "Tourist Award, Trade Leaders Club" 24.11.89; Zambia National Tourist Board, 4.1.90, scans; Comment: We were unable to collect the trophy as our application for travel and existence allowance was refused.

unrest and harassment that was everywhere and in spite of the difficulties in obtaining food supplies in the country. Without the methods we had used from the start to improvise and be as self-reliant as possible we would never have survived. Restaurants and shops were being stormed into by UNIP cadres demanding to see UNIP cards and bullying staff and shop owners. UNIP had lost its way and ugly incidents were occurring, for example when President Kaunda was to address a public meeting or there was a UNIP political rally to be held in a marketplace, UNIP cadres would come into our as well as other restaurants and shops, order people out and shout us to close the premises. Officials from UNIP were also going into shops 'requesting' contributions for extensions to the UNIP Freedom House building; a request which it would be foolhardy to refuse.

Corruption in the misuse of funds, common in the Government and parastatals, had now been exposed in the United Church of Zambia [UCZ] causing President Kaunda to make a public statement of his dismay, sadness and anger at the UCZ leadership. He rebuked the clergy and accused them not only of letting the State down, but of bringing shame on the country. To the populace, however, his words were hollow. Anger with UCZ was there, but the pointing of fingers when his own house, i.e. the Government, was responsible for far greater thieving only drew more attention and condemnation of his own activities.

The machinery I had brought from New Zealand had tremendously improved our restaurant in Cha Cha Cha Road. This small business had made it possible to finance an expansion of our farming activities, as well as the purchase of The Garden Restaurant, and in this year of 1988 against all the odds we finally paid off every debt that we had with the bank and debts that related to the failed transport venture. In

Personal Story of Sylvester M. Chisembele

September, we cleared the mortgage on the Filalo Farm in Chisamba[132] and the following month, we also cleared the last outstanding debt, the balance of the mortgage on our house in Buckley Township. This house Sylvester had bought in 1966 on a 20-year mortgage. Immediately after independence, the Government had housed Cabinet Ministers, but not Parliamentary Secretaries who were advised to purchase homes for themselves and to facilitate this directive the Government arranged to guarantee mortgages which would be issued by the National Building Society. Chisembele and several of his colleagues did so, but during the intervening years we had re-mortgaged the house in order to pay off recurring commitments and to finance farming projects.

I was invited by my sister to spend Christmas with her family in New Zealand and so I left on the 1st December, again my trip was financed by my sister and her husband. A month later whilst I was in Wellington I received a letter from Sylvester informing me that he had purchased two hundred and fifty breeding goats which were now on the farm. Our daughter Christina, who was studying veterinary science at the University of Zambia, advised that this would be a good move particularly because goats were not as susceptible to disease as chickens which need very careful monitoring, especially in view of the still problematic supply sources for the Newcastle Disease vaccine.

We did not realise at the time that we had made a terrible mistake to clear off all our debts and by doing so we left ourselves open for a later corrupt, vindictive government to remove all the properties we owned, one by one; the restaurant businesses and the farm, with the exception of our house in Buckley Township and our personal vehicles.

---

[132] "History of Farm ZSIC loan"; "History of Buckley Township", scans

Zambia – The Freedom Struggle and the Aftermath

1989 – 1990

The political situation was continuing to deteriorate. The food prices were decontrolled and though, in theory, mealie meal was exempt from the decontrols, the price for this staple food soared to more than double. There was a corresponding increase in outbreaks of rioting leaving property destroyed and police resorting to violent measures to disperse crowds, especially on the Copperbelt. One day in July 1989 youths en masse looted and destroyed property in all the towns in the province, to which the police responded with teargas crushing the uprising within a day. The riots were to spread quickly to the northern regions and other districts in the country.[133]

The unrest in the country was intensive, especially in the towns and cities, the measures that President Kaunda enforced failed to bring the situation under control. The call from all parts of society was for the reintroduction of multi-party politics. To counteract this, the President had descended into repressive methods on a scale unseen before in Zambia. Paramilitary police seemed to be everywhere. Roadblocks which had been part of the landscape on main roads for years, were now appearing in town centres mounted by soldiers and paramilitary brutalising ordinary people. The paramilitary were even marching into shops, banks and offices slapping the counter assistants and workers around and where they found a business establishment was not displaying a portrait of the President in full public view, then that establishment was closed down and the people within beaten. This blatant, open bullying behaviour had not been there before; it appeared to have started after the food riots began in 1986.

These measures of intimidation which President Kaunda used completely failed in their objective to subdue the people.

---

[133] Ibid. Fn.84 Chisembele, "Constitution Contribution for Public Awareness", 2005, pt 2 "Corruption and Moral Decay of 1980's".

The President resisted for as long as he could, but the rapid deterioration in the ability of his Government to hold in check a situation which was fast moving towards anarchy, was beyond control.

In an effort to quieten the country and counteract the growing calls for multi-party democracy, President Kaunda announced that he would set up a referendum on the One Party State. However, this did not pacify his many critics and the referendum was not followed through. President Kaunda was forced by the state of affairs in the country to finally accept that he had no other choice but to reintroduce multi-party politics. Following this decision he appointed the Mvunga Constitution Review Commission.

Zambians were to express their opinions regarding the formation of a new Zambian Constitution and the Commission was to receive written contributions as well as verbal which were easily ignored if that was the will of the members of the Commission. Chisembele contributed a written document and the campaign which had for so long been underway, was intensified against dictatorship.

The Chiluba Years

Chapter 10
1991 – 1995

1991

This was the year of the historic elections that removed Kenneth Kaunda from power after 27 years of sole control of the affairs of Zambia. The Mvunga Commission after a relatively short time had issued their recommendations early in the year and although it paved the way for the Zambian Constitution to be amended to end the One Party State and restore multi-party elections, it did not touch on the absolute power still to be held by the Head of State.

After bickering and threats of boycotts between the opposition and the Government, the Zambian Constitution was formally amended in August two months before the 1991 General Elections were due, opening the way for a presidential challenge.

Once the restriction had been removed, several political parties were formally registered. Frederick Chiluba, who was the Chairman of the Zambia Congress of Trade Unions, was now President of an opposition party, the Movement for Multi-Party Democracy. Frederick Chiluba together with Valentine Kayope came several times to The Garden Restaurant for consultations with Chisembele; he sometimes came with a group of his close advisors and supporters. These meetings were not always in total accord in that Frederick Chiluba, had names in mind of former UNIP office-holding leaders whom he intended to bring into a new government, which was showing positive signs that the MMD would be elected to form. Chisembele spoke openly and named the individuals who whilst serving in Kaunda's Government had proved themselves corrupt, putting self-interest first, and some of these individuals were among those whom Frederick Chiluba was now closely associating with. He advised Chiluba that this was a great chance for the Nation to shake off corruption and start to develop solely, cleanly for the benefit of the people. Frederick Chiluba initially thanked Chisembele for the advice, but then went on to say that the individuals concerned were the ones helping him build up MMD. Chisembele advised that even so, it would be imperative for a successful, effective government to begin and continue with clean hands Chiluba said that he would bring Chisembele into his new administration when the elections were over. However, Chisembele whilst thanking Chiluba for his consideration said that he would not rejoin the Government in any capacity mainly for reasons of health and the need to continue the establishment of a sound future for his family.[134]

True to form, President Kaunda when the momentum was obviously with MMD and power slipping away from him, sent several of his top aides, former colleagues of Chisembele and family members as well as groups of UNIP officials from Freedom House to the restaurant to solicit Chisembele's support. A rumour was circulating within the UNIP hierarchy that as there was a family connection between Chisembele and Chiluba, Chisembele was the organiser behind the scenes for Chiluba. This was not true. The fact was that although Sylvester Chisembele's sister, Victoria, was married to MMD President Chiluba's uncle of the same name, Frederick Titus Chiluba, who had been a fellow seminarian

---

[134] Sophena Chisembele, excerpt of letter to my sister, Sheila Ahern, 1.08.91, scan

and had married Chisembele's sister, Victoria, before independence was achieved, his nephew, the future President of Zambia, was not close to the Chisembele family.

The truth was that the majority of the citizens of Zambia desperately wanted change from the open corruption and dictatorship of Kaunda's regime and Chisembele and those who understood the danger incorporated in the Zambian Constitution placing all power in the Head of State as it did, had hope and expectation that this was the golden opportunity for the Constitution to be corrected under a new, clean government.[135] Although Chisembele advised the president-to-be on a future government he did not actively support or campaign on behalf of Frederick Chiluba or the MMD.

The Movement for Multi-Party Democracy was voted into power, as expected, with huge country-wide support. The victory was celebrated en masse. Unfortunately, the new President did not heed advice and among the new leadership he tolerated previously known corrupt politicians. His own history had been questioned, but he had a strong Zambia Congress of Trade Unions [ZCTU] background and the populace had faith in him and in his promises. Hopes and expectations were again very high in the country.

In December, Chisembele received a telephone call informing him that he had been called to State House as the President wanted to see him. Mr Kayope came on the appointed day to take him to the meeting. Kayope had been given a ministerial appointment in the new Government by President Chiluba, initially as a Minister of State and later brought into the Cabinet. The call for Chisembele to see the President turned into a debacle. They were refused admittance by the State House security officials at the main gate and all efforts made by Minister Kayope to secure

---

[135] *Times of Zambia* (Ndola), 24.1.91, scan.

admission were unproductive. Chisembele urged Kayope to come away and leave it be because, he said, from his experience of security at State House to continue arguing with the security officers would place them in a dangerous situation.

1992

In March Chisembele received a telephone call from the Deputy Minister of Local Government & Housing, Valentine Kayope, informing him of another invitation extended to him to see President Chiluba; this was followed by a letter of confirmation written by the minister. However, Chisembele declined the invitation citing the earlier incident when he had been called and then refused admittance as well as the fact that the invitation had not come directly from an official State House source. Thereafter, on the 23rd March Chisembele received a telephone call from State House asking why he had not attended the meeting at 9 a.m. scheduled with the President. Chisembele explained that there must be a misunderstanding because the meeting had not been confirmed by him for reasons given at the time of the invitation which had been relayed to him by Valentine Kayope.[136]

A placid relationship existed between Chisembele and the new Government, although signs of corruption within the MMD were already emerging. The dire effects of the introduction of the economic austerity measures taken together with the corruption so quickly evident in some of the leaders and officials in the new MMD Government caused people, particularly in the towns, to question the behaviour and actions of party and government officials.

---

[136] Letters from Valentine Kayope to President Chiluba 16.3.92, SMC 17.3.92; Diary excerpt, scans

Dr. Kaunda was determined to take back control of the country. One tried and tested universal method was the splitting of votes. UNIP under the direction of President Kaunda tried to organise this by implementing the covert formation of several smaller political parties, regionally oriented, which were believed to be financed by funds held by Dr. Kaunda. A few months after UNIP had so roundly lost the election, a group of Luapula leaders, Lusaka based, who had held various positions in previous Kaunda administrations came to The Garden Restaurant several times to persuade Chisembele to join them in setting up a new political party.[137] Chisembele had no interest in participating in any such endeavour, even though among the visitors were respected politicians and friends. It appeared that these political party groupings were being formed along provincial lines. It seemed evident that some among the groups had knowledge of Kaunda's involvement and motives and had received assurances that when the former President regained power through this method of vote-splitting they could then either rejoin UNIP or give support on a coalition basis to a Kaunda administration. He would then appoint them into government positions. Some of these leaders still had grassroots support pre-dating independence, and those that were elected as Members of Parliament could always cross the floor at an appropriate time.

During the course of the year, a rumour was spreading along the line of rail of the existence of a plot to overthrow the Government. This plot was called "Zero Option" and was said to be the brainchild of the UNIP hierarchy to put Kenneth Kaunda back into power. Many rumours of plots were circulating, but this one seemed to be the most credible, it was certainly predominant.

---

[137] Letter from ex-Ministers Mambwe and Mumba re New Political Party, 18.06.1992 scan

Personal Story of Sylvester M. Chisembele

1993

As was his way, Chisembele was always available for advice, if needed,[138] and in spite of the political differences that had emerged between the MMD Government and Chisembele and the debacle of the aborted appointment at State House in December 1991, Chisembele, in time of difficulty, was still being called upon for counsel.

On Sunday 14 March, Kayope arrived early in the morning. I quote the entry in my diary for that day:

> As we were leaving for Church, Kayope arrived I dropped SMC at his house. SMC returned around 10 pm. It seemed President Chiluba had telephoned Kayope in morning about Security and Zero Option. SMC was dragged into a meeting with Kayope, Mr Lembalemba of Mufulira the uncle of Leonard; Comas Maunga; SMC and John Chalwe (deputy registrar UNZA). President Chiluba again telephoned and Kayope was to take group to State House. SMC refused to go, but was persuaded to remain at Kayope's to hear results. They wanted advice from SMC on how to investigate secret reports of 60 people taken to Iraq for training for a coup. The whole issue and Chiluba's reactions seem premature to me ... diplomatic relations broken before evidence of wrong found.

The comments I made in my diary were, of course, foolish and made in ignorance. The relationship between President Kaunda and the Iraqi President, Saddam Hussein, was known to be very strong. "Zero Option" was now openly said to be a plot instigated by Kaunda and UNIP to overthrow the Government, and it was imminent. Rumours and speculation were rife and security reports were said to have confirmed the existence of such a plot which would involve assistance or even the covert participation by Iraq and perhaps even Iran.

---

[138] Sylvester M Chisembele, "A Brief History 1991 – 2000", p 1

Zambia – The Freedom Struggle and the Aftermath

Zambia's Foreign Affairs Minister publicly accused the Governments of both Iraq and Iran of funding plots to overthrow the MMD Government by Kenneth Kaunda and UNIP. The alleged "Zero Option" plot was taken very seriously by the Government and a good number of people were detained including Wezi Kaunda, son of the former President.

President Chiluba declared a State of Emergency at the beginning of the month, and two weeks later on 18 March 1993 there was a riot in Lusaka claimed by MMD to have been engineered by UNIP, but that would only have been part of the reason, many people were feeling disillusioned with the new Government and some were prepared to demonstrate alongside UNIP cadres.

A vicious circle of claim and counter claim began. Unfortunately, corruption was not diminishing under the MMD Government, it appeared to be widening with an added dimension of an avarice that extended beyond the apparent broad boundaries of the previous regime in that properties were being seized on flimsy or fabricated grounds from individual ordinary people. We were not to be immune.

On 28 April, the whole country was shocked to learn of the plane crash in the sea at Gabon when the Zambia National Soccer Team perished. 30 people died. The following day the Government inferred that a bomb had been placed on board, this was to counteract accusations by opposition parties that they had provided a worn-out aeroplane for use by the National Soccer Team. Finger-pointing ensued, but people in general were too shocked and upset to allow the tragedy to be brought down to the level of political scoring. The whole country mourned.

In June of this year 1993, I was very unwell and eventually went to the hospital on 21 July. A specialist at the University Teaching Hospital [UTH], Lusaka told my husband to take me back immediately to England because I had had a serious heart attack and they did not have the facilities to treat me in Lusaka. We left for London on 28 July. My sister and her husband were in the UK at the time, she had been invited as guest speaker for the William Harrison four hundredth anniversary celebration. She had links with Radwinter which went back for some years and indeed we had visited together the parish where the Rev. William Harrison had been Rector. She had written an article on William Harrison which had appeared in the December 1992 issue of the Essex Journal.[139] I was admitted into the Harefield Hospital in Middlesex, for treatment and whilst there our daughter Christina, who had been selected by Irish Aid for work experience in Ireland, was able to visit me in the hospital.

Chisembele remained with me in the UK until October when he returned to Zambia. He found that during his absence the farm, which had been left in the care of our son Mwale, assisted by a large group of workers, had been destroyed and the livestock was gone. The damage was not that of ordinary thieves, it was extensive with even the main house, which was a double-storey building with stone exterior walls, totally destroyed. It had taken enormous effort to break down this house and the farm buildings which now lay in ruins. The headman of the village closest to us came to inform Chisembele that government agents were responsible. He reported that the villagers had been threatened and the farm workers had run away. Mwale had been in Lusaka to spend some days assisting the restaurants manager organise supplies and to attend the hospital clinic because he was feeling unwell. This was a terrible period which Sylvester faced alone for our son Mwale was ill and I was still away.

---

[139] Letter from John Ahern, 5.04.93, scan.

This disaster was to be followed later by the forced removal of the restaurants one by one and the eventual seizure of the farm as well.[140]

The first restaurant to be removed was The Garden Restaurant for which we had international recognition for excellence. I quote an excerpt from "A Brief History 1991-2000" written by Sylvester Chisembele:

At this time my son was dying, my wife was still in London awaiting a major heart operation, my fighting spirit had left me and the question of losing my big Garden Restaurant became nothing. I decided to let the restaurant go without resistance. I had been in it for 8 years. I purchased the lease from Mr Theo Bull when it had been collapsing and I built it up to the standard where it was. I said God if this is your wish, let it go and I closed my eyes and my mind.

1994 – 1995

I remained in the UK for a considerable time. The treatment was long and I was waiting to be admitted for an operation. I was advised by my doctor that I should remain and live in the UK and not return to Zambia. This was a bitter blow, followed in March by the tragic loss of Mwale who died after an attack of cerebral meningitis in March. In June, Chisembele came to the UK and spent a month with me. Of course, I had been informed of the death of Mwale, but Chisembele told me nothing of the difficulties he was facing in Zambia.

I was feeling better. I had undergone a procedure in Harefield Hospital and I made a decision to return to Zambia which I did on 9 February 1995.

---

[140] Ibid , Fn.102 Folder "Filalo Farm Destruction & Seizure", documents and photographs;   Ibid. Fn.138 Chisembele, "A Brief History 1991 – 2000"; "Sequence of Events".

Personal Story of Sylvester M. Chisembele

In May, Sylvester was informed that a group of previously staunch supporters of Kenneth Kaunda which included Alex Shapi and Chikako Kamalondo had decided to approach President Chiluba. Following this and in view of the forthcoming General Elections and the fact that activities of the former President were causing concern to the ruling party, Sylvester was called again for advice to yet another MMD leaders meeting which included Kayope; B. Chisenga; K. Konsolo, Permanent Secretary Legal Affairs; M.K. Mufwaya; Kamamba and others. In the light of the actions taken against us, I could hardly believe that MMD officials could still approach Chisembele for advice.

Towards the end of the year in November, President Chiluba announced the formation of a Constitution Review Commission, which would be chaired by John Mwanakatwe and known as the Mwanakatwe Constitution Review Commission. The Terms of Reference for this Commission were far-reaching.

I went back to the UK with Sylvester in August for a medical review and we returned together to Zambia at the end of the same month. From now on I had no choice but to make regular visits to the UK for health reasons, which I did.

The build-up for these coming elections saw again visits from UNIP delegates and politicians representing various parties endeavouring to involve Chisembele in their electioneering. UNIP Freedom House representatives talked of the need to preserve the patriotic party of independence which was UNIP.

Ex-President Kaunda was tirelessly trying to regain control of the considerable ground lost. Following his usual tactics he sent a delegation to our house in Buckley Township on Sunday 10 September, they were preceded by an extended family member who worked in the Bank of Zambia, Mrs Monica Chitoshi, she came with a group of UNIP politicians and others. They spent some considerable time trying to persuade Sylvester to re-enter politics on behalf of UNIP. The suggestion was that if he would accept, an aeroplane would be provided so that he could fly around various parts of the country to campaign. However, Sylvester, polite as always, refused and I quote from my diary:

... but SMC left them in no doubt of his opinion of Kaunda.

A week later on 17 September Mrs Chitoshi came again this time with a group of family members, they spent all afternoon with us but the part of the visit touching on politics went to no avail. Another similar visit was made to us the following Sunday, 21 September.[141]

The Mwanakatwe Constitution Review Commission presented its report. It appeared that the over-riding purpose of the MMD Government in appointing this Commission was to block Kenneth Kaunda from contesting the 1996 Presidential Election by introducing a third generation citizenship requirement for presidential office. This change would be effected the following year.

---

[141] Comment: - Mrs Monica Chitoshi has read this paragraph and has given me permission to quote her name.

Chapter 11
1996 – 1999

1996

At the beginning of the year, in January the parastatal Zambia National Building Society from whom we leased the premises for our small Ethel's Restaurant, out of the blue, came to close down the restaurant. We were shocked at this action because we had been leasing the premises for 16 years with no problems from our side. Chisembele embarked on a series of meetings and attempted meetings with ZNBS officials to clear the situation but to no avail. We were locked out of the premises, never compensated for the property within or reimbursed for years of maintenance which the ZNBS had repeatedly promised to refund. We were denied access and we were not, therefore, able to recover all of our restaurant machinery, furnishings or equipment. A few months later a fire gutted the ZNBS headquarters in Cairo Road destroying all documents and this incident became the reason ZNBS would not honour their commitments as they now had the legitimate excuse that there were no records. The shop premises removed from us were then given to another trader. We were not, of course, the only concern affected by this fire at the ZNBS.

Just over a year previously The Garden Restaurant had been removed under the pretext that the Christian Council from whom we rented the premises wanted to use it for themselves as a Staff Canteen, whereas, in fact, they actually rented it out to a European concern. These events were inexplicable.[142]

Presidential and Parliamentary Elections were held this year. There was a very uneasy atmosphere with several smaller parties actively seeking support. Intimidation and corrupt practices continued widespread. The sweeping in of the MMD in 1991 had fired the hopes and expectations of the populace, but these expectations showed no sign of being met, confusion and disappointment were turning into apathy. The spread of corruption was far worse under the MMD Government than it had been under Kaunda. When Kaunda was in power he and his cronies were the main beneficiaries of the corrupt practices in place, but now under the MMD administration the corruption was extensive and it appeared to be a 'free-for-all' for government leaders, party cadres and civil servants, that is those without scruples.

The Constitutional Amendments which followed the Mwanakatwe Constitution Review Commission Report were rushed through Parliament and effected in 1996. Prior to the parliamentary debate, the MMD National Chairman, Sikota Wina, MP issued a press statement with which he released official documents confirming that Kenneth Kaunda had held Malawian citizenship, which he had not renounced until 12 June 1970, when he was granted Zambian citizenship. A fact that would later be used in a challenge to his citizenship.[143]

Under the adopted Constitutional Amendments former President Kaunda was disqualified from contesting the Presidential Election to be held in November 1996, an action which caused UNIP to boycott both the Presidential and Parliamentary Elections. The ongoing unfruitful visits to Chisembele ceased. Regrettably, the important changes that

---

[142] Ibid. Fn.138 Chisembele, "A Brief History 1991 – 2000".
[143] K.D. Kaunda Citizenship documents, scans

were needed to move away from One Man Rule through the absolute power held by the Head of State were not touched, as far as this was concerned, the status quo remained; also a recommendation that the Constitution be adopted through a Constituent Assembly and National Referendum was ignored.

The amendment omissions under the Mwanakatwe Constitution Review Commission were a great disappointment. One achievement had been made and that was to limit the presidential term of office to two terms, but not the most important change needed to correct the situation of one individual holding sole power under the Constitution.

The boycott of the elections by UNIP, the main opposition party, ensured a victory for the MMD and for President Frederick Chiluba. A few smaller parties did contest both Presidential and Parliamentary Elections, the strongest of these being the Zambia Democratic Congress [ZDC], led by Dean Mung'omba, but their results even collective were negligible for they had made little impact on the electorate.

In what appeared to many to be a 'tit-for-tat' ploy, UNIP and the smaller opposition parties rumoured that the election to the presidency of Frederick Chiluba was an illegality because, they claimed, he was not a Zambian but had been born in the Democratic Republic of the Congo. This rumour turned into open accusations that would eventually become a Court case challenging the legitimacy of President Chiluba's position.

Zambia's first Vice-President Reuben C. Kamanga died on the 20th September. He had remained a personal friend. We attended the State funeral at the Holy Cross Cathedral on the 24th September 1996. After the service groups of mourners had assembled in the Cathedral grounds en route to the Old Leopards Hill Cemetery where Reuben Kamanga was to be buried. After greeting the various dignitaries, we passed on to greet Dr. Kaunda, one of his aides standing alongside him said *"Ah! Chisembele, if we had six Chisembeles to campaign for us, we would not have lost the elections".* He was, of course, referring to the 1991 elections.

1997

In May, Chisembele was again called to see President Chiluba. He was assured that no problems would be met at the gate. No reason was given for the call, but this would be an opportunity to inform the President directly of the corruption surrounding the removal of our restaurants and destruction on the farm. However, when Sylvester was called in to see the President, President Chiluba, after initial greetings, immediately said that he had heard about the farm and that all the restaurants had been removed and he asked what plans Chisembele now had.

During the course of the meeting the President asked Sylvester how much money he would need to restart his farming projects and replace the machinery, losses, etcetera, caused by the destruction of the farm and removal of the restaurants. On not receiving a suggestion from Chisembele, the President followed up by saying he would give him three million kwacha.

The offer of three million kwacha was derisory, if it was intended as compensation, because this amount would have barely replaced a single piece of the agricultural machinery destroyed or removed from the farm; or even a few pieces of commercial machinery for use in a restaurant, and if by asking Sylvester how much money he would need to expand his farming projects a question that was not met with a request but with a diplomatic evasion, then the meeting amounted to little less than an attempt to compromise Chisembele.[144] In the event, the President did not call Chisembele back to

---

[144] Comment: - In 1989 the exchange rate was K21 to the £1 sterling; by 1997 the exchange rate was K2200 and rising to the £1 sterling.

receive the proffered three million kwacha, nor to continue the discussion on the case Chisembele was trying to pursue against the Government for compensation, as he said he would.

Two months later, in July, Chisembele received a letter from the Commissioner of Lands stating that he had discovered that there was insufficient activity going on in Filalo Farm owned by Sylvester Chisembele and that unless the farm was reactivated, the Government would re-enter and give it to someone else. Chisembele went to see the Commissioner of Lands and told him of the activities which were currently in place on the farm and the Commissioner advised him to put the details in writing and a letter was accordingly written in October detailing events and developments on the farm. This threat coming so soon after the dubious, unjustifiable actions taken to remove both of our restaurants caused us considerable concern. However, nothing more was heard and we continued with the farming projects and re-building programme which we had in place.

In the same month of October a coup attempt was made by a small group of Zambian Army soldiers led by a Captain Stephen Lungu, who called himself "Captain Solo". He walked into the ZNBC radio station in Lusaka, ordered the staff aside and then addressed the Nation saying that he had taken over the government of the country.

After the initial shock and fear caused by the announcement made by Captain Solo, and when the facts became known, the 'coup' attempt became an object of derision and laughter. It emerged that Captain Solo and his group had first fortified themselves in a local bar before their attempted coup and if not actually drunk they were well on the way. This was not the first time a coup attempt had been made in Zambia. In the past there had been a few failed attempts to overthrow the Government which had faded from the scene fairly quickly, but this attempt led by the self-styled

"Captain Solo" was notable not just for the repercussions but because of the farcical aspect at the beginning of the episode.

Regardless, the Government was obviously far more informed and took this coup attempt very seriously. A few weeks later it was the grounds on which they then arrested several opposition leaders, including former President Kaunda. President Chiluba had declared, without the support of all the Christian Church denominations, Zambia to be a Christian country in 1991 and now he had taken an action to arrest Kenneth Kaunda on Christmas Day. This fact, if for nothing else, drew sympathy for Kaunda from many quarters. He was released a few days later and placed under house arrest.

1998

A coup plot involvement charge was brought against the former President in January, but this charge was dropped some six months later in June. A few weeks afterwards, Kenneth Kaunda announced that he would resign his position as President of UNIP and he put forward his son, Wezi, a former army major, to take over the leadership, ostensibly to be his successor. However, this proposition was not met with sufficient acceptance from within UNIP and a spate of wrangling and engineering for positions ensued until 2000 when a new leader was selected.

UNIP together with several smaller opposition parties which included Dean Mung'omba, President of the Zambia Democratic Congress, now joined together in presenting a petition before the High Court to have Frederick Chiluba's election as President nullified on the grounds that he was not a Zambian.

However, the issue was clear, Frederick Chiluba was definitely a Zambian and as it was a matter of principle which if not put to rest would cause a spate of challenges and disturbances within families and the society at large, on request, Chisembele contacted his brother-in-law who was also the President's uncle, Frederick Chiluba, in Mansa who agreed to make a television appearance to clear up the matter. However, at a meeting of MMD officials in State House chaired by the Deputy Minister, Josiah Chishala, it was decided that other methods of proof already in hand would suffice. Eventually in November 1998 the High Court threw out the petition which challenged President Frederick Chiluba's citizenship.

In August, Chisembele received another letter from the Office of the Commissioner of Lands referring to the letter Chisembele had written in October 1997 concerning Filalo Farm; the Commissioner wrote that Chisembele was given an 18 month extension to complete his building projects on the farm. We had no idea of what was going on in the Ministry of Lands. It was open knowledge that there was a great deal of corruption and disorganisation within the Ministry.

1999

President Chiluba and his close associates were engaged in an attempt to have Kenneth Kaunda deported for they were convinced that he had been the instigator of the "Zero Option" coup attempt in 1993 and since then that he was involved in other plots to overthrow the Government. A petition challenging the citizenship of the former President came before the Ndola High Court in March when Mr Justice Sakala ruled that Kenneth Kaunda was a stateless person and that he had held the post of Office of the President of Zambia illegally. The fact that he had not renounced his Malawian citizenship until 1970 which was well after Zambia's independence, fed the accusation that he was, in fact, a foreigner and had no right to contest any election in Zambia at any time. The place of Kenneth Kaunda's birth was also disputed with many asserting that he had actually been born in Nyasaland (Malawi).

In October we were shocked to receive a Notice to Re-Enter on our Filalo Farm in Chisamba from the Commissioner of Lands, it was backdated to 16 July 1999 giving Chisembele three months to make representation as to why a Certificate of Re-Entry should not be enforced. This caused us total confusion and after a series of 'come back tomorrow' visits to officials in the Ministry of Lands, eventually Chisembele saw the Commissioner of Lands who assured him that it had all been a misunderstanding, and that everything was in order and there was no threat to repossess the farm.

In November 1999 occurred the awful incident of the murder of Major Wezi Kaunda. This crime sent waves of shock throughout the country. The majority of the people may have rejected and hated the corruption associated with the Kaunda family, but they had no ill will to the extent of wishing them physical harm. Although the murder was put down to robbers, this explanation was not accepted and it was widely believed that it had been politically motivated. Following this ugly incident, a few months later, the attempt to deport Kenneth Kaunda collapsed and was withdrawn. His Zambian citizenship was restored to him by the Supreme Court of Zambia.

We were very surprised in November to receive a visit to our home of a Mr Vangelatos, a businessman and Managing Director of Dar Farms & Transport Limited. We had no previous knowledge of or association with this gentleman. Vangelatos told Chisembele that the Commissioner of Lands was intending to remove Filalo Farm from his ownership and then it would be given to the Minister of Commerce & Industry. Vangelatos went on to say that it was common knowledge that politicians and officials in the MMD Government were busy grabbing land and businesses from people and, in fact, we knew that this was the open truth. The interest of Vangelatos was to buy the farm himself immediately because, he said, the Commissioner of Lands was his personal friend and he would have no trouble with the minister concerned grabbing the farm from him. He asked to go with Chisembele to the farm even though he was told by Sylvester that he had no intention of selling the farm to anyone.

As this was now obviously a political issue with echoes of the route taken to remove both restaurants, Sylvester went to see the Deputy Minister, Valentine Kayope and he informed him fully about the farm issue. Kayope asked for everything to be put in writing. This was done and on the same day they went together to State House to deliver the letter, and there they were given a promise that an appointment would be arranged for Chisembele to see the President. Kayope was insistent that the President knew nothing of the issue and that President Chiluba would in no way close his eyes to such open corruption.

Shortly after leaving the documents at State House, Kayope left on a mission to Europe. Chisembele received no response from State House and so he went to discuss the issue with the lawyer, A.J. Lungu of Chilupe & Company to whom he gave copies of all the documentation. The advice given was that in view of the imminent threat to repossess the farm, Chisembele should see the Vice-President, Lt. Gen. Christon Tembo, as President Chiluba was away on holiday and would not be back in his office until the New Year.

The Vice-President proved impossible to see. Visits made at suggested times and telephone calls and promises of return calls were fruitless. The Vice-President, Lt. Gen. Christon Tembo, later when out of office and President of a new political party, Forum for Democracy & Development [FDD] formed in 2001, made serious accusations against his former colleagues regarding the seizure and illegal allocation of land by ministers in the MMD.

On Christmas Eve, Vangelatos again made contact and as Chisembele was not free to see him that day, asked if he would visit him immediately after the Christmas holidays.

Chapter 12
2000

2000

UNIP leader, President Kaunda, finally stood aside and the leadership of the party passed over to Francis Nkhoma. Francis Nkhoma was a former Governor of the Bank of Zambia, he had a dubious history, with charges of corruption and abuse of office levelled against him.[145] However, he remained for only a few months in the position. His short-lived UNIP presidency was difficult and at one point in 2001 he was expelled from the party. He was replaced by Kenneth Kaunda's son Tilyenji, who had taken over the Kaunda political dynasty when his brother, Wezi, had been murdered.

In January, Chisembele kept the appointment with Vangelatos, who was eager to buy the farm. Vangelatos then informed Chisembele that as the Commissioner of Lands was on holiday, he would give him the Commissioner's private cell phone number and home address so that Chisembele could ring the Commissioner or go and visit him. When telephoned the Commissioner of Lands asked Chisembele to come and see him in his office. The same morning Chisembele had received a Certificate of Re-Entry to the farm. The Commissioner of Lands told him to ignore the certificate which he said he would cancel, but he said that he was under

---

[145] Ibid. Fn.84 Chisembele, "Constitution Contribution for Public Awareness", 2005, pt 2, p 28.

a great deal of pressure because the Deputy Minister, A. Nkole, had told him that the seizure of Chisembele's farm could not wait for the effective date of the Certificate of Re-Entry in February, but must be done immediately.

From the Commissioner of Land's office Chisembele went straight to see his lawyer and he informed him of these further developments, and that following the advice previously given he had tried to book an appointment to see the Vice-President but this attempt had been stonewalled.

The lawyer was still sure that the matter could easily be settled at the political level and suggested contacting the Press Secretary at State House. Chisembele followed this advice but again was stonewalled, in that after much difficulty, he was given an appointment, but when arriving at State House to keep the appointment he was told that his name was not on the list and informed that the Press Secretary was out and that no message had been left.

When these events were relayed to the lawyer, he decided that he would make the contact himself which he did. The lawyer later informed Chisembele that he had left copies of the documentation with the Press Secretary who had come back to him with the information that Chisembele's case would be the first item on the President's agenda when the President returned from holiday. The lawyer also said that he would make direct contact with the Commissioner of Lands.

Nothing materialised and there followed a series of 'run-arounds' with Chisembele directed from one office to another. He met with the lawyer several times and then on 15 February when he saw him again, Chisembele told him that history was repeating itself; the issue was following the same course as that of the restaurants where he had been given the same 'run-around' before both had been taken away from him. The removal of the restaurants had also been political and again all efforts he had made to book appointments at ministerial or presidential levels had been blocked or rebuffed.

The lawyer said that even so Chisembele should exhaust the political and administrative channels before going to the Courts and, he said, the person who could take action to correct the situation as far as the farm was concerned was the Minister of Lands. Knowing that we could never afford the Court process which in any case was no guarantee of a fair and just hearing,[146] Chisembele agreed and after the lawyer had tried and failed to get through by telephone to the Minister of Lands, who was attending an MMD caucus, he suggested that Chisembele should go and wait in the minister's office. This he did.

The secretary of the Minister of Lands refused to make an appointment for Chisembele stating that the procedure was that he first saw the Deputy Minister and then if he were referred to the minister he could be given an appointment. He then went to the Deputy Minister's office where the secretary told him that he would be contacted by telephone on that or the following day.

Hearing nothing, Chisembele went again on 23 February, this time he was told by an official that the Deputy Minister had referred him back to the Deputy Commissioner of Lands.

Chisembele had been patient to the extreme and now he went, as directed, to a meeting with the Deputy Commissioner of Lands. During the course of this meeting, he finally lost his temper as it became obvious from the treatment he was receiving that there was no intention by the Government to correct the issue, and he was being treated as a fool. I quote from "A Brief History 1991-2000, Chisembele":

Then I was taken to see the Deputy Commissioner of Lands, Mr Malunga, who asked me 'what can I do for you Mr Chisembele?' I was provoked and felt this to be an insult to me and I retorted that I did not come to see you to start with

---

[146] "Judiciary Not Free", Post Newspaper, 6.5.2002, scan.

as I am on Appeal, it is the Deputy Minister I came to see but his secretary told me that the Deputy Minister is not around but he has already made arrangements for me to see you about my Appeal. This is very confusing, why should I be referred to you the Deputy Commissioner, I asked, your senior the Commissioner of Lands, Mr Zulu, has already told me that what you did by issuing the CERTIFICATE OF RE-ENTRY on my farm was wrong and that the CERTIFICATE OF RE-ENTRY is invalid and he assured me that he was going to instruct you to cancel it, but you didn't. Why? I asked him.

I went on to say 'you people what you are doing to Zambians is horrible, you have no right to be grabbing lands from farmers for nothing because you are so greedy; you are not even ashamed of what you are doing, this is very unfortunate. This behaviour has contributed to the damage of this country's reputation and honour, which we had built after independence. The Zambian passport was a paper of honour and respect, today it carries no respect and holders are subject to harassment at international ports, nobody gives respect to Zambians today, it will take great courage and effort to bring back the standard of honour which we had. Our policy then was to create as much impetus as we could when it came to agriculture and land development so as to attract as many Zambians as possible to settle and develop the land, not as workers but owners of the land, but you people you are doing the opposite and don't you expect people like me a freedom fighter to watch you grabbing lands from Zambians and treating them like pieces of dirt and do nothing. No wonder there is an outcry in the country, I told him, I am going to join the progressive forces to fight MMD Government until it is out. My colleagues freedom fighters who have already answered the Lord's call could not be happy to see the human rights and dignity they fought and died for being abused by you people, don't make a mistake that because I retired from politics in 1983 so the people have forgotten me and they will not respond to the call ... watch my words.' The Deputy Commissioner of Lands in reply said he was sorry he had made a mistake in issuing the CERTIFICATE OF RE-ENTRY.

Then I asked him if you have made a mistake then why didn't you cancel it. He said he had no power only the Commissioner of Lands has power to cancel the CERTIFICATE OF RE-ENTRY. I said this is incorrect because your Commissioner, Mr Zulu, said the same power you used to issue the CERTIFICATE OF RE-ENTRY is the same power you will use to cancel it. Then he said 'Mr Chisembele don't be worried, everything is going to be alright' I challenged him straight away that this was the same appeal you made to me with your Commissioner on the 29th November 1999 when you promised me that you were going to write me a letter after our discussion over the farm which I told you was developed and I briefed you on what I was doing further in the field of development, and you were advising me not to worry but to concentrate on what I was doing, but 3 days later your Commissioner, Mr Zulu, went on leave and you, Mr Malunga, issued me the CERTIFICATE OF RE-ENTRY, how can I trust you, I asked. Then he said, 'No! Mr Chisembele what should be done is that you should come back in 2 days' time on Friday 25th February at 15.00 hrs and we shall go together to see the Deputy Minister, by that time the Deputy Minister will be waiting for us'. I left.

This crucial meeting must have been reported to State House for very early the following morning Valentine Kayope telephoned; he spoke to me and told me that President Chiluba had rung him that morning. Kayope was very concerned about the incident and Chisembele's reaction and he asked me to calm my husband. I explained that Chisembele's back was against the wall and he would do what he thought was right with my full support. Kayope did not speak to Chisembele at the time, but later that day he rang again and informed Sylvester that an appointment had been made for him to see the President at 16.00 hrs. A telephone call was also received from State House asking whether transport should be provided. I could not understand the rationale behind the politics and the actions taken against us. I knew that President Chiluba was displeased with Chisembele for his refusal of a post in the Government or the diplomatic service which had been on offer from the President. Chisembele had even been tentatively approached by his sister, Victoria Chiluba, on this issue.

Chisembele went to the arranged meeting with President Chiluba who assured him that all would be well and that he would be handling the matter from then on. During the meeting, the President had telephoned, in apparent anger, to the Minister of Lands and told him that Chisembele had been unfairly treated. Chisembele told the President that there was a pre-arranged meeting for the next day with the Deputy Minister of Lands and the President agreed that Chisembele should still keep the appointment.

The following day, 25 February 2000, Chisembele went to the Ministry and saw the Deputy Minister, Nkole, who expressed ignorance of Chisembele's previous day's meeting with the President. Nkole's behaviour during the meeting was belligerent and in the course of their discussion he said that he wanted to visit the farm to see it for himself. It was agreed that they would go together the following day. However, the visit did not take place and the Certificate of Re-Entry was cancelled the next day.[147]

During March the lawyer had advised that there was a good case against the Government for compensation, but he suggested that as there was a proven political dimension to

---

[147] Diary entries, pp 21 - 26 February 2000, scan

the affair it would be best to discuss the issue with the President first and settle the matter out of court.

President Chiluba had promised Chisembele during their meeting in February that a further meeting would be arranged to discuss the issues of the restaurants removal and farm destruction, but this meeting never materialised. At the beginning of April, a letter was received from the President regretting the treatment Chisembele had received, reading: [148]

Dear Mr S M Chisembele,

I was happy to learn from your letter of the 29th February 2000 to Hon A Nkole, MP, Deputy Minister of Lands whose copy I was availed that after our discussion in my office, the Ministry has finally written to cancel the Certificate of re-entry into your farm No.2563 at Chisamba effectively bringing to an end a protracted dispute about the status of your farm.
I am glad that inspite of the obvious anxiety and psychological torture you were subjected to, the matter has been laid to rest and you have retained ownership rightfully of a property on which you have spent all your time and resources to develop.

May our God keep blessing you always.
Yours faithfully,

Frederick J T Chiluba
PRESIDENT OF THE REPUBLIC OF ZAMBIA

In the course of the next months Chisembele had several meetings with the Minister of Agriculture, M. Sikatana and the Minister of Energy & Water Affairs, K.R. Lembalemba, to

---

[148] Letter from President Chiluba to Chisembele, 31.3.2000; "Summary & Comments on the Brief History 1991 - 2000", Chisembele, 2002, scans

discuss with them the issue of compensation for the illegal seizure of the farm and the destruction as well as the removal of both restaurants; this they assured him was in hand. He had also tried during the year to hold President Chiluba to his promise of a meeting to discuss the matter of the farm, restaurants and the issue of compensation.

In July 2000, we were surprised when Michael Sata on a Heroes Day programme broadcast on ZNBC TV talked about Sylvester Chisembele's heroic role in obtaining Zambia's independence. The surprise was partly because among many of the freedom fighter leaders Michael Sata was held in a degree of suspicion and distrust, not just because of his sometimes colourful behaviour, but because he had been a policeman, working for the British, during the freedom struggle. After independence, President Kaunda had brought him into leadership when he was courting support from the traditional leaders, for Michael Sata's father was an influential headman in Chitulika Village in Mpika, Northern Province.

President Chiluba in the meantime, contrary to the amendment to the Constitution limiting to two the presidential terms of office in 1993 under his MMD administration, was engaged in an attempt to gain support for a further change in the Constitution to allow him to serve a third term in the Office of President. This move was not supported by Chisembele and was almost universally opposed with even many members of President Chiluba's Cabinet reluctant or openly opposed to any such change. One of his colleagues, however, Michael Sata, did actively campaign on behalf of Chiluba in his bid to remove the two-term limit on the presidential office and he tried, unsuccessfully, to build up support for this amendment. Behind the scenes, in return for this backing President Chiluba was rumoured to have told him that he would name him as his successor.

The Mwanawasa Years

Chapter 13
2001 – 2003

2001

At the beginning of the year, President Chiluba, accepting that his bid for a third-term was a lost cause, abandoned the attempt. In August he appointed Patrick Levy Mwanawasa to be his successor. Mwanawasa had previously been his Vice-President but had resigned because, he said, the MMD Government was allowing corruption to flourish. Michael Sata, assured that he would be appointed Chiluba's heir, was furious at the deception and he left the MMD to form another political party, the Patriotic Front [PF]. Allegations later were that President Chiluba had promised several people confidentially and in private that he was going to appoint them his successor and so when the announcement was made that Levy Mwanawasa had been selected it caused bitterness, dissension and resignations in the MMD party.

There had been no action or response other than verbal from the Government regarding Chisembele's claim for compensation. The matter was still unresolved by the end of the year. The lawyer continued to advocate patience advising Chisembele that issues of this type take time to be investigated.

At the end of the year, the General Elections were held and Mwanawasa claimed victory with the narrowest of margins. The EU Observation Mission and other international observers failed to sanction the elections stating that they could not be confident in the announced results. Anderson Mazoka of the United Party for National Development [UPND] was the favourite to win and his narrow defeat was received with incredulity and widespread allegations of fraud and vote-rigging. During the run-up to the elections both parliamentary and presidential there was a climate of apathy and intimidation.

A period of unrest followed the announced result of the Presidential Election with riots in the cities and a police raid on the offices of the United Party for National Development where several party activists were arrested. The UPND President, Anderson Mazoka, along with several opposition party leaders alleged vote-rigging, but their attempt to challenge the election in the High Court was refused and their application dismissed.[149]

2002

A few months after taking Office, President Mwanawasa in a successful move designed to increase his popularity, which had never been particularly strong, instigated the process to remove the immunity from prosecution of his friend and benefactor, Dr. Frederick Chiluba. This was a popular move and in July 2002 the immunity from prosecution of the former President was revoked making way for charges of corruption to be brought against him in 2003. The various corruption cases against Dr. Frederick Chiluba dragged on for years until he was eventually acquitted in 2009; he died two years later.

There was no evidence that corruption was diminishing in the Government. President Mwanawasa, in turn, disappointed the country during his time in Office. He too had made many promises that he would stamp out corruption, but it proved to be rhetoric. On the international scene President Mwanawasa was being praised as a 'corrupt free'

---

[149] BBC News, 16th January 2002, scan

leader. This view was not shared within the country. He was soon embroiled in accusations of corruption with rumours abounding of involvement in huge sums of money passing through dubious companies.

In March, Chisembele was still having non-productive meetings with ministers, Lembalemba and Sikatana, over the farm issue which was continuing to drag on unresolved. He prepared a summary of the events surrounding the issue which has been recorded in "Summary & Comments on the Brief History 1991 – 2000". It was now obvious that nothing was being done by the Government to investigate or consider compensation for the destruction of the farm or the unjustified removal of the restaurants and so Chisembele attempted to take up the issue with President Mwanawasa who was one of the post-Kaunda era of politicians with whom Chisembele had no personal contact. Chisembele went to State House to seek an appointment and was advised by junior officials there that there were three ways to book an appointment to see the President: through a Cabinet Minister; through a personal friend of the President; and by a personal letter to the President. Chisembele tried all three methods, all of which proved futile.

In June Chisembele went to see the newly appointed Ambassador of the Republic of Zambia to the UN, Love Mutesa, a mutual friend of both President Mwanawasa and Chisembele, he expressed shock at the treatment Chisembele had received from the Government. Ambassador Mutesa was given documents which he personally took to the President who told him that he would grant an appointment to Chisembele.

Four months later in October, Ambassador Mutesa contacted Chisembele to tell him that he had again seen the President who informed him that he had passed the documents to his officers to study. Then again in December at a further meeting, Love Mutesa informed Chisembele that the President had stated that he would make an appointment for Chisembele soon. In the event, the attempts of the Ambassador to secure an appointment for Chisembele to discuss the issue directly with the President, failed.

During the course of this year, we heard reports on the BBC of various groups established in several countries seeking justice and restitution for abuses suffered at the hands of governments. This followed the example of the Jewish people who made successful claims against the German Government for atrocities committed against them in World Word II. The Aboriginal people in Australia took out an action against the Australian Government for the forced removal of their children and for their land rights. In fact, claims were being made by many dispossessed people all over the world. Here in Africa, the family of Patrice Lumumba had put in a court action against Belgium to claim compensation for the atrocities he had suffered and for his eventual murder; in Kenya ex-Mau Mau freedom fighters had also started to demand restitution for atrocities and imprisonment suffered at the hands of the British Government in their fight for Kenyan independence; and in South Africa, under an indigenous Government, demands were being made for restoration of land to black South Africans who had been forcibly removed from their homes and lands during the apartheid era.

2003

Chisembele thought about these various claims for restitution that we had heard about on the BBC and then of the many still-living freedom fighters, most in abject poverty, here in Zambia, many of whom had been maimed, imprisoned, and dispossessed. No provision had been made by the various Zambian governments to assist these aging freedom fighters. President Kaunda had made promises to act on their situation but had done nothing. Under the governments of Kenneth

Kaunda, FJT Chiluba and Levy Mwanawasa the aging freedom fighters were paid lip service on Heroes Day and Independence Day, but as far as their welfare or their rights were concerned these were just ignored.

This new world era of Human Rights and Justice for indigenous peoples was a challenge to us that surely we must also put in a claim against the British Government, instead of just complaining among ourselves that here in Zambia no one had ever been held accountable for the atrocities people suffered in their just, heroic struggle to bring Zambian independence.

In June, Chisembele decided that he would make a claim on the British Government which would, in effect, be a test case and when successful, as we were sure it would be, would give hope and open doors for others with justifiable cases to claim compensation. Chisembele started to prepare supporting documents for the claim and later in the month he personally delivered the claim documents together with a covering letter to the British High Commissioner in Lusaka.

On 30 July, Kayope came to visit and when told by Chisembele that he had made a claim on the British Government for atrocities suffered and wrongful imprisonments during the freedom struggle, Kayope was very interested and pleased. As they were meeting the following day for the funeral service of Kayope's grandchild, he suggested that Chisembele provide him with a set of documents for the Zambia Human Rights Commission [ZHRC] which he would and did take direct to the Human Rights Commissioner, J.C. Sakulanda.

A week later Kayope came again, I thought it was about the claim on the British Government, but it was actually concerning Dr. Kaunda. At this time Dr. Chiluba and his wife were accused by his chosen successor of corruption, and numerous serious charges were brought against them. Many people were questioning the obvious, why were charges brought against Zambia's second President but leaving the first President of the Republic, Dr. Kaunda, untouched. Therefore, a group of friends and supporters surrounding Dr. Chiluba were trying to use this fact to protect Dr. Chiluba and/or to include Kenneth Kaunda in the so-called promise of a crackdown on corruption, which if fairly applied should have included many others. An edited excerpt from my diary concerning this visit reads:

> *I thought Mr Kayope had come about SMC's claim on BHC but No! he came with papers and letters he intends to send to the governments of Germany and America about money stolen during the Kaunda period. He wants SMC to read and help. I spoke very frankly to him and I said 'people will say you are only doing this now because of your connection with Dr. Chiluba - they will say why didn't you pursue corruption when you were in power'.*
>
> *I went on to say that I thought plunderers should be pursued and all money stolen under the administrations of Chiluba as well as Kaunda should be recovered for the poverty-stricken Zambians. Mr Kayope confirmed that he thinks ALL plunderers should surrender their stolen money. He was adamant that Mwanawasa's Government is only selective in its Task Force. No doubt this is true.*

A few days later Kayope came again this time bringing with him papers regarding the corruption issues surrounding the administrations of Dr. Chiluba and Dr. Kaunda. My diary for the 14 August 2003 records:

> *Hospital – Physiotherapy - All ready to leave when Mr Kayope arrived. He brought papers with him for SMC to read. Anyway, we explained the position and he said he would bring them back later this evening. We all left together. I personally think it could be significant that Mr Kayope was*

with Dr. Chiluba this morning in the Court and came to us afterwards. While we were waiting for SMC, Mr Kayope asked my opinion. I was very frank and said plunderers should be followed up. I also said I had no respect for Dr. Chiluba for the way he had behaved towards SMC. I said he had insulted SMC when he offered him K3 million - a marketeers money. I also said we had firsthand experience of the corruption in Dr. Chiluba's Government and I said the President had taken no action on Nkole even when it was proved to him that the man was corrupt. I said Dr. Chiluba tolerated corruption in his Government. Mr Kayope asked me if SMC held the same views. I was diplomatic (I think!) and said I spoke from a non-political emotional view, but SMC was a politician and his views would be based on reason and proof.

On 28 August, Kayope came to tell Chisembele that the Zambia Human Rights Commission would take up Sylvester's case against the British Government. An appointment was made and Chisembele went to see the ZHRC Commissioner in September. Very oddly the Commissioner offered Chisembele one hundred and fifty thousand kwacha, which he then increased to two hundred thousand kwacha. Chisembele said the amount was too low and in any case his claim was against the British Government and not the ZHRC. The Commissioner then asked for a background report and, he said, he would take up the matter with the British High Commission. I wrote in my diary on 20 September 2003:

... up until 3 a.m. I worked on SMC's Background to Assassination Attempt. Finished it. It was interesting and I enjoyed typing it out. Managed to finish it in time, ran off a copy for him to take to Mr Kayope at 3 p.m. as arranged. It was a rush job to see if SMC could photocopy and, hopefully,

Personal Story of Sylvester M. Chisembele

Mr Kayope could give to Mr Sakulanda before the Commissioner sees the BHC. In the event, Sylvester went to Mr Kayope and found him gone. Apparently, Dr. Chiluba had gone there early in the morning and picked up Mr Kayope to go to Ndola for the funeral of Bishop de Jong.

Later, on his return from Ndola, Kayope took the documents to the Zambian Human Rights Commissioner, Sakulanda, and Chisembele also delivered duplicate documents to the Ministry of Foreign Affairs in Lusaka. There was a Freedom Fighters Association with headquarters in Lusaka and Chisembele also gave them a set of documents, and although they were very pleased with the action taken by Chisembele they were unable to participate or take any meaningful part in the claim, lacking the funds and the manpower.

By September there had been no response from the British High Commission and so in September Chisembele decided to contact Dr. Rodger Chongwe. Dr. Chongwe had been involved in an incident in 1997 when he had been travelling in a car with former President Kaunda and police had fired bullets at the vehicle seriously wounding Dr. Chongwe. He had instigated a claim against the Government who refused responsibility. Eventually he took the case to the United Nations Commission on Human Rights [UNCHR] who supported his claim and eventually he was awarded damages against the Zambian Government. We, therefore, decided that Chisembele should take the same course and find out from Dr. Chongwe the procedure to follow.

I telephoned Dr. Chongwe on 18 September, an excerpt from my diary reads:

Rang Dr. Chongwe at 6.45 pm he was very nice spoke good words about SMC. He said 'Who could forget the humanity of Mr Chisembele.' Said he would be pleased to help in any way.

Zambia – The Freedom Struggle and the Aftermath

Arranged that SMC would go to his office. I asked him to provide us with the address and contact of the Human Rights Organisation that helped him with his claim.

And on the 22nd September, an excerpt reads:

He saw Dr. Chongwe and Amock Phiri. Got the address, which turned out to be the same as the one I had. He said he had written, no reply in 3 months so he wrote again and again. Eventually, he heard from them that the reason for the delay was because they were investigating and had written the Zambian Government with no response. Eventually, they gave the GRZ 6 months to respond ... they didn't ... so they gave them a further 2 months ... they still did not respond, so they awarded damages over US $2 mil to Dr. Chongwe. Dr. Chongwe said correspondence should only be addressed to the Chairman.

Dr. Chongwe and Amock Phiri who was a friend and colleague and had been a former Zambian High Commissioner to Britain and in 1969 a member of the Committee of 14, were extremely interested in the claim that Chisembele was pursuing against the British Government and offered to assist in any way they could. Dr. Chongwe advised that he too when pursuing his claim had made an approach to the Zambia Human Rights Commission which had proved fruitless. Following this advice, Chisembele wrote to the United Nations Commission on Human Rights and to the EU Commissioner for Human Rights sending details of the claim submitted to the British High Commission. Copies of the claim documents were also sent to the British Institute of Human Rights and the Commonwealth Parliamentary Association, but no response was received from either of these two Associations.

Personal Story of Sylvester M. Chisembele

The Zambian Human Rights Commissioner, Sakulanda, informed Chisembele during a telephone conversation that he had made an appointment with the British High Commissioner to discuss the issue in two days' time, on 11 October. Sakulanda later informed Chisembele that he had been told by the British High Commissioner that they had referred the matter to Whitehall. The issue as far as the Zambia Human Rights Commission was concerned slowly petered out as Sakulanda did not respond to follow-up correspondence.

Chisembele had still received no answer from the British High Commissioner to his letter of 16 June 2003. Then in October, after he had sent the British High Commission several reminders and faxes, he eventually received a reply from the High Commissioner, Tim David, stating that the events were long ago and he believed were possibly barred after the lapse of time. The High Commissioner suggested, however, that Chisembele ask his Government to take action on the claim through the Zambia High Commission in London.[150]

Following this advice, Chisembele wrote to the Zambia High Commission in London sending them a full set of claim documents by registered post on 31 October 2003. In spite of follow-up letters, no response was received from the Zambia High Commission in London until the following year.

On the internal claim against the Government for the removals and destruction of the farm and restaurants, a year had now passed without the promised appointment to discuss the issue with the President materialising.

The recently appointed Vice-President, who had no political background and was personally unknown to Chisembele, was a Dr. Nevers Mumba, a pastor and founder

---

[150] Folder, "BHC – Claim Correspondence" : - British High Commissioner, Lusaka letter to Chisembele, 29.10.2003, 20.08.03, scan

of an evangelical ministry called Victory Bible Church. Pastor Mumba had become famous or infamous, depending on the point of view, through the "Miracle Crusades" he held where hundreds of people were said to have received miraculous cures. These assertions and other various miracles he claimed to have performed boosted his congregation and popularity, and Levy Mwanawasa appointed him as his Vice-President against this backdrop in 2003.

On taking up his Office as Vice-President, Pastor Nevers Mumba issued a statement published in *The Post* newspaper on 8 June 2003 appealing to the Nation to come to him if they felt aggrieved or had suggestions or complaints regarding government policies. He said he was open to all and had instructed his officials of this policy. Chisembele, with this in mind, wrote to request an appointment with the Vice-President on 29 October 2003 enclosing a set of farm and restaurants claim documents, a follow-up letter was sent on 14 November 2003. A telephone call was received a few days later from the Vice-President's Senior Private Secretary saying that an appointment would be made after they had had sufficient time to study the documents.[151] The appointment was never actually granted, however, the office of the Vice-President referred the matter to the Solicitor General.

Reports of widening corruption were now appearing in the press and pressure was mounting on President Mwanawasa to explain his acquisition of land and farms previously owned by government institutions and parastatals. Lt. Gen. Christon Tembo, President of the Forum for Democracy & Development, his former colleague, in a statement published in *The Post* newspaper called on Mwanawasa to return land belonging to the University of Zambia [UNZA] which he had corruptly acquired during his term in Office as Vice-President of Zambia. Lt. Gen. Christon Tembo attributed this factor to

---

[151] Ibid. Fn.70, Chisembele, letter to Vice-President, 29.10.03.

the President's failure to act on the land scandal involving the lands Minister, Judith Kapijimpanga and Copperbelt Deputy Minister Webby Chipili.

A few days later another former colleague, Lusaka lawyer, Sakwiba Sikota issued a statement in the same newspaper claiming that Mwanawasa had sold the UNZA land. President Mwanawasa responded by stating that he had surrendered the land, but this statement was challenged by Simon Zukas who had held the post of Agriculture Minister during the time the UNZA land had been acquired by Levy Mwanawasa. Zukas stated that in fact the UNZA land had only been surrendered after President Chiluba had forced the then Vice-President, Levy Mwanawasa, to do so. The issue of the UNZA land, in particular, was widely publicized.[152] President Mwanawasa and several of his ministers were accused of acquiring farms by 'allocation' whose previous owners had been removed for various dubious reasons or 'given' land that belonged to government institutions which had been unilaterally re-assigned without justification or following through legitimate procedure.

Countrywide, the Zambian Constitution remained a burning issue with many people disappointed in the failure of each successive government to accept a devolvement of the total power still held by the President. The signs clearly indicated that President Mwanawasa was running an elitist, scandal-prone Government and this was a cause of disquiet. The President had in April 2003 appointed a Constitution Review Commission to consider amendments to the Zambian Constitution. This Commission whose members he had appointed was to tour the country and was known as the Mung'omba Commission. President Mwanawasa would not listen to any of the calls regarding the composition of the Constitution Review Commission. Chisembele on being

---

[152] *The Post* newspapers, 17.11.2003; 25.11.2003; 22.12.2003, scan.

approached by various groups including the press made his views known that any Constitution Review Commission selected for the purpose of amendments to the Constitution must include representative members of all the groups of people making up the society of Zambia ... in other words a constituent assembly of elected and selected individuals representing the society at large.

Chapter 14
2004 – 2005

2004

In January following on the letter sent to the EU Commissioner for Human Rights in September 2003, regarding the claim against the British Government for compensation for atrocities suffered during the freedom struggle, Chisembele received a letter informing him that his correspondence had been passed to the European Court of Human Rights [ECHR]. In the following month of February, the ECHR agreed to consider the case and sent application forms which were completed and submitted to them on 29 April 2004.[153]

Within Zambia there had been no movement and no response had been received from the Zambia High Commission in London or from the Ministry of Foreign Affairs in Lusaka. Therefore, Chisembele decided that whilst waiting for the result of his application to the European Court of Human Rights, it would be correct to write direct to the British Foreign Office in London. I telephoned the British High Commission to obtain the right address and I spoke to a sympathetic British High Commission official, who advised a different course of action, recorded in my diary on 29 January 2004 which reads:

---

[153] Ibid. Fn.4 Folder, "ECHR – Claim Correspondence".

Personal Story of Sylvester M. Chisembele

I telephoned BHC for the address of the Foreign Office. A Lynn Shaw rang me back. She asked if it was in connection with the claim. She was extremely helpful and expressed surprise that the Zambian Government had not acted. She suggested SMC see the Zambian Minister of Foreign Affairs. Then she said she would contact Kenya to find the name of the British Lawyer representing the Kenyan women. She rang back with details of a lawyer, born in Zambia, who had represented many Africans. He is a Mr Martyn Day and she gave me full address details.

She said they had been in touch with the Foreign Office, and it was the Foreign Office who advised that the claim should be submitted through the Zambian Government, and she said no point in writing to the Foreign Office as they would refer the matter back to Lusaka, and we would be going around in circles. She was very kind and helpful.

Following this advice, Chisembele wrote the same day to the Minister of Foreign Affairs sending a further set of full documentation, with the request that they be passed through to the British Government. He also wrote to the UK lawyer, Martyn Day, as had been suggested by Ms Lynn Shaw.

In February, a response was eventually received from the Zambian High Commissioner in London, stating that he had referred the matter to the Ministry of Foreign Affairs in Lusaka. Officials in the Ministry of Foreign Affairs were, of course, aware of the issue and had been for some months, but had not responded.

In March, we heard another report again on the BBC that the lawyer, Ed Fagin, who represented Jewish victims of the Nazis and also Apartheid victims was now representing a group of black American descendants of African slaves transported to America in the 19th century in a claim against the slave ship insurers, Lloyds of London, for the terror and suffering caused to their ancestors,[154] Chisembele, therefore, decided to write also to his law firm, in the hope that he might be prepared to assist. However, no response was received.

Chisembele decided to make direct contact with the Minister of Foreign Affairs, Dr. K.T. Mwansa, and on telephoning his office he was informed by the secretary that the minister was out of the country. But later on the same day when a daughter rang the office, without stating a reason, but to find out when Dr. Mwansa would be back in the office, she was told that he was there and she would be rung back later, which she was. A letter of complaint at this disrespectful treatment was sent by Chisembele to the minister who then granted him an appointment. A meeting was held with Dr. Mwansa on 18 March 2004.

Chisembele had this meeting with the Minister of Foreign Affairs and discussed in full with him the justification of his case against the British Government for restitution for wrongful imprisonment, atrocities and destruction of property suffered by him during the freedom struggle for the independence of Zambia. But although the Minister of Foreign Affairs spoke very nice words about Sylvester personally, he was more concerned that such a claim would, I quote, *"open the floodgates"*. Chisembele in reply to the minister told him that it was the right of freedom fighters to seek for restitution and he went on to tell the minister that Britain is a rich country and there is no reason why poor freedom fighters should not be assisted by their Government to make legitimate claims for restitution. The minister said that he could not be involved although he did pass the issue on to the Attorney General. However, no government assistance was forthcoming and eventually months later a

---

[154] "Some Important Diary Notes & BBC Quotes - 2003 & 2004", Sophena Chisembele – 2004

Personal Story of Sylvester M. Chisembele

letter dated 5 August 2004 was received from the Minister of Foreign Affairs enclosing a copy of a letter he had received from G. Kunda, Minister of Justice and Attorney General, stating that it was *"a private matter"* and *"the case should be pursued through a Private Lawyer and Government will not get involved"*.[155]

Chisembele's case was a lost cause as far as any assistance from Zambian institutions was concerned and after following through various stages with the European Court of Human Rights, finally Chisembele received a letter dated 25 October 2005 enclosing a copy letter dated a year earlier, 25 October 2004, stating that the Ruling of the three Judges of the European Court of Human Rights in Strasbourg that heard the Case was that the events of the claim happened before the Convention came into force in respect of the respondent State, i.e. Great Britain and was, therefore, inadmissible.[156] Chisembele had no option but to accept the decision, but we did not understand why a time limit was in force as far as events in a previously British colonized country in Africa were concerned, whilst much older atrocities suffered by people in other areas of the world were being successfully pursued, albeit using various paths closed to us. It was also difficult to understand the attitude and refusal of the Zambian Government to support the claim or be involved in any way and as far as the suggestion that we take up the issue privately through lawyers this was an impossibility for we had no funds available to us to take such a course.

In contradiction to the ruling of the European Court of Human Rights on Chisembele's case, the BBC on 26 March 2004 carried a report of a ruling made by a Judge that the ten-year time limit on claims in previously occupied countries

---

[155] "Minister of Foreign Affairs – Meeting Notes" 18.3.04; "Letter from Minister of Foreign Affairs", 05.08.04; Chisembele "General Comments on Freedom Fighters", July 2004
[156] "Letter of Ruling from European Court of Human Rights", 25.10.2004.

could not apply where the violation of human rights was concerned. This ruling made it transparently clear to us that universal human rights 'justice' is selective.[157]

We had sought assistance from various quarters and Chisembele had even written with full documentation to the Secretary General of the UN, Kofi Annan, UK lawyer Martyn Day, USA Lawyers Michael Hausfeld and Ed Fagin, British Institute of Human Rights, and the Commonwealth Parliamentary Association but all these approaches were ignored, except in the case of Martyn Day, who wrote to decline to assist. Therefore, this attempted claim against the British Government came to a full stop as there was no avenue left open to us.

The case regarding the destruction of the farm and restaurants removal was still unresolved. At the end of January 2004 Chisembele had received a letter from the Solicitor General stating that the matter had been referred to him by His Honour the Vice-President. Chisembele wrote to the Solicitor General sending him a complete set of documents regarding the case which were acknowledged.

A meeting was held with the Solicitor General on 5 March 2004. The Solicitor General, S.B. Nkonde, appeared to be unaware of the issue, in spite of the fact that previously a letter had been received from him in which he wrote that he had received and read the documents. He asked several times during the course of the meeting if the farm still belonged to Chisembele. The attitude of the Solicitor General was dismissive of both Chisembele and the claim. A few days after this meeting we were astonished to receive on 10 March 2004 a letter from the Commissioner of Lands with a notification that our farm would be repossessed, allowing for a 14-day time limit in which we could challenge the decision.

---

[157] Ibid. Fn.154 "Some Important Diary Notes & BBC Quotes - 2003 & 2004", Sophena Chisembele – 2004.

Personal Story of Sylvester M. Chisembele

The letter was dated 25 February 2004 with a post-date stamp on the envelope of 7 March 2004 and so the 14-day expiry date was the next day. Chisembele replied immediately copying the correspondence to State House, the Solicitor General and to the Chibombo District Council which covered our area.[158]

Also in March, Chisembele received a telephone call from the District Secretary of the Chibombo District Council to say that the Council would speak on behalf of Chisembele to the Commissioner of Lands and he requested full information on the issue, which was sent to him. However, he said that the problem of farm repossessions in the Chibombo District area for disputed and doubtful reasons was commonplace nowadays.

As far as the case of Chisembele was concerned, the Government was obviously not intending to solve the problem and by this latest action to repossess the farm, with a Notification which gave an already expired period of appeal, was intent on a preconceived decision to remove the farm and hand it to an individual or concern waiting in the wings.

On 5 April 2004 the claim against the Zambian Government for the farm destruction and restaurants removal was formally rejected and a letter to this effect was received by Chisembele, to which he responded counteracting the reasons given for the rejection in a letter he wrote in reply to the Solicitor General on 16 May 2004.[159]

Chisembele had continued with his attempts to discuss the issue with President Mwanawasa until it became quite evident that the President had no intention of granting him an appointment and so to implement the advice of the lawyer that the only feasible option was to settle the matter out of court directly with the President was impossible.

---

[158] "Solicitor General – Meeting, 5.3.04"; Ibid. Fn.102 Folder, "Filalo Farm": "Commissioner of Lands", correspondence.
[159] Letter from Solicitor General, 5.4.04, scan; Letter to Solicitor General GRZ, 16.5.04.

Zambia – The Freedom Struggle and the Aftermath

In the face of the outright rejection and refusal by the Government to settle the issue, in June Chisembele assembled a set of documents referring to this claim he was trying to pursue with the Government around the farm and restaurants issue for the purpose of seeking further advice. He went to see Dr. Rodgers Chongwe on 11 June 2004, my diary reads:

SMC went to see Dr. R Chongwe. I am delighted with his reaction. He showed great interest and asked SMC to leave the documents with him as he wanted to study them. He said Mwanawasa has made a mistake, he should have handled this himself, it is a political issue. He said it should be exposed. Wanted SMC to see him again on Tuesday, but SMC explained my journey, so they agreed to meet on Thursday. This has greatly cheered me as I read the whole thing during the afternoon and it seems a strong case to me, but now Dr. Chongwe's reaction has confirmed it. SMC came with a letter from State House, Special Legal Assistant to H.E of outright rejection. Worked on reply to State House Legal Assistant and final letter to H.E.

I left for the UK on 15 June, but before doing so I prepared a set of documents for Chisembele to send to the UN Commission on Human Rights which was followed up later with reminders, but no response was received from them.

Over the next few months the set of documents that concerned the farm and restaurants issue was distributed to all Members of Parliament, the Chief Justice, leaders of Political Parties, Chiefs, Church and State Institutions. This country-wide document distribution was done for the purpose of exposing the corruption rampant in the Government and the MMD.[160]

---

[160] Ibid. Fn.102 Folder, "Filalo Farm: Distribution Cover Letter – 2003".

Personal Story of Sylvester M. Chisembele

In response to the distribution of these documents many people made contact and some tried to actively assist, among them: government ministers, The Archbishop of Kasama and the Secretary General of the Zambia Congress of Trade Unions [ZCTU].

The Secretary of the ZCTU wrote to the President on 23 September 2004 regarding Chisembele's case and his deputy informed Chisembele on 15 November 2004 that his case would be raised at a scheduled meeting with President Mwanawasa and the ZCTU Executive Board to be held at the end of November. The Secretary General of the ZCTU wrote to Chisembele on 6 December to inform him that this meeting had been postponed by State House until 17 December 2004. However, after later postponements the meeting between the ZCTU and the President did not materialise.

The Speaker of the National Assembly wrote regretting that neither the Hon Mr Speaker's office nor the National Assembly as an institution had jurisdiction to render any meaningful assistance, but he advised in his letter that Chisembele should *"relentlessly pursue"* the claim. A letter was also received from Archbishop James Spaita who wrote of his regret at the action taken against Chisembele.[161]

Following persistent rumours, during September another scandal involving the illegal transfer of farms to politicians after they had been re-entered by the Ministry of Lands was brought into the public domain. This time the accusations involved the Vice-President, Pastor Nevers Mumba, whom it was said had been given a farm in Chisamba belonging to Zambia Railways. The press carried reports on the issue and when questioned, the Permanent Secretary in the Ministry of Lands stated that the Minister of Lands was the best person to

---

[161] Letters from "Zambia Congress of Trade Unions – 23.9.04, 15.11.04 and 6.12.04"; "Speaker of National Assembly - 25.8.04"; "Archbishop James Spaita, 11.10.04", scans; various other letter scans in Folder, Ibid. Fn.102 "Filalo Farm".

answer questions over the transaction. Following the disclosure by *The Post* newspaper, the farm was withdrawn from the Vice-President and restored to the legal owners, Zambia Railways.[162]

Our Filalo Farm was also situated in Chisamba, an area which before independence had been the reserve of white settler farmers and, therefore, after independence a popular and sought after district because it had an existing infrastructure including roads both tarmac and gravel, and was just 60 miles from the capital, Lusaka. It was now an apparent prime location targeted by corrupt MMD officials and MMD politicians for the acquisition of land or farms, seized from others.

On 16 October 2004 we received a visitor, Cuthbert Mumbi Kolala, representing the Office of the Vice-President, he was accompanied by a family member, Ernest Chisembele. The purpose of their visit was to inform Chisembele that President Mwanawasa would bestow an Honour on him during the Independence Day celebrations later in the month. Chisembele immediately declined the Award giving the reasons for his refusal. He fully informed them of the case that he was pursuing against the Government concerning his farm and properties which involved corruption and the misuse of power within the Government. A case, he informed them, which was widely known as he had distributed documents not only to the President and government officials but to various organisations in the public sector. He stated that to accept an Award under the circumstances would impugn his integrity. An excerpt from my diary of 16 October 2004 reads:

This evening around 6 pm Cuthbert Mumbi Kolala came here bearing a Business Card from the Office of the Vice-President

---

[162] *The Post* newspaper 10.09.04, scan.

Personal Story of Sylvester M. Chisembele

to see SMC. He said he had come to arrange for SMC to go to the VP Office to discuss the Honour which would be bestowed on him on Independence Day. He talked of Kaunda and said how he had made it seem that he, Kaunda, alone had brought independence to Zambia. He said Kaunda would be shamed now by the honouring of real freedom fighters whom he had denied and now SMC would be honoured by Mwanawasa.

Mr Kolala was made aware of the situation and the rejection and treatment of disdain that SMC has received from Mwanawasa and his Government. He was given a set of documents. He told SMC he would not have come if he had known of the treatment SMC had been receiving from Mwanawasa. SMC told him 'Mwanawasa is too big to see me – he has refused to meet me because he is too big'.

A few days later on 22 October, Ernest Chisembele came again this time with a James Kekana:

Ernest came around 12 noon with a Mr James Kekana said to be brother to the Vice-President. They came to persuade SMC to accept the Honour from Mwanawasa. They were here until almost 4 p.m. but SMC refused. Mr Kekana said just let them take a photo and some historical notes and then the Award can be collected by a son or daughter! – SMC refused. Kekana said what they could do was to go through a Mr Sakala at the Bank of Zambia who is brother* to Maureen Mwanawasa and she can ask her husband to see SMC!

After they left, I was worried about Ernest collecting the Award (can we trust him?) so I rang Bwalya Matilda and asked her to get him to ring me immediately. He did and I told him forcefully that SMC's NAME MUST NOT BE USED and no member of the family must collect an Award on his behalf. Later in the evening Christina rang to say Caristo Chitamfya will come on Friday to interview Dad for the ZNBC TV. I reacted to say 'NO'. She spoke to Dad who

refused. Later Bwalya Matilda rang to persuade, again we said NO.
*Later information corrected this to nephew of the President.

And on 22 October an excerpt from my diary reads:

Ernest brought Killie* in the evening. Whilst they were still at the door after coming in, I asked if the Award business was cleared. Ernest said 'maybe, I think so, they might do a photo with some information about the struggle' I reacted instantly with real anger. I told them both that if SMC's name is used in any way, we will put rebuttal advertisements in all the newspapers and 'you people will pay for it, we are not paying for it' I went on and on as is my wont. I was trembled. SMC then talked to them explaining again the reasons in his calm, measured way - I just walked off.
*family nickname for Christina Chisembele

The two Government agents, Cuthbert Kolala and James Kekana, tried several arguments to persuade Chisembele to accept the Award stating that the compensation issue could easily be dealt with and that an appointment could be obtained for Chisembele to see the President after the Award had been received. Chisembele thanked them for coming and stated clearly that there was no way in which he would accept an Award from the Government. The State representatives regretted his decision, and assured Chisembele that his decision would be respected and his name removed from the Honours list. However, as a result of this latest visit, Chisembele to be sure decided to contact the Vice-President's Office direct and on doing so he received a third assurance that his name had been removed from the list of people to be granted Awards during the Independence Day celebrations.

Personal Story of Sylvester M. Chisembele

On the same day, 22 October 2004, a telephone call was received from Brig. General Godfrey Miyanda, a former Vice-President under the MMD administration and now leader of the Heritage Party [HP], to acknowledge receipt of the documents sent to him concerning the farm claim. Two days later he made a surprise visit to discuss this issue. He like so many others was shocked not so much because of the corruption involved, for the corruption existing in the Government was widely known, but because the Government had extended its grabbing of land from leaders known for their integrity and role in obtaining independence for Zambia.[163]

We thought the issue of the Award was closed, but we were astounded on 25 October 2004 to be told that Chisembele was named in the media as having been present and that he had been awarded the 4th Division Order of the Eagle by President Levy Mwanawasa during the Honours Ceremony at State House. The Award was published in Government Gazette Notice No.629 of 2004.

The following day Chisembele went to see the Cabinet Secretary, Dr. J.L. Kanganja, who said that he had been misinformed. The Cabinet Secretary said that he had been told that the whereabouts of Chisembele were unknown, but the decision was still made to include him on the Honours list even without confirmation of acceptance. Meetings and letters followed but yet again no action was taken to correct the situation and in spite of the commitment made by the Cabinet Secretary that he would degazette the Notice of Award, this was not done.[164]

On 2 November, family member Ernest Chisembele came again this time saying that he had been sent to arrange a meeting with Chisembele and the nephew of President

---

[163] Letter from Big. Gen. Miyanda, 21.10.04, scan.
[164] Folder, "Award Issue".

Mwanawasa, Simon Sakala a Director of the Bank of Zambia.[165] Two days later Simon Sakala came to the house to see Chisembele. Surprisingly he never mentioned the Award issue at all. He wanted to learn the details surrounding the farm and restaurants. After discussion with Chisembele, he was given a full set of documents. Sakala's reaction was sympathetic and he promised that he would do everything he could to assist Chisembele to obtain compensation and that he would inform his uncle of the full facts.

Simon Sakala discussed the issue direct with his uncle, the President, whom we were told had indicated that he would settle the matter and, Sakala said, the President had been convinced of the veracity and justification of the claim by the evidence which had been given to him.

In the meantime, we were engaged in seemingly endless correspondence and contacts in an effort to rectify the untrue media coverage of the Award supposedly presented to Chisembele. He attended meetings with Dr. Kanganja, Secretary to the Cabinet, who made promises of degazetting the Award and a correction published in the media; promises which were never kept.

In view of the impression that this Award presentation announcement gave of a lack of integrity on the part of Sylvester Chisembele; on the one hand accepting an Award from the Government and on the other accusing the Government of corruption, Chisembele prepared and sent a 'rebuttal' letter to all the organisations, institutions, and individuals to whom he had just a few weeks earlier sent full documentation regarding the claim he had made against the Government for the farm destruction and restaurants removal. This issue he continued to publicize believing that the exposure was of importance not just of this personal issue, for which he was seeking assistance in pressurising Government,

---

[165] "Sakala S - Diary Notes 2004-5"

but was also a potent illustration of one of the many instances of Government victimisation and the unbridled corruption in the country.[166]

Meanwhile the Constitution Review Commission which had been appointed the previous year was in progress under the chairmanship of Wila D. Mung'omba. When this Mung'omba Commission had been set up the action was met with initial hostility from some quarters particularly because the presidency itself was still in question with challenges pending in the Supreme Court. However, notwithstanding critics President Mwanawasa went ahead to initiate the Mung'omba Constitution Review Commission which, as with previous Commissions, was to tour the country to hear and record the views of the populace. There was widespread apathy as it was feared that even a majority view, if it did not meet the administration's requirements and approval, would be ignored as previous Commissions had shown. But the opportunity and hope that perhaps this time the Government would heed the wishes of the populace made the matter of the Zambian Constitution again a hot topic. The participation of the Oasis Forum, a body set up by the Churches to peacefully agitate to change and democratize the Constitution, was a welcome development. Chisembele too had started working on his paper "Constitution Contribution for Public Awareness", a document that he would submit when finished to the Mung'omba Constitution Review Commission.

In December 2004, a letter regarding the compensation claim for the farm and restaurants issue was received from Hon. Rose Banda, Deputy Minister in the Office of the Vice-President, in which she wished Chisembele God's blessing, but stating that no documentation was done during the new culture administration, a term used to indicate the Dr. Frederick Chiluba's MMD administration, and so, she wrote,

---

[166] Ibid. Fn.164 Folder, "Award Issue" "Rebuttal Letter – 27.10.04".

there was no written evidence. This letter was in response to a letter sent to her in August. Chisembele replied on 31 December and referred the minister to the full documentation which he had sent to her in August, but apart from an acknowledgement no further contact was received from the Deputy Minister.

In contrast, a few weeks later a letter was received from her colleague, Cabinet Minister Rev. Gladys Nyirongo, Minister of Sport, Youth & Child Development in which she stated that Chisembele should insist on a meeting with President Mwanawasa who was, she stated, the only person able to address the farm and restaurants claim issue. This advice echoed that of the Speaker of the National Assembly and Chisembele's lawyer, A.J. Lungu of Chilupe & Co.[167]

Also in December a visit was received from Ernest Chisembele who came with some others to tell us that if a statement was made and signed by a witness present at the destruction of the farm then this would be sufficient for the Government to grant compensation. Chisembele said that such a witness could not be produced because the farm workers present at the time had all run away in fear. The response was that this did not matter, anyone could write and sign the statement. As this suggestion was tantamount to fraud, Chisembele refused outright. A few days later a message was received from Simon Sakala, President Mwanawasa's nephew, the details of which from my diary of 17 December 2004, read:

> *Ernest rang in the morning to say that Mr Sakala had telephoned him to ask again for a statement to witness the destruction of the farm - he said it was a mere formality that would not be followed up and even Ernest himself could make*

---

[167] Letter from Deputy Minister, Office of the Vice-President, 9.12.04, scan; Letter from Minister of Sport, Youth & Child Development, 21.1.2005, scan.

the statement. SMC told him NO! it must be above board and no lies from our side must be told. I said I would prepare photos and give him those. This could be a trap - if we make a false statement the Government could then issue a press release to discredit SMC and cancel out his publicity by saying Government had investigated and found that Mr Chisembele had made a fraudulent statement and therefore Government had rejected his claims. Michael Sata is saying 'Mwanawasa has fallen into my trap' - there is no way we will tell lies and fall into a Mwanawasa trap!

Chisembele did, however, write the same day to Simon Sakala explaining the reasons why a statement from a witness could not be given and he sent some photographs for his scrutiny. Ten days later Simon Sakala made another visit and he was given a full set of photographs detailing farm development and of the destruction that followed. He said that the President would return to Lusaka in January, following the Christmas break, and he would then take the photographs personally to the President and he would make further contact with Chisembele in the middle of January. A few days later I telephoned Ernest, who informed me that Sakala was impressed with the farm photographs; I recorded in my diary on 29 December 2004:

I telephoned Ernest late morning. He said he was about to telephone us. I asked what Mr Sakala's reaction to the photos was. He said Mr Sakala said it is enough. He said Mr Sakala was doubting, but now he is satisfied. He said Mr Sakala had rung him yesterday to say he is going to Copperbelt with the President and will contact us middle January. Ernest said Mr Sakala was impressed with the photos. This news cheered me up and gave me the spirit to start working on all the old files.

2005

Chisembele was ill towards the end of the previous year and we were told that it was recurring malaria, he was prescribed medications, but they were ineffective. In January, Archbishop James Spaita came to visit him and during the time he spent with us discussed at length the issue of the farm destruction and, he said, he would raise the subject of the farm with the President at their next meeting. Several government ministers responded to the documentation they had received from Chisembele on this issue, and he had individual meetings with them to discuss the matter, but none were forthcoming with any concrete suggestion or were able to assist in settling the issue.

In February, we received a telephone call from Fr. Miha based in the Copperbelt who informed us that in the next issue of *The Challenge* news magazine they would cover the subject. A telephone call was also received from Alfred Mudenda, Deputy Secretary General of the ZCTU, to say that they, the Union, had a meeting arranged with the Vice-President and Chisembele's case would be discussed with him. Certainly outside support was there and many efforts made to assist, but with those in positions of power to act within the Government there was no action. A feasible possibility, at least to arrange an appointment with the President, lay with the President's nephew, Simon Sakala.

Chisembele was working with an urgency to complete the "Constitution Contribution for Public Awareness" which was finished later in the year and submitted to the Mung'omba Constitution Review Commission. He was working late into the night writing even though he was unwell. The issue of the Zambian Constitution was uppermost in his mind during this last year of his life. A few months after his death in 2006 this work was serialised in the *Weekly Angel* newspaper.[168]

At the start of his undiagnosed illness he told his daughter, Bwalya Matilda, that the battle of the Constitution he had engaged in might get him killed, but, he said, those who work for God do not fear. As the illness progressed he believed and said that he had been poisoned.

In view of Simon Sakala's visits and his discussions with the President, we were shocked to receive another Repossession Order on the farm, dated 8 March 2005. Of late we had not received any communication from Simon Sakala and so on 29 March Chisembele wrote to inform him of the turn of events, and in the letter he outlined the substance of their previous meetings. This letter was hand-delivered by Bwalya Matilda who later informed us that she had had a meeting with Sakala who told her that he had a conversation on Good Friday with the President, but that the President had not yet had sufficient time to read the documents.

Sakala had also said that he was upset with Chisembele's letter of 29 March 2005; we were sorry to hear this because that was not the intention for we were appreciative and thankful to Simon Sakala because he had shown seriousness in trying to get some action regarding restitution and compensation for the farm and restaurants issue. The following day Sakala informed Bwalya Matilda that he had seen the Commissioner of Lands and during the meeting the Commissioner said the Repossession Order on the farm would be revoked.

Chisembele had submitted his "Constitution Contribution for Public Awareness" to the Mung'omba Constitution Review Commission and following this, he was approached

---

[168] "The Vitality of Constituent Assembly" The *Weekly Angel* (Lusaka) serialised between issue No. 0069. 10.04.2006 to issue No. 0083, 25.10.2006, scans; Ibid. Fn.84 "Constitution Contribution for Public Awareness", 2005.

to speak at various forums on this topic, which to him was the most important issue facing Zambia. *The Post* newspaper also organised a forum at which he spoke extensively and this was followed by an interview broadcast on Yatsani Radio, which he gave even though he was very ill at the time.

The Yatsani Radio reporter asked a question during the interview regarding the Committee of 14 which had been established in 1969 and banned by President Kaunda the following year. He asked if Chisembele thought that he and the Committee of 14 leaders had failed in their attempt to bring democracy to Zambia. This is a question that others have asked.[169]

It has been stated by one UK historian that the aim of the Committee of 14 was *"tribal balancing to oppose Bemba influence in UNIP"*. This is not correct and does not take into account the fact that Luapula, a prominent member of the Committee of 14, is a Bemba-speaking Province, as indeed are the Copperbelt and Northern Provinces. Tribal balancing, therefore, is not at all the same thing as equal provincial representation, and, in fact, President Kaunda had paid token tribute to the idea of tribal balancing, which in itself would be a difficult if not impossible achievement when there are over 70 tribes in Zambia. The difference was that the Committee of 14 wanted the provincial representative UNIP Members of the Central Committee to be equal in number and elected within the individual provinces, thus ensuring a democratic process, and not be subject to the approval or selection by the Head of State, so that whatever influence might exist in the governing of the country should at least be spread across all the provinces that made up the Nation. There is certainly nothing strange or new in this concept, everywhere people want to be

---

[169] Ibid. Fn.75 Yatsani Radio, sound file "S.M Chisembele interview with Yatsani Radio" 22.11.05; *Sunday Post* (Lusaka), 20.11.05; Letter from. Kayope April 2012; National Assembly Debates 30.1.74, col.691, 692, scan.

represented by elected members of their own community who obviously would know and appreciate their wants and aspirations.

It has also been alleged by the same UK historian that the grassroots structure was *"a vibrant but rather uncontrollable mass movement"*. This statement too is incorrect in that it is from the organised grassroots structure that the freedom fighters emerged who through sacrifice and dedication eventually achieved independence. The grassroots structure that existed in Luapula Province, Northern Province and the Copperbelt, the foremost provinces in the fight for independence, was by and large well organised, controlled and effective throughout the period.

As far as the leadership of Luapula Province is concerned which includes the extensive presence of Luapulans in the Copperbelt and elsewhere, I know that I am not alone in stating total belief that the leadership of the Luapula veteran freedom fighters was not only vital to the establishment of Zambia as a Nation but successful and sound. And in particular Chisembele's guidance after independence along the path of peace whilst working towards the time when the importance would be realised by the majority of people in all the provinces of Zambia of the need to correct the mistakes in the imposed Zambian Constitution, which gave all power to one man and thereby established dictatorship right at the start of Zambia's independence. His approach was correct in that, as was the raison d'être for the establishment of the Committee of 14, it avoided the destruction, terror and slaughter inflicted on the peoples of too many African countries by sectional interests, coups d'état and counter-coups.

At no time did Chisembele or the Luapula leadership support the dictatorship enforced by President Kaunda and their lonely stance against One Man Rule began before independence and continued thereafter, hence the hatred that

Zambia – The Freedom Struggle and the Aftermath

President Kaunda held for Chisembele and the early Luapula leadership, that is those who did not accept to become 'bootlickers' or participants in corruption, which was a tool President Kaunda used to ensure control.

Chisembele and the Luapula leadership apart from the strategy they employed, before and after independence, which included the successful dissemination of information for non-violent action also kept in mind that when dealing with an implacable enemy, such as Kenneth Kaunda, the use of the tactics of the Bemba proverbial mouse which nibbles at your toes and then breathes cool, soothing air and goes away and comes back again and so on until, without your realization, you are crippled. This proverb and the previously mentioned proverb 'when the elephant fight, it is the grass that suffers' were quoted to me by Sylvester Chisembele and particularly on one occasion when I expressed frustration at his refusal to go along with suggestions from some leaders that they should take direct action and organise demonstrations when he was suspended in 1971. Chisembele knew the time was not right and the cause was not sufficient and he did not trust Kaunda to refrain from using the paramilitary police to shoot and kill unarmed civilians.

I quote an excerpt from a letter I received written by Valentine Kayope in response to a section from this brief history which I sent to him for perusal:

The Para may stand as written. The Committee of 14 leaders did not fail in their attempt to bring democracy to Zambia. It was a start in the effort to influence change but the country and the people were not ready and Kaunda was stubbornly adamant. Sylvester Chisembele had foresight not to force the way as acting otherwise would have resulted in Kaunda happily unleashing paramilitary police on defenceless people under pretext of maintaining law and order like he brutally did before to the ex Lumpa uprising when he was Prime

Personal Story of Sylvester M. Chisembele

Minister. The 'when the elephant fight, it is the grass that suffers' becomes most relevant and appropriate to this forbearing patience.[170]

In spite of the obvious displeasure of President Mwanawasa and the threats that he made against those who did not agree with his views on a proposed new Constitution for Zambia, I found President Mwanawasa's rebuff of Chisembele astonishing in view of Chisembele's personal political history. Chisembele had had difficult relationships with previous administrations, but not such obvious, open rejection at a personal level.

So many people had made direct approaches to President Mwanawasa on behalf of Chisembele, believing his case to be just and deserving of a hearing, among them government ministers past and present; the Zambian Ambassador to the United Nations Love Mutesa; Secretary General of President Mwanawasa's own party the MMD; the Zambia Congress of Trade Unions; Archbishop James Spaita; leaders of other political parties including Enoch Kavindele who had served as Vice-President under the MMD administration during the period 2001-2003; and including President Mwanawasa's nephew Simon Sakala.

In fact, Enoch Kavindele during a meeting he had with Chisembele informed him that he had been given a compensation payment of over one billion kwacha for a case he had against the Government and he expressed shock at the treatment Chisembele had received. Enoch Kavindele was absolutely sure that he could arrange a meeting for Chisembele with the President, as were the Zambian Ambassador to the UN and others who had access to the President through their positions or familiarity.

---

[170] Letter from W.V.C. Kayope, 29.6.12, scan

I was confounded by the refusal of the President to meet and discuss the issue with Chisembele who though not a particular acquaintance of his was neither a friend nor a personal enemy, making the reason for his refusal inexplicable.

This issue of the threats to Chisembele's ownership of the farm and the compensation claim re the farm and restaurants alongside the Award debacle were still outstanding and unresolved at the time of the death of Sylvester Mwamba Chisembele on the 5th February 2006. When he was dying in hospital he asked me the heartbreaking question *"is the farm safe"* I told him untruly that it was.

Chapter 15
2006 – 2009

2006
Sylvester Chisembele died on the 5th February in the Government University Teaching Hospital. His death was traumatic. He had been admitted to the University Teaching Hospital and put in a side ward which was bare, containing only a bed and a dilapidated side-locker. The room was dirty with broken windows and there was scant staffing. We made efforts to improve his surroundings taking in bedding, a mosquito net, a chair and sheets of cardboard which we fixed as best we could over the broken windows. Representation was made to the Minister of Health and when no response could be obtained we contacted by letter and personally, led by our eldest daughter, Bwalya Matilda, various organisations requesting assistance in pressurizing the Government to transfer him to a section within the hospital which catered for private patients and government sponsored patients, and where the conditions and medical treatment were to a high standard. The private wards were open to those who could afford the additional very high costs. Within the public and these private wards, the medical treatment and surroundings were worlds apart.

All our efforts were to no avail; the Government was impervious. We had made physical representation to the Ministry of Health where efforts to see the Minister, the Permanent Secretary or their deputies were fruitless. We approached the political wing of the Government, going around from office to office and when the situation was becoming desperate I wrote directly to the Minister of Health on 29 January 2006, but the letter went unacknowledged. We were not asking for something unusual or particularly preferential, for others who had served Zambia in the past and present were assisted in time of medical need.

When near death he was transferred to the Intensive Care Unit, Kenneth Kaunda came to visit him. Two serving Government Ministers, Vernon Mwanga and Dr. K.T. Mwansa came to the intensive care unit to visit another patient, and on being approached by a family member they stopped by Chisembele's bedside. When they left the ward on their way out I spoke to them and requested Government assistance, but my approach was brushed aside and I was told that the Minister of Health had seen my letter, but she was away and that the Permanent Secretary would deal with the matter. When I challenged this statement by referring to the unsuccessful and unacknowledged attempts made by family and others for assistance to be given to Sylvester Chisembele, it angered Minister Vernon Mwanga and he and his companion turned heel and walked away.

Even at this late hour, Valentine Kayope, unwell himself at the time, tried again, unsuccessfully, to get for Chisembele the Government assistance he needed. Others had also tried, but the Mwanawasa Government was implacable. It was a commonly known fact that it was a practice of the Government to provide medical treatment, even overseas, for 'friends' of the Government and here was Chisembele who had never sought or asked for privileged treatment from any government, denied even basic assistance.

In spite of Sylvester Chisembele's immense, unsurpassed contribution to the attainment of independence and his service to the Nation, in the end he was left to the mercy of God to die in what can only be described as squalor and neglect. As a family we could not raise the exorbitant funds needed to pay the fees to transfer him to a private ward within the hospital where facilities and medical care were infinitely better.

After his death, as was the custom, a wake was held during which there was a meeting of the family elders to discuss arrangements for the funeral, the issue was raised of the siting of the grave in church grounds. This was discussed with the Archbishop of Kasama, James Spaita, who travelled down from Kasama in the Northern Province, arriving at our home after darkness had fallen. Archbishop Spaita gave the opinion that we should go ahead with the burial in Leopards Hill Cemetery and at a later stage, after consultation with other authorities in which, he said, he would participate, we could see about arranging reburial in Cathedral grounds, given the contribution and character of Sylvester both in public and in private and his lifelong Catholic faith.

Sylvester Chisembele was buried in Leopards Hill Cemetery on the 9th February 2006. His Grace the Archbishop of Kasama, James Spaita, travelled down again from Kasama to conduct the Funeral Mass and interment. During his homily he spoke of the humility and self-effacing nature of Sylvester and of his endurance during the days of the freedom struggle.[171] His words were uplifting followed by eulogies from Valentine Kayope and family members. Notification of his death and funeral had been sent to Cabinet Office, but no representative of the Government attended.

On 6 March 2006 I wrote to President Levy Mwanawasa informing him directly of the death of Sylvester Mwamba Chisembele and enclosing copies of (a) the letter I had written to the Minister of Health, (b) the general letter seeking assistance, and (c) the meeting notes of Hon. Vernon Mwanga's visit to the UTH. The purpose of my writing to the

---

[171] Sylvester M. Chisembele, "Funeral Mass", 05.02.2006, composite photographs

Personal Story of Sylvester M. Chisembele

President was to inform him that I would continue to try to get some justice from the Government for my husband. This letter too went without response or acknowledgement. Later after the publication of the Obituary for Sylvester Chisembele in the *Weekly Angel* newspaper, I sent a general distribution letter to various institutions and individuals with which I enclosed copies of this letter that I had sent to the President and its attachments.[172]

The previous week I had also written to Simon Sakala sending him copies of correspondence surrounding the death of my husband and informing him that I would continue the claim for the restitution for our farm and compensation. I also sent a photocopy of the Certificate of Re-Entry to our Filalo Farm. I received a telephone call from Simon Sakala on 8 March expressing his condolences.

We prepared an Obituary for Sylvester Chisembele which originally the *Zambia Daily Mail* had promised to publish, but later their spokesman came back to us and regretfully declined. The other government newspaper the *Times of Zambia* also regretted that they could not publish the Obituary. The independent newspaper *The Post* also faded away in spite of initially suggesting they would also carry an additional piece on the life of Sylvester Chisembele.

The Obituary was eventually taken to the *Weekly Angel* newspaper, an NGO [non-government organisation] and published in their edition of 13 March 2006.

The attitude of dismissal and total lack of respect shown during his illness and following his death caused in me anguish to turn into fury and in the week following the publication of the Obituary, a further article covering the events surrounding his death entitled "VJ Lets Down Politician's Wife" was published in the same newspaper on 20 March. I had been warned by the editor of the *Weekly*

---

[172] Letter to President Levy Mwanawasa, 6.03.2006; Folder "Obituary Documents".

Zambia – The Freedom Struggle and the Aftermath

Angel newspaper to expect a hostile response from the Government. On 30 March 2006, a few days after the publication of the second article, the editor came to inform me that the newspaper had been blocked from publication.

In the *Weekly Angel* edition published on 20 March 2006, the newspaper carried an editorial titled "Tribal politics" detailing the effectiveness of Sylvester Chisembele's implementation of the "One Zambia One Nation" slogan, which read:

> *Anyhow, this issue was ably tackled during the Kaunda era through the One Zambia One Nation slogan that was made effective by then Western Province* (Barotseland) *minister and freedom fighter, the late Sylvester Chisembele who would later head the Copperbelt, and yet he was a long time Chembe Member of Parliament in Luapula Province. Thus, the people of this region are sometimes despised as tribalists together with their traditional cousins the Tongas because they were the only Zambians to have supported the opposition wholeheartedly.*[173]

There was a strong public reaction to the publication of the Obituary and the account of the hospital treatment Chisembele had received. The coverage of these events in the *Weekly Angel* resulted in stories appearing in the other newspapers and TV discussions on the neglect of freedom fighters, to which I received several invitations to participate. I received telephone calls from Michael Sata, the President of the Patriotic Front, and from other political parties as well as another call from Simon Sakala, President Mwanawasa's nephew. I did not accept any of the requests to appear on TV

---

[173] The *Weekly Angel* "Death of a Hero", 13.3.06, Issue 0066, The *Guardian*, "Other Lives", 8.12.06.; The *Weekly Angel* "VJ Lets Down Politician's Wife", Issue 0067, scan; The *Weekly Angel* "Editorial", 20.3.06, Issue 0067, scan

discussion panels and as far as invitations from various political parties were concerned there was no way that I could allow the name of Sylvester Chisembele to be used for any purpose which he had not sanctioned.

This was an unnerving time for me with inexplicable, unsettling events occurring around me. The editor of the *Weekly Angel*, Shadreck Banda, who had been imprisoned in 2002 by the Mwanawasa Government alongside three of his journalist colleagues for allegedly insulting the President, advised me during a conversation that I should go to the British High Commission to 'watch my back'. I knew this advice was sound and I did so on the 23rd March 2006. During this visit to the British High Commission I was advised by officials to return as soon as possible to the UK, this was not advice that I could at that time follow, but I felt more secure after the visit.[174]

Within the week of the Obituary appearing in the press Kenneth Kaunda called a press conference and gave a radio broadcast speaking of the plight of freedom fighters. Mainza Chona too issued a statement on the same issue, and following the *Weekly Angel* article covering the Government treatment during the hospitalization of Sylvester Chisembele, Dr. Kaunda in an apparent attempt to justify his own treatment and neglect of freedom fighters announced at a press conference that he would be sending a team around the provinces to look into the conditions of still living freedom fighters (I have no idea whether he actually fulfilled this promise, I think he did not). President Mwanawasa reacting to the charge of neglect of freedom fighters called a press conference at State House on 31 March and issued a warning to former President Kaunda advising him to *"keep quiet"*

---

[174] Sophena Chisembele, "A Brief History – 2006 onwards", Shadreck Banda was shown this document when written in 2008 and gave permission for references to himself to be included; Sophena Chisembele, Diary Excerpts for 2006, scan; Dr. M.W.C. and Mrs B. Barr, emails to and from Sophena Chisembele, April 2006.

saying that he (Mwanawasa) had *"done enough for the people who fought for the country's independence"* and he also referred to the wealth of Kaunda and the good living he enjoyed.[175]

Voices which had been silent regarding the issue of freedom fighters and for that matter on the issue of the indulgence and corruption in successive governments were now coming out eager to make statements condemning the neglect of freedom fighters, and even Grey Zulu, a former Government Minister and Secretary General of UNIP, was reported in *The Post* newspaper of 28 March 2006 as declaring himself a pauper who had to sue the Government in order to obtain his gratuity of K40 million. Two days later, Enoch Kavindele, who was now making a bid to take over the leadership of MMD of which he was Vice-President, purchased a vehicle for Grey Zulu for which he was given publicity in the mass media for his largesse. Receiving the vehicle on 10 April from Kavindele, Grey Zulu threatened to mobilise former freedom fighters to fight for their retirement benefits from Government. These good intentions of Grey Zulu even if they had been fulfilled would only have benefited a select few, i.e. only those who had worked in the Government.[176]

However, as with Kenneth Kaunda's promises to look into the plight of freedom fighters, the pledges by others of action to help still living freedom fighters who had sacrificed so much for Zambia and who were now living in abject poverty, lapsed.

Shadreck Banda, The editor of the *Weekly Angel* when discussing with me the article on the Government treatment of Sylvester Chisembele, had also discussed with me the possibility of me writing further articles for the newspaper

---

[175] *The Post* newspaper, excerpt March 2006
[176] *The Post* newspaper, excerpts March and April 2006

and this I started to do, but later I was told that they had been stopped from publishing anything further written by me.

On 27 March I received a telephone call from State House informing me that President Mwanawasa would grant me an appointment to discuss the seizure of our farm which I was told could easily be sorted out. I said that a family member would be available to attend the meeting, but because of the circumstances and closeness of Sylvester Chisembele's death, I personally would not attend. Apart from the consideration of the mourning period which I knew would be understood, my thinking was that my husband of infinitely more worth and entitlement than me, had been refused an appointment to see the President in the months leading up to his last illness when he was fighting to prevent his farm being illegally confiscated and, therefore, I felt it would not be right for me to attend any appointment. I suggested that a family member should attend the offered appointment and this was agreed.

The President's nephew, Simon Sakala, informed me that the President had requested that I resubmit copies of the documentation and so I did this again with a covering letter dated 30 March 2006, and these papers were delivered by hand the same day. However, a day later I was informed that Levy Mwanawasa had had a stroke and had been flown to London. In the ensuing months, I was informed several times that the illness was delaying the proffered appointment, and after a period of time the issue of any meeting with President Mwanawasa died away and there was no official communication from the Government. Nonetheless, as a family we were mindful and thankful for the efforts that Simon Sakala had made on our behalf.[177]

---

[177] Chisembele correspondence with Simon Sakala, December 2004 and March 2005; Letters from Simon Sakala to President Mwanawasa, Commissioner of Lands and Sophena Chisembele, April 2006, scans

However, I felt duty bound to continue the fight for the farm and this I did until I had exhausted my capabilities. I was also trying my level best to continue Sylvester's efforts to rectify the fictitious announcements carried in 2004 by the ZNBC TV, the press and media of his acceptance of the Award which was also published in Government Gazette No. 640 of 22 October 2004. Eventually, after a challenging telephone call that I made to the Office of the Secretary to the Cabinet, I was called to Cabinet Office to a meeting with the Secretary to the Cabinet, Dr. Kanganja, to discuss the matter. The atmosphere in the meeting held on 24 April 2006, was intimidating and the Secretary to the Cabinet, was contentious from the start.[178]

On 16 April, the week before I had this meeting with the Secretary to the Cabinet, the first installment of Chisembele's "Constitution Contribution for Public Awareness" was published in the *Weekly Angel*. Again I was informed by the editor, Shadreck Banda, that there had been an immediate, appreciative reaction to the publication and that it had been very well received. However, at the end of April the editor came to tell me that again the *Weekly Angel* would be on hold, this time for a month or so and the reason given by the owners was that new printing machinery would be installed. After an interim period, the newspaper was back in print and the serialization of Chisembele's "Constitution Contribution for Public Awareness" continued until it was completed towards the end of the year. It was still in the process of being serialized until after the General Elections were held in September 2006.

In the first week of May, the Minister of Lands made a statement on ZNBC Radio that there was corruption in her Ministry which, she said, she would investigate as she had found that officials were corruptly giving away state lands

---

[178] "Account of Meeting with Cabinet Secretary – 26.04.06".

and lands that belonged to other people. The following day President Mwanawasa appeared on the main ZNBC TV news saying that the Ministry of Lands was the most corrupt ministry in his administration. These statements, whilst accurate, seemed very much at odds with the individuals making them for both had been accused of acquiring land illegally. Later, the following year, the Minister of Lands, Rev. Gladys Nyirongo and her Commissioner of Lands were sacked for corruption. In November 2003, her predecessor the former Minister of Lands, Judith Kapijimpanga, together with the Commissioner of Lands, Chipili, were reported in *The Post* newspaper as having been strongly condemned by the Chairman of the Lands Tribunal at the hearing of a case brought against a Company, owned by the Minister of Lands, the Commissioner of Lands and the Attorney General, for irregularly allocating themselves land. President Mwanawasa, too, had many accusations leveled in the press against the methods used in his own acquisition of several farms owned by him plus the acquisition of land belonging to the University of Zambia.[179]

There was a reporter, Solomon Zulu, working at the *Weekly Angel* who had been a great help to me, introducing me to their editor, Shadreck Banda, and facilitating the publishing of the Obituary and the serialization of Chisembele's "Constitution Contribution for Public Awareness" in that newspaper. Later he made several visits suggesting I should follow up the publicity gained by appearing on some TV channels. Solomon Zulu was a regular on several TV programmes appearing as a Political Activist. In fact on one occasion I was not happy when he quoted passages from Chisembele's "Constitution Contribution for Public Awareness" with no mention of his name, but then later when it became obvious that several people were doing the same, I

---

[179] Ibid. Fn.152, *The Post* newspapers, 17.11.2003, 25.11.2003.

realised it was immaterial whether or where credit was given. The important thing that Sylvester would have cared about was the enlightenment of the public especially regarding the need to change the Zambian Constitution and the reasons why.

Solomon Zulu had been instrumental in not only helping publish the Obituary but in taking copies of this and Chisembele's "Constitution Contribution for Public Awareness" around to political and NGO groups. He had taken copies of these documents with him to various political rallies up and down the country which he circulated. I wanted to widen the exposure of Chisembele's "Constitution Contribution for Public Awareness" and to facilitate this, I made a tape-recording of the Obituary for Yatsani Radio Station which they were prepared to broadcast. Zulu then suggested that I made several tapes which he would distribute to other radio stations.

In May, Solomon Zulu contacted me regarding a well-known businessman based in the Copperbelt who was interested in establishing an NGO to push for changes in the Constitution and, in particular, facilitate the removal of a certain existing clause so that children born in Zambia to parents, who were not necessarily Zambians, could contest presidential elections. Solomon Zulu was interested to hear what I thought about the issue. I told him that I did not think it was a good idea and not one that I would support, quoting him the example of the South American (Peru) ex-President Fujimori who after being indicted for corruption fled the country, claimed and was granted Japanese citizenship based on the fact that his parents were Japanese, this was then the basis for the Japanese Government to refuse a request to extradite him to Peru to face the criminal charges brought against him.[180]

The following day, Solomon Zulu rang to say that the Copperbelt businessman whom he had spoken to me about was in Lusaka and he wanted to see me. I was collected and taken to the Lusaka residence of "Mr X" and had a very interesting discussion. He told me that there was a group of white farmers who would be prepared to assist me in my attempt to recover our farm in Chisamba from the Government. However, later during the discussion he spoke of the Constitution and the fact that under present restrictions the children of non-Zambian born citizens were barred from contesting presidential elections. This clause he and like-minded people wanted removed and an NGO would be set up for this purpose. He asked my opinion and so I reiterated the views that I had expressed to Zulu the previous day; I said it was not something which I would or could agree with or support. Mr X was also in favour of the establishment of a Constituent Assembly, but its make-up was, in my opinion, not sufficiently representative, my diary for 12 May 2006 reads:

Mr X had a paper with the make-up for a Constituent Assembly. From memory it read: 27 seats Chiefs (each chief with 2 selected people) 3 seats each for the following: Army, Air force, National Service, Judges, Church Mother Body, Oasis Forum, Disability Groups, Trade Unions Federation, Students Union, NO POLITICAL PARTIES. It seemed unbalanced to me because many of the organisations cover appointed people and/or paid by Government. I said that some

---

[180] Comment: - Ex-President Fujimori fled Peru in 2000 but five years later he was arrested in Chile, extradited to Peru and sentenced to prison for 6 years for corruption. Some years on, other charges including violation of human rights were brought against him, for which he was found guilty and given further sentences of imprisonment.

Zambia – The Freedom Struggle and the Aftermath

were vulnerable. He replied not all. I said too the Armed Forces were appointed, he again defended saying only the top one not the rest. His interest is with the whites, Indians and coloureds. Said as British Government was responsible for imposing a wrong Constitution, they should be included along with the UN to correct the Constitution. I said maybe the UN in an advisory capacity to assist on protecting HUMAN RIGHTS as Zambia had signed the protocols, but as far as the UK Gov. was concerned, I didn't think so ... He appeared conciliatory. He said money is no problem. He dropped a lot of names. Said KK came and sat where I was sitting, said Paramount Chiefs were his guests, said he saw Mwanawasa and told him about corruption in State House and said to the President 'Shall I go on?' and H.E. said 'No! Let's discuss the Constitution'. Said he was the one that wrote a particular, critical political article that was published by Mission Press. I said I was impressed! Said he speaks on Icengelo, Phoenix, newspapers - in other words he is a big shot. Said Chiluba was going to appoint him Minister of Home Affairs, and had given him a list of people he must not touch. The list had the names of the drug barons. Said he would not take the post because of that and Dipak Patel had been appointed. Said the problem was that when they started MMD they had to use the drug barons because they had the money. Said that Chiluba told them that the drug barons would step down after 5 years, but they didn't.

Told me he could get plenty of money. Said he was offered US $20 million to start a political party, if he could get twenty good people, but the problem was to get clean people. Said he could easily get money for my cause because it was the type of clean cause his group was interested in. Said he wanted to help me. Said at the meeting of White farmers he wants to invite me to come and speak because money is no problem to fight my cause. I said I would not touch money, but if help was offered to reproduce and circulate Sylvester's

Personal Story of Sylvester M. Chisembele

'Constitution Contribution for Public Awareness' I would be happy. BUT SMC's Constitution document is exactly the opposite of their interest. I said even if we had opposing views, it would not make us enemies because that is what democracy is about - put out the views and let people make their own decisions - he said yes, that's right. I told of my visit from Archbishop and did a bit of name dropping of my own! Told of H.E's offer of a meeting. Left the H.E; Kanganja; and Distri letters, but not the newspapers as he said he had them. He gave me the impression they want me in a party; they want the name and the cause which is so clean. He said several times, money is no problem; he can easily get help for me!

However, I also explained to Mr X that I was only concerned with publicizing Chisembele's views on the needed Constitution changes and that, in fact, I had no basis in politics or citizenship to give me the right to participate on a personal level.[181]

Africa Freedom Day was near and on the same day of my meeting with Mr. X, I was told that freedom fighter and former Cabinet Minister Lewis Changufu had been reported in the press, and had been on the radio, stating that he would never accept an Award from the Government because he was disappointed over the way Sylvester Chisembele had been treated by the Government. Later I was informed that several people had followed suit among them Alexander Chikwanda, later to be appointed Cabinet Minister by Michael Sata.

After this meeting with Mr X, Solomon Zulu contacted me again to say that the Muvi TV station would broadcast a tribute to Chisembele and I was asked to appear. I was reluctant because I had taken on board the advice given me by Valentine Kayope and family members that I should avoid political groupings or appearances on TV or radio stations

---

[181] Ibid. Fn.174 Sophena Chisembele, Diary Excerpts for 2006, scan.

except Yatsani Radio, which is a Catholic Church broadcasting station. However, fearing that my refusal was cowardice on my part and because this was an exception in that it was a Tribute to my husband, I said eventually that I would do it.

On the arranged day, 24 May 2006, Solomon Zulu came to collect me and shocked me by telling me that Anderson Mazoka, leader of the UPND political party, was dead. He said that we should first go to the funeral house. When we arrived there were many people, politicians and individuals present. We spent some time at the mourning and in greetings. Eventually we met up with Mr X who told me he was a founder of UPND. The producer of the Muvi TV programme came over and said that we should leave shortly for the studio, but further conversation proved that the programme was not just a Tribute but also would cover political topics and a panel discussion. I expressed my disquiet to Solomon Zulu who accepted that this was not what I was prepared for. I decided I would not appear on the programme and he accepted my decision although both Mr X and the Muvi TV producer tried to persuade me that I should.

Anderson Mazoka had made several accusations against the Government. Apart from reiterating the widespread belief that the 2001 elections were fraudulent, he had claimed that he had been poisoned by government agents, and among his supporters this story had caused anger. Notwithstanding this and other factors, several MMD officials attended the mourning, among them government representative, Minister Vernon Mwanga, who was also a prominent MMD official, the following day he was shown on the ZNBC TV with a stiff arm and a bruised head. According to the reports carried in the Zambian media he had been beaten up at the funeral house. His presence had outraged party cadres who felt his attendance inappropriate. I did not feel as sympathetic as I should have done. The family of Anderson Mazoka apologised to the President for the incident. An Official funeral was held for Anderson Mazoka with the Service in the Cathedral of the Child Jesus, Pope Square, Lusaka, which had been completed and dedicated on 30 April 2006. Pope John Paul II had celebrated Mass on the site in 1989 on his historic and successful papal visit to Zambia. The Pope had blessed the foundation stone of this to-be-erected cathedral.

In June, following a family discussion an appointment was made for me to see A.J. Lungu of Chilupe & Co. who was the lawyer from whom Chisembele had been receiving advice re the claim for the farm and restaurants issue and who held Chisembele's Will, which we needed in order to finalise affairs. Together with Christina Chisembele I went to see Lungu on 11 June 2006, taking with us some selected documents and photographs and with the intention of giving him a CD covering the claim issue as it currently stood. The interview was hopeful and he asked that I send him hardcopies of all the documents rather than on a CD. He said that the matter could go to the Human Rights for Africa in South Africa after everything else was exhausted. He was very helpful and said he was Sylvester's friend and that the cause was just. Lungu said we should come again and see him the next week. We delivered a full set of hard-copy documents the same day.

The following Tuesday I went again accompanied by Christina to the given appointment. The lawyer was not as welcoming as he had been previously, but he telephoned the Commissioner of Lands in our presence to make an appointment. This appointment never materialized and although we telephoned the lawyer's office several times we failed to speak with him again and the contact ceased.[182]

By the end of July the campaigns for the General Elections were in full swing and I knew that it was time to completely

---

[182] AJ Lungu, Notes re Meetings, 2006

distance myself from politics. But I was told and I believed that Chisembele's issue was a burning one for on 28 July the Government announced that they had signed an agreement to build the Chembe bridge to span the Luapula River linking the Copperbelt, via the Democratic Republic of the Congo, to Luapula Province, something promised by previous administrations over the years, but which had always been shelved for one reason or another. Chembe was the constituency which Sylvester Chisembele had represented for 20 years.

In August Victoria Chiluba died. It was a shocking development and totally unexpected. Her funeral was held on 7 August 2006 with the Funeral Mass in the Cathedral of the Child Jesus, Pope Square, Lusaka. On this day Christina informed me that Dominic Chisembele had discussed the farm issue with Michael Sata and she told me that he would inform the family gathering of his action. The traditional meeting of elders after the funeral reception for Victoria Chiluba was held in Dominic Chisembele's house and although it is usually a male dominated grouping, I was able to brief the elders on the current position regarding the farm. Dominic's assurance of his active participation from this time on was welcomed.

Some days later Dominic came to visit in order to discuss various issues with me. I explained that I was continuing the fight with the Government over the farm and Award issues, but that as far as the farm was concerned, I was handicapped on several levels, and I did not have the financial or physical resources that were needed. We decided that he would take over the issue of the farm and I would continue to handle the Award issue.

Dominic Chisembele discussed the farm with his lawyer, Pikiti & Co. who expressed surprise and disappointment at the way the matter had been handled by the Government. The lawyer advised that it would be a long drawn-out process, but the case was important enough to be worth the effort and the wait involved.[183]

The Presidential and Parliamentary Elections were duly held, and on 2 August 2006 following the announcement that Patrick Levy Mwanawasa had been re-elected, riots broke out. At this election President Mwanawasa's main rival was Michael Sata of the Patriotic Front Party. The former party front-runner, the United Party for Democratic Development had formed an alliance with two other parties, the Forum for Democracy & Development and UNIP. There was a great deal of dissatisfaction with the result which was received with disbelief. The opposition announced that the elections had been fixed and the figure given for President Mwanawasa's vote share of 43% hugely inflated. Even in our suburban area of Lusaka riots were so bad that most vulnerable residents remained indoors. Shops in the city were closed and barred, now a normal practice when riots started.

The issue of the unaccepted Award was still unresolved and so we had continued to make representation to the Secretary to the Cabinet, Dr. Kanganja, to have the fictitious Award announcement rectified. Eventually on 2 September I received a single piece of paper carrying at the bottom of the page a date stamp of 8 May 2006 entitled "Gazette Notice No..... of 2006 Honours and Awards: Amendment to the Addendum",[184] this was un-numbered and undated. I wrote to the Secretary to the Cabinet querying its validity, but this letter and further attempts to clarify and confirm the implementation of the Gazette correction went unacknowledged and unanswered. I felt that I had reached the end of the road as far as the Award issue was concerned, and that I would just have to accept the piece of paper as it was in the hope that it was valid.

---

[183] "ACC. DM Chisembele and Pikiti & Co." folder.
[184] "GRZ Gazette Notice No.... of 2006".

Zambia – The Freedom Struggle and the Aftermath

I spent the rest of the year and the next concentrating on the "Constitution Contribution for Public Awareness", printing out hard copies for binding and then distributing widely throughout Zambia, with the help of others: family members and politicians who believed in the project and considered it important.

2007

By January it was heartening to learn that Chisembele's "Constitution Contribution for Public Awareness" was being very well received and I was particularly happy to receive a letter from the President of the Federation of Free Trade Unions of Zambia [FFTUZ] to inform me that they would circulate the document to their members and that they considered it invaluable.[185] The Zambia Congress of Trade Unions too informed me that they were very pleased to receive the document from me. I was later informed that the President of the FFTUZ was quoting from it at various meetings within the country.

Although I had handed the farm issue over to Dominic Chisembele, which was a great weight off my shoulders, I remained involved on the sidelines providing information and copy documents as and when needed. Then on 7 April I received a telephone call from our daughter Christina telling me that an official of the Zambia Anti-Corruption Commission [ACC] had telephoned her to say the ACC wanted to see us to discuss the farm. Christina said she had taken some documents in to them, and we arranged that I would prepare a complete set. She also telephoned Dominic Chisembele to inform him of the approach by the ACC. I wondered later if there could have been a connection to the ZNBC TV interview in 2005 with the then Minister of Lands, Judith Kapijimpanga, who was questioned on a live TV

---

[185] Letter from President, FFTUZ – 12.01.07, scan

programme and asked to give details of the farms that President Mwanawasa had acquired since taking office; she named three farms but then said that of the farm in Chisamba she did not know the details.

On 9 April 2007, I went with Dominic Chisembele and Christina to an arranged meeting with the Anti-Corruption Commission where the repossession of the farm was discussed at length. Nothing concrete came of the meeting, although the following day a telephone call was received by Christina from the Permanent Secretary for Central Province informing her that ACC officials had been to his office to investigate allegations and rumours that President Mwanawasa was involved in grabbing the farm from Chisembele. The Permanent Secretary said that he knew of the matter and told her that there were several farms in the area which had been seized from their owners. He also told her that we should expect a telephone call from State House.[186]

At this point in time, I decided that our daughter, Christina, should distance herself from our fight with the Government, because at that time she, an epidemiologist, was working in the Civil Service and as National Project Coordinator of Avian Influenza under the Food and Agriculture Organization of the United Nations. She held a Master of Science degree in Tropical Animal Health obtained from the Institution of Tropical Medicine, Antwerp, Belgium, and had undertaken several NGO sponsored courses in various countries. The fear I had was that her job with the Zambian Government might be put in jeopardy and, in turn, perhaps affect her future career.

During the course of the past few years the stance that President Mwanawasa had taken of insisting that the adoption of any amendments to the Constitution under the Mung'omba Commission which he had inaugurated in 2003,

---

[186] Anti-Corruption Commission – Meeting 9.04.2007

should be in the hands of an appointed elite assembly who would then pass their draft Constitution to Parliament for ratification, caused a chorus of dissension which had continued growing in intensity. Now, the President reacted with fury threatening to charge with treason any individual who expressed views which he considered were nonsense bordering on malice. This warning made in October did nothing to silence his critics, but swelled their ranks. The threat was made on a ZNBC TV programme and covered extensively in other media; it was also included in a broadcast on BBC World on 10 October 2007.[187] President Mwanawasa's words on the Zambia State television programme were *"Any more nonsense bordering on malice, they are going to be arrested and charged with treason. As you know, treason is not bailable"*.

2008
In the many months following the death of Sylvester I had been trying to arrange a re-burial in the grounds of the Catholic Cathedral of the Child Jesus in Pope Square, an aim which had been supported by the Archbishop of Kasama, James Spaita. I wrote several letters to pursue this optimum plan, but it was not to be. I was informed by the Secretary of the Archbishop of Lusaka in January that they were investigating and awaiting a response from the Lusaka City Council to their application, but eventually I received a letter from Fr. Lazarus Mwansa, Secretary/Chancellor of the Archbishop of Lusaka to inform me that the Lusaka City Council had refused their request stating that they would only allow the Church to inter bishops within the Cathedral grounds.[188]

---

[187] "Treason charge threat in Zambia", scan BBC News, 10.10.2007, scan
[188] Letter from Fr. Lazarous Mwansa, Secretary/Chancellor of the Archdiocese of Lusaka, 8th May 2008, scan.

Personal Story of Sylvester M. Chisembele

In August it came as a shock to hear that President Mwanawasa had died. He had not been appearing in public and in spite of the rumours concerning his health, his death was unexpected. The Vice-President Rupiah Banda became the Acting President.

2009
Dominic Chisembele died on the 28th May 2009. At his funeral both former Presidents Kaunda and Chiluba, as well as representatives from State House, government officials, past and present government ministers, and presidential hopeful, Michael Sata, were present at the funeral. At the burial service on 31 May, former President Kaunda and Michael Sata gave eulogies.[189] Dr. Kaunda preceding his eulogy with the waving of his famous white handkerchief, but not getting the same roar of response to his usual slogans; his era was definitely past.

During the earthing of Dominic's casket, Michael Sata had put out a hand to assist me across the uneven ground and he drew me across to former President Kaunda saying to him *"do you know Mrs Chisembele"* the reply was terse *"Of course I do"*, we exchanged polite words. I hoped the incident did not publicly indicate an alliance with Michael Sata's Patriotic Front Party, which did not exist, for Chisembele on retiring from politics did not support publicly any particular political party, rather his time and concern was with the Zambian Constitution and the rampant corruption in the country. On leaving the burial ceremony, Dr. Kaunda was courteous and with a smile and a wave of his handkerchief he bid me goodbye.

---

[189] Comment: - Dominic Chisembele had for a long time a respectful relationship with President Kaunda; his wife, Mary Katongo, for years had been employed as personal nurse to President Kaunda and remained for some time working for President Kaunda after the lost election in 1991.

Zambia – The Freedom Struggle and the Aftermath

During this last year of his life, Dominic Chisembele in a Court appearance concerning the farm reported to the family that *"I told the judge that the farm that the Government has re-entered is of a big freedom fighter who should be untouchable in aspects like these, if there were two biggest freedom fighters in Zambia, my brother is one of them, if there was one, my brother is the one"*.

A few years before, in April 2006, I had an inspirational meeting with a priest, who is a historian, and who had spent many years in Zambia. During the meeting I told the priest that Sylvester had said to me that he had been poisoned, I expected skepticism bearing in mind that the priest was European, but to the contrary he did not doubt. He said that poison and witchcraft were still in use in Zambia. He gave me counsel and it was his encouragement and suggestion that I should write a record of events pertinent to Sylvester Chisembele's life, which he deemed to be of great importance.

After this meeting I started writing down a few memories, paying heed to advice to take a low profile and concentrate on writing. However, I did so spasmodically because I considered the main task to be the distribution of the "Constitution Contribution for Public Awareness" which we continued to send out, together with copies of the Obituary and article covering the final days of Sylvester Chisembele in the University Teaching Hospital. I decided to extend the distribution to include the museums and universities in Zambia and I was very pleased to receive requests from those institutions to send them additional material. Their reaction corroborated the view of the priest and encouraged me to eventually take on the task of writing this brief political history surrounding the events of the life and times of Sylvester Chisembele.

Earlier, in March 2006, I had been advised by security officials at the British High Commission (where I went after the editor of the newspaper that published the Obituary and

Personal Story of Sylvester M. Chisembele

the article on the neglect my husband suffered during his last days in hospital, told me to 'watch my back') that it was not safe for me to remain in Zambia and that I should return to the UK.[190] However, I had started circulating copies of the Obituary and other documents within and without Zambia and so I remained.

I was living in virtual isolation, alone in a big house with a garden of four and half acres, mainly of fruit and flower trees affording restricted vision, and with just a schoolgirl who came in the evenings from the relatively nearby Linda compound to sleepover in the house with me.

On 11 March 2009 early in the morning, I was attacked in the house by masked men; I was tied with ropes to a chair and threatened with knives; I underwent another frightening experience.[191] I remained, however, for another six months, but it was with a great sense of disquiet and unease and when I left for the UK for a break with every intention of returning, the friends with whom I stayed, Dr. Michael and Mrs Beryl Barr, urged me to remain this time, advising me that I could just as easily write the planned history of Sylvester Chisembele from the UK in peace and security. They offered me a temporary home for as long as I needed. A few months later with the aid of their daughter, I secured a small flat.[192] I returned to Zambia to explain my decision to the family, which was well understood and supported.

I left Zambia with nothing of the material possessions which we had worked for and accumulated over the years. The farm was repossessed by the Government and no

---

[190] Ibid. Fn.174 Sophena Chisembele, "A Brief History – 2006 onwards".
[191] Zambia Police, "Police Statement", 11.3.09
[192] Comment: - Dr. Michael Barr and his wife Beryl Barr, friends I had met in Zambia in 1968; both working for the British Crown Agents; Beryl my fellow stenographer and Michael working for the Geological Survey Department of the Zambian Government.

compensation ever paid,[193] the house was left to the family, the ownership of which could in any case have been disputed under customary law, and had I wanted to sell it, which was never my wish, I could not have done so. But I came away with what was far more important to me: the papers, diaries, photographs, letters, etcetera, that have enabled me to write this brief political history on the life of Sylvester Mwamba Chisembele.

Finally, in the hope that it will not appear arrogant for surely I am well aware of my own limitations and failings, I would like to say that although this history may appear pessimistic in that it partly details the corruption that has been evident in administration after administration, I believe this to be part of a process moving through an era of corruption, which is a result of the politics of poverty. This era will pass and when people in the so-called third world are able to exercise their right of equality, and hold their leaders to account, then democracy will naturally follow, and though this will never eradicate corruption completely at least governments will be better held to account, and a decent standard of living will not just be the prerogative of the elite.

What can happen now or in the future cannot be predicted, but Chisembele and others with similar thinking were right, a change did come in Zambia by a groundswell of public rejection which brought an end to the rule of President Kenneth Kaunda, and Zambia has been spared the coups d'état that have occurred in many African countries that have brought so much misery, famine, death and destruction on so many people.

I thank God for the privilege granted to me to have spent the greater part of my life with Sylvester Chisembele. There are men and women of great ability and achievement who

---

[193] The corruption surrounding the seizure of our farm was so blatant that it defied belief: Ibid. Fn.102 folder "Filalo Farm".

live by principle and maintain a code of ethics throughout their lives, Chisembele was one of these. He was a courageous man who lived by faith and I thought it necessary and right to record, even if only a little, his great contribution to Zambia both during the struggle of the indigenous people for independence and later in Government, and in the continuing fight for a real democracy and a move away from dictatorship.

I know that one can only speak with authority on one's own experiences and that some people, like my husband, go through their lives with integrity, courage and commitment, but still seeming to suffer injustice to the end; but then we do not know what comes after. I only know that for me some unpleasant experiences have years on become an essential part of a pattern, which in the end makes up a life. I hope that I will face my death with faith in the promise of Jesus Christ that I will be forgiven for my own transgressions and be reunited with the people I love.

Appendix A

Article contributed by The Hon. Valentine W.C. Kayope

BA MAYO BANA CHISEMBELE

LUAPULA PROVINCE'S CONTRIBUTION TO POLITICAL INDEPENDENCE AND DEMOCRATIC GOVERNANCE

Once more my sincere condolences for the tragic loss of Dr. Christina Chisembele whom you raised together with your late great husband Sylvester Mwamba Chisembele. I share fervently your deep loss especially the agony you experience in gathering and verifying information about your dear husband who had a wealth of information about the struggle for Zambia's independence because he was greatly and deeply involved in it.
You have an edge over Dr Larmer in the sense that you witnessed history in making as you lived under the same roof with the man at the centre of it all while Dr Larmer, with all the wealth of information before him to which he had ready access by virtue of his physical presence in a University, knows what he was told and had read what was written by those who heard what had gone on and those who wanted history written as they wanted it to be recorded. But Dr Larmer's observations are meant to help sharpen your perception and assist to correct the distorted political history of our country. In the process he is also learning from you what he did not know before about facts concerning Luapula's unique position in the struggle for independence. In history writing he is

entitled to his interpretations of situations as he read and heard of them.

Both Kapwepwe and Kaunda share a common social background namely from the tribal Chinsali village as childhood friends to the primary school classroom in a strange urban set up. Sylvester Chisembele came from a seminary where philosophy was intensely taught and went into the world of business in an urban set up where he abandoned a lucrative and successful business to venture into the unknown. The perception of life as well as the degree of sacrifice cannot be the same as that for the two. He was a down to earth political organiser: an effective grassroots operative as he had entered politics with greater confidence than the other two men who had no benefit of the wisdom of British liberal thinkers. This Chinsali relationship greatly determined the influence Kapwepwe had on Kaunda and their attitude therefore towards elective leadership.

Dr Larmer made objective observations on the Musakanya Papers which he ably discussed and edited. Incidentally I went to the same secondary school in Southern Rhodesia now Zimbabwe where the late Mr Valentine Musakanya had been a few years before. Both Mr Musakanya and I remained faithful to the school motto "Esse Quam Videri" he made an impression on the administration in Zambia and I left an imprint on the Zambian Parliament regarding democracy and free debate which Sylvester Chisembele stood for from 1962 up to the time he died.

In an unwritten history, Western Province now the Copperbelt Province was an extension of Milambo Myelemyele's realm and today Mufulira where Simon Mwansa Kapwepwe won a Parliamentary seat without being physically present to campaign in the area known and generally referred to by all Bemba speaking people as "Kwa Milambo" and Kaunda had before him similarly won his first Parliamentary seat in Luapula. History cannot easily overlook this fact of Luapula Province factor.

In relation to Northern Rhodesian politics Luapula Province was specially ranked. The British colonial administration made it a point that all senior administrators at senior provincial commissioner level invariably had first to serve in Luapula Province before being posted to the Western Province now Copperbelt Province. This Dr Larmer should know.

Regarding the importance and influence of Sylvester Mwamba Chisembele to the struggle for independence in comparison with both Kapwepwe and Kaunda one should look at the fact that the Chief Secretary who was in charge of the day to day running of the administration of Northern Rhodesia travelled all the way from Lusaka to Samfya in Luapula Province to meet and discuss with Sylvester Chisembele at the time the struggle for independence was hottest. This privilege and honour was never extended to any other freedom fighter by the Chief Secretary of Northern Rhodesia.

It was only in Luapula Province where three chiefs were dethroned and restricted outside the Luapula Province for their active involvement in the struggle for independence. These are Chiefs Milambo Chilyapa, Kasoma Bangweulu and Mulakwa. Coincidentally Senior Chief Milambo Chilyapa was grandfather to Paulina Milambo, Sylvester Chisembele's first wife. Senior Chief Milambo Chilyapa refused government overtures to be reinstated in his position after independence on ground "it did not make sense to rid ourselves of foreigners, the British as our rulers because they were white and to agree and accept to be ruled by another foreigner, a Nyasalander because he was black".

By its close proximity to Luapula Province, Copperbelt Province drew more of the Bemba speaking people from Luapula when mining of copper started. The Bemba spoken on the Copperbelt is the same as the one spoken in Luapula Province and the pattern of politics followed that of Luapula in terms of militancy and purposefulness. The numerical strength of the people of Luapula origin on the Copperbelt is best understood by this fact: In their social corporate responsibilities mining companies organised clubs around which football was organised. Most footballers selected in the national team came from Luapula as for example the victims of the Gabon Air Disaster over 2/3 that perished were from Luapula Province including the football association President Michael John Mwape from Kawambwa who like Kalusha Bwalya, also was of Luapula origin. From Sylvester Chisembele's home district, Mansa four players are featured presently in the national team and 2 of them scored a goal each in the last Africa Cup of Nations competition. The ratio cannot be by accident but by demographic reality.

Long before the independence struggle started Africans owned and operated bus services in competition with Thatcher and Hobson which was later named Central African Road Services (CARS) between the Copperbelt province and Luapula Province. All these Bemba speaking people: Nsemukila, Kalyafye, Mwemena, Chongo, Mwenso and Luka Mumba were all from Luapula Province.

Throughout the struggle about 99.9% of the inspiring Bemba songs for freedom sang on the Copperbelt were composed in Luapula and Copperbelt Provinces by people of Luapula origin and bear the accent of Bemba spoken in Luapula

Province. At the last independence day celebrations, 24th October, 2011 at State House President Sata honoured a choir from Samfya in Luapula Province for composing the political songs that helped and saw the P.F elected as the Government of Zambia.

Kapwepwe was an acknowledged leader of the Bemba speaking people and wielded enormous influence in as far as he was closest to Kaunda. But Kapwepwe and Kaunda saw Bemba speaking people as coming from the Northern Province only. In a way their attitude towards people from Luapula Province was believed to trace its origin from the advice said to have been tendered to Kaunda by a reputable colonial administrator, Ewen Cameron Thomson when he was Senior District Commissioner at Kawambwa. He is said to have told him to be careful with the people from the Luapula Province because among others they were intelligent, frank and courageous and above all far better organised. But Kaunda needed no such advice because he worked with one such person in the name of Titus Mukupo from Kawambwa who was his deputy when he was General Secretary for the African National congress. And Luapula had been personified by one single person, Sylvester Mwamba Chisembele.

I have been most impressed by your position with regard to difference in opinion between you and Dr. Miles Larmer, the author of the Musakanya Papers with particular reference to Luapula Province's contribution to Zambia's political liberation and particularly to democratic governance under the gifted unequal political leadership of Sylvester Mwamba Chisembele.

Luapula was politically marginalised and its people totally excluded from appointments to senior party and government positions. It was for this reason I refused a transfer to Mufulira in 1968 to go and run Parliamentary Elections. I was summoned to Lusaka to be persuaded by the British Administrators that I should go to Mufulira because in their opinion I was the only District Secretary they thought could run elections in a politically troubled District. Wamunyima Mubita whom I was to succeed had been removed, literally sacked but because of the presence of his cousins Sikota and Arthur Wina in Cabinet he was instead sent into Foreign Service in India I did not see any Luapula influence both in the party and government and my point was appreciated but I had to go to Mufulira. Gazette Notices show that successive Kaunda Cabinets between 1964 and 1968, the turning point, excluded political personnel from Luapula, despite her unequal contribution to the struggle for political independence. I succeeded to run the elections impartially largely because I found on the ground at grassroots level UNIP being led mostly by people of Luapula Province. It was the same in the ANC. The most senior person at the UNIP Regional office of Luapula origin was a driver, a simple driver who had no influence on politics. Joseph Mutale from Kasama and Sinkamba from Isoka both in Northern Province were in charge of the party. I was lucky I had key people in the district all British; Officer Commanding, Engineering Squadron Major Niblok, Mufulira Town Clerk and Mufulira Copper Mines General Manager. I had a fine professional Officer Commanding, Police the late Mr Chambwe and the Director of Elections was British. With these I was able to work out security arrangement that guaranteed peaceful elections.

But after the elections, following the shooting of an innocent person by a successfully elected candidate in a convoy celebrating victory in an illegal procession, there was wholesale widespread violence in the district with nearly all houses in townships belonging to Mufulira Copper Mines damaged mostly window panes shuttered. The man, the newly elected killed came from the Ng'umbo area of Samfya District in Luapula Province. I recorded 72 hours of continuous work to restore order while the Officer Commanding Police Mr Chambwe recorded 79 hours of no sleep. After restoring order I hosted a reception at my residence funded from the meagre monthly entertainment allowance I supplemented with my own personal savings.

It is an inconvertible fact that in 1962 at the UNIP Magoye Conference Luapula Province stood alone in agitating for democracy in opposition to a political dictatorship which Kaunda and Kapwepwe conceived and sought to entrench and indeed did entrench. No other province sided with Luapula in rejecting an appointive political system. Delegations from 7 provinces fled into the bush as Luapula delegation in its effort to instil milk of human understanding chased up everybody except national leaders. Chisembele's order to the Luapula delegation to follow up everybody except national leaders was obeyed to the letter. In my debate to parliament on 4th December 1991 after Mr Chiluba also of Luapula origin came into power, I justified that action as evidence I cited in Luapula's consistency in its urge for the establishment of democratic system of governance. My complete speech is emailed and can be seen at the 1st paragraph on page 109 of the Parliamentary Debates.

Mr Chisembele resumed in earnest the fight for Democracy in the party and for equality of political representation in parliament in 1968. Copperbelt Province where people of Luapula origin were in majority was exclusive. Aran Mulwe, a UNIP Constituency Chairman in Kabushi, Ndola for 7 years was appointed UNIP Youth Regional Secretary Ndola, a third position after Regional Secretary and Women Regional Secretary. Northerners openly rejected him and leaders from Northern Province who included **Kapwepwe and Justin Chimba** were up in arms stating "we cannot be led by batubulu – foolish fishermen". This insult fuelled anger among people from Luapula Province. My maiden speech to the

Personal Story of Sylvester M. Chisembele

Third Parliament at page 688 on 30th January, 1974 e-mailed refers to this marginalisation of Luapula Province politicians by Kapwepwe and Kaunda the special reason vindictive for the opposition to the 1962 entrenchment of a Nominative Political System. It was sad to learn from the correspondence between you and Dr Larmer that the Committee of 14 was specifically formed to weaken the Northern Province grip on power. How could we have come along with that which excluded us from participation in all organs of power? Let him read paragraph I at page 690 of my maiden speech to parliament on 30th January, 1974. The House of Commons in London has debates from all commonwealth Parliaments. Kaunda did not dispute the claim that Luapula was leader in nationalism and that Luapula had paid the highest price in the struggle for independence.

The greatness of Sylvester Mwamba Chisembele is seen in what transpired at the Magoye Conference and during the 1973 General Elections. That national leaders were spared of the ordeal orchestrated by the order to castigate explains the respect the Luapula delegation had for their leader, Sylvester Chisembele. His first wife who was granddaughter of a great chief Milambo Chilyapa the one the British dethroned for being a hard core nationalist was President Kaunda's candidate in Chembe. Wilson Chakulya a leading trade unionist husband of the niece of Dr. Kaunda Mama Nyamhango who was also from Nyasaland was UNIP official candidate in Mansa and Chikako Kamalondo, a British trained lawyer who was the first UNIP representative in London during the struggle was the preferred candidate in Bahati where I stood. Central Committee member, Cabinet Minister,

Provincial Political Secretary, District Governor and 3 Regional Officials, in charge of the entire party machinery campaigned for the official candidate in Mansa District where all 3 of us stood as people Kaunda did not want elected. Petronela Kawandami, Mrs Chisanga was specially assigned as leader in the central committee to carry out the campaign there. We had, between ourselves to cover 3 parliamentary constituencies, only 1 vehicle a Peugeot 404 van which I owned. The decision Mr Chisembele took was for us to run the party and make Dr. Kaunda and his officials completely and totally irrelevant throughout Luapula. All of us allied to Mr Chisembele were elected. In an arrogant show of power Kaunda refused to invite any of us into his Government and this included Clement Mwananshiku who had been promised appointment as Solicitor General: Clement Mwananshiku was selected unopposed and was not in the country away to the United Nations General Assembly when we made Kaunda and his men politically irrelevant in Luapula. This election was covered in Luapula by a young lady researcher from a British University. In return I asked Honourable Kaushi elected member for Mansa on a tour to accompany me to cover all the 3 constituencies in Mansa to show people how between 1964 and 1968 Kaunda and Kapwepwe had marginalized Luapula Province politically and the recent exclusion gave added ammunition. Kaunda on my tour of 3 constituencies to gauge reaction of the people to our exclusion in his post 1973 election Government placed 8 intelligence officers. Honourable Kaushi backed out after a hot meeting at Mibenge my tribal Chief's headquarters and I personally asked Chiefs, to stay away from my meetings. I was accompanied on that tour by a highly nationalistic young lady a resourceful and highly courageous person built in Sylvester Chisembele's mode, an official based at Muwanguni Joyce Mapoma as my secretary. I was armed with gazette notices, showing composition of President Kaunda's Governments since 1964 in which he excluded people from Luapula province. I made it clear that I would go to speak in Parliament according to the reaction of the people and I delivered my maiden speech fearlessly the first time it was ever done in a one party political dictatorship. So hot was the reaction to my explanations that one man in annoyance misquoted the Bemba proverb "Ukusengela uwetako likulu kukupoka icifulo" meaning "to allow a person with big buttocks to share a seat with you is to deny yourself space on the bench" and said instead "ukusengela uwebolo likulu kukupoka icifulo" meaning "to allow a person with a big testicle". Nobody laughed including Joyce Mapoma who enjoyed recording tough language used by the people for my purpose in Parliament. When the man asked after tempers calmed simply said what he said was what he wanted to say and there was no need to amend his proverb about being taken for granted or to apologise for the language used. Kaunda never allowed me to stand for elections any more vetoing me 4 times in 1978, 1979, 1983 and 1988 on all four occasions people invited me to stand.

It is not true and in a way therefore a distortion of history to record that Alex Kaunda Shapi presided over the torture or persecution of UPP members in whatever capacity he was. His appointment, as

Secretary of Defence and Security was cosmetic and did not carry with it the functions of office. He did not, for example, exercise the powers that Grey Zulu performed when he held the same office.

It is important to note that it was not by accident that Kaunda and Kapwepwe conceived for independent Zambia a system whereby political leaders were to be appointed by Kaunda to elective political offices what Chisembele's Luapula Province delegation first rejected at Magoye conference in 1962. Each leader had his own reason. For Kaunda the sense of insecurity that he was a Nyasalander and born in Nyasaland and Kapwepwe for his future political purpose. Both men were not very well educated. Before the breakaway from the African National Congress there was about August, 1958, a provincial conference of the African National Conference held by political leaders in Northern Province at Matumbo in Chinsali when Kaunda was outside the country. Kapwepwe was asked to lead the party that was to be formed after the planned breakaway. He said he wanted Kaunda to do so first but would take over later. They told him that it would be impossible to remove him once he became President. Before the Northern Province Provincial Conference of the ANC took place Sylvester Chisembele, Justin Chimba and Sikalumbi had persuaded Kapwepwe in vain to lead the party to be formed. About three times the three talked to Kapwepwe who preferred Kaunda to lead. He flatly refused. Harry Mwaanga Nkumbula from whom they were to break away, had also told Kapwepwe that if they were to breakaway let Kapwepwe lead the new party to be formed. The reason was the same that Kaunda was not indigenous to Northern Rhodesia. But the British were smarter. They enshrined his name in the 1964 independence constitution as the first President of the independent Zambia.

Three contributions I made to debates in Parliament 30/ 01/ 74, 04 / 12/ 91 and 07/ 05/ 96 which are e-mailed will help to clarify points of your disagreement with Dr Larmer. Clement Mwananshiku dubbed my maiden speech to parliament on 30th January, 1974 as the Luapula Declaration. Every politician from Luapula Province religiously followed Chisembele's 1962 Magoye Conference position which I articulated throughout my Parliamentary career and which Frederick Chiluba also from Luapula stood for when he restored Democracy to Zambia. It would be hypocritical of me and for me to think and believe and then state that Chiluba was truly liked by Northern Province politicians. He was not even before the MMD was formed Dr Larmer has to know that the immediate cause of rupture in relationship with Northerners was the insult. "batubulu" foolish fishermen over the appointment, as Youth Regional Secretary at Ndola, of Aram Mulwe in 1968. If other Provinces had their interest Luapula's interest was Democracy and equal representation in Government.

VALENTINE W. C. KAYOPE

Appendix B

Part Autobiography of Sophena Chisembele

Move to Zambia 1968:
I had been working as secretary to Dr. Gordon Latto who with his brother Dr. Douglas Latto ran a private surgery in Great Cumberland Place, Marble Arch, London. Dr. Gordon was at that time physician to Sir Francis Chichester, the yachtsman, who credited Dr. Gordon with curing him of cancer, which later proved to have been remission. Dr. Gordon used treatment methods biased toward diet change and included natural medicine. He was at that time President of the Vegetarian Society of Britain and later became President of the International Vegetarian Society. Both doctors were eminent vegetarians and campaigners for animal welfare.

They also accepted to treat, without charge, patients who were financially strapped. During the years I worked there, there was one young couple in their twenties who came to the surgery; the husband had been diagnosed with inoperable stomach cancer and Dr. Gordon was treating him with a regime that included diet change, with the object of shrinking the tumour so that it might be possible for an operation to be performed to remove it. We were three office staff, Maggie Pfaff, secretary to Dr. Douglas, Maggie Loffstadt who was a young, bright receptionist and me. In time we learnt that this couple was struggling to pay the fees. The patient's wife was working full time as well as caring for her husband who, unable to work, was making knitted soft toys which they sold in order to help with the medical expenses. We decided that Dr. Gordon should be informed, so being the senior member of staff I approached him and told him of their circumstances. Dr. Gordon from that time on waived his fees. Periodically the young man would be sent to see Mr Conrad Latto, a third brother, who was a Consultant Surgeon at the Royal Berkshire Hospital, he also waived all consultation fees. At the time I left the employment in 1967, the young man was still undergoing treatment; it was long past the estimated life-expectation that his condition had imposed upon him. His appearance and vigour were vastly improved.

The Doctors treated their staff almost as extended family. During Wimbledon fortnight one or other of us in the office, would be given a precious ticket to Centre Court and be sent off to watch a tennis match when pressure of work did not allow Dr. Gordon to attend. Dr. Gordon was a keen coin collector and Dr. Douglas a philatelist and even today I still have in my possession a few British coins, of little value, that I collected on a foray with Dr. Gordon to a coin and stamp market in Notting Hill Gate, London.

I spent odd weekends with Dr. Gordon's family at his large house in spacious grounds in Reading where he had an outdoor trampoline and there were small cottages in the grounds which were for the use of their sons and daughter. Dr. Barbara, Dr. Gordon's wife, made a particular bread with stone-ground flour which was moist and unusual to me. Dr. Gordon always brought in his lunch made with this bread. Dr. Douglas lived immediately opposite his brother in a similar property. He had a swimming pool so that both families could interact at leisure. On a weekend visit to Reading I particularly remember a meeting of the Reading Vegetarian Society, which I attended with Dr. Barbara, and which was addressed by Dr. Gordon. Although I did not become a total vegetarian, my time with the Drs. Latto had a lasting influence on my lifestyle. All three Latto brothers were committed Christians.

One day in 1967 Maggie Pfaff came into the office with a newspaper showing an advertisement by the British Crown Agents with the caption "WANTED SUNSHINE GIRLS" they were recruiting stenographers to be sent out to the newly independent country of Zambia. Neither of us knew exactly where in central/southern Africa Zambia was, and so we got

Zambia – The Freedom Struggle and the Aftermath

out an atlas to pinpoint the ex-colonial territory of Northern Rhodesia. Maggie challenged me that *"you are always talking about the right of self-rule for colonial territories, this is a chance for you to put your words into action and go for a real adventure at the same time, why don't you apply?"* I did, and was called for an interview and was later accepted for a posting.[194] However, then I got cold feet. At that time Rosemary Latto, daughter of Dr. Gordon, was making arrangements for a trip she was planning to Australia and she was going alone. I said that she had courage because if I decided to go to Zambia I at least would be going out to a job; but Dr. Douglas said I should think it through very carefully because there was a great deal of difference between travelling to Australia with a list of contacts in your pocket and going alone to Africa where I knew no-one, and had no rich parent to bail me out. On a weekend home visit with Maggie Pfaff to her parents in Folkestone, her father (who was then a Bank Manager, I think of the National Westminster Bank) said that he would never allow one of his daughters to do such a thing. However, I was living with my mother and she said that if I really wanted to, I should go, and though she would miss and probably worry about me, the contract was for 2 years and I would

---

[194] With friends I had joined protest marches outside the Belgian Embassy in London during the period of the arrest, imprisonment and later assassination of the first elected Prime Minister of the Democratic Republic of the Congo, Patrice Lumumba. I had taken part in a mass protest rally outside the Belgian Embassy in London in February 1961 which was described as a riot but, in fact, was not as far as we demonstrators were concerned; rather the disturbance was instigated by mounted police who charged towards us causing panic and injuries. At this rally one of the speakers was Kenneth Kaunda who had taken refuge in London in 1960-1961. In Northern Rhodesia at that time there was a freedom fighter held in prison, named Sylvester Mwamba Chisembele, I never imaged then that I would one day meet and marry this imprisoned freedom fighter in a free Zambia or live in a house in Ndola, Zambia in which at one time the hero whose murder we had protested in demonstration, Patrice Lumumba, had taken refuge;
"Christian Ogbu – Farewell Party, 1962", photograph. Christian Ogbu on returning to Nigeria became involved in the Biafran civil war in Nigeria (1967-1970) and lost his life.

295

have to promise her that I would then come home. My brothers and sister also thought that I should go for the experience, as long as I came back after two years.

With all these different views to think about I continued to dither. Some six to eight weeks on, I was informed by the British Crown Agents that if I did not take up the offer of the post within a certain stated time limit, then they would remove my name from the list of accepted candidates.

I had a Ford Cortina car and during that year, 1967, I had had two accidents neither of them my fault. One accident had been caused by ice and sleet which had resulted in the car sliding across the road and banging into the central barrier, I was driving from Boreham Wood early in the morning with alongside me my sister-in-law, Fiona Alison, (she and my elder brother Peter met when they were both on the stage, he a singer and she a dancer; she is now a professional photographer specializing in child portraiture; my brother Peter died in 1996). The second accident had been caused by a car pulling out of a slip road and crashing into the side of my car. I made a perhaps childish pact with myself that if I had another accident, I would go to Zambia. I also asked God to show me clearly if I was meant to go.

Some days later, I was sitting in my car in the centre lane of Marylebone Road waiting for the traffic lights to change, when a red fire engine came racing along the road with its bells clanging; it rushed past me completely taking off the door on my side of the car. I sat stunned and shaken but as with the other two accidents, I was unharmed. I took this as a sign that I should go to Zambia and so I did. I left the UK on the 21st February 1968 to take up the post offered to me.

Before leaving for Zambia, I met some of my fellow stenographers when I attended some induction meetings organised by the Crown Agents; the speaker was a British civil servant, I remember her name as Mrs Buchanan, she was on secondment to the Zambian civil service and at present on

Zambia – The Freedom Struggle and the Aftermath

leave in the UK. I left a bitterly cold, rainy London the week before my 32nd birthday, I thought there would be some recruits travelling with me, but no, I travelled alone. The most exciting moment of the flight was when the pilot announced over the intercom that we had just crossed the equator. I will never forget landing at Entebbe airport in Uganda for a stopover and stepping onto the aeroplane ladder, at around midnight, and feeling a sudden wave blast of hot air with an earthy smell which was so strange and ancient, and hearing an all-pervading noise which later I discovered was that of African crickets.

I arrived in Zambia in the morning shortly after daybreak and I was met by three representatives of the Establishment Division of the Zambian Government. I was taken to Longacres Hostel and for the first time met a whole group of fellow expatriates from several countries working, on contract, for the Zambian Government in various fields.

This momentous arrival was not merely the beginning of an exciting experience, but the beginning of the future path of my life.

Earlier:
We were living in Stepney, East London, but at the onset of the Second World War in 1939 my elder brother Peter, my sister Sheila and I aged nine, six and three respectively, were lined up with a large group of London children, with labels pinned on our chests, and taken by train to Brighton as evacuees. My younger brother, Edward was still a baby and so he remained in London with my mother. My sister and I were billeted with an elderly couple living in Ladysmith Road and my brother elsewhere.[195] The London house we had lived in was destroyed; fortunately my mother and brother were not there at the time. Some years later, we were reunited as a

---
[195] Brighton photographs, 1939 and others, scan

family and sent to Royston in Hertfordshire along with other evacuee families.

At the end of the Second World War we left Royston, where we had lived for several years. I was 10 years old. It was 1946 and we had only been back in London for some months when my father, still serving in the RAF, died aged 42.

The house we had lived in had been bombed and so on moving back to London we were housed on the third floor of Havelock Close, a five-storey block of flats, one of many blocks of flats in the White City Estate, Shepherds Bush. Our block had a large centre courtyard in which we children played rounders and similar games. Parts of the estate were still being developed and there were lines of temporary pre-fabricated houses along the edge of the complex. The Labour Party was in power and they were embarked on a massive project of housing the poor and dispossessed, and those whose original homes had been destroyed during the war were among the first to be placed in housing estates constructed around the country. The house we had originally lived in, 42 Christian Street, Stepney E.1, was among those completely flattened during the bombing raids on London.

The most exciting part of this estate was a large area of scrub land along the back boundary of the buildings. This scrub land was full of boulders and land holes, probably caused by bomb damage, in which we children played and which we called "the Chinese Jungle". It was a common playground for children from all around the estate in spite of strictures from parents and the wooden "Danger - Keep Out" signs erected at various points along the barbed wire fencing. From time to time we would be chased out by watchmen but this too was part of the fun. Years later, this derelict land became the BBC Television Centre.

Whilst we were in Royston, my sister, Sheila, the clever, studious child of the family, had done extremely well in her 11 plus exams but could not obtain a place in a grammar school, which, in any case, was beyond the purse of my mother. But my mother was an intelligent, dedicated woman and my father in letters home had urged her to make sure the children were educated. She contacted a Lady Newman in Royston who was involved in an organisation concerned with the welfare of the evacuees to Royston. Lady Newman had already shown an interest in my mother and her family and through her direct intervention my sister was given a place in Letchworth Grammar School and the RAF Benevolent Fund was brought in to finance the cost of her schooling, travel between Royston and Letchworth, and the fees for school uniforms and other incidentals.

On returning to London, my sister was granted a place in Burlington School for Girls, a grammar school in Wood Lane, Shepherds Bush. My younger brother, Ted and I were put in Ellerslie Road Primary School, nearby was the Queens Park Rangers football ground, from there we were placed in the North Hammersmith County Secondary School.

There wasn't much overt colour prejudice in the girls division of the secondary school, although there was a bit of stigma attached to girls coming from the White City Estate, but in spite of coming first and never below the top three in my class exams, I was never advanced to a higher level class.[196] Shortly after I left school my sister who was by this time doing a teacher training course was sent to my old school, North Hammersmith Secondary, as a stand-in teacher. In the staff room she was questioned on her surname and told that they had had a pupil of that name in the school, my sister replied that *"yes, she is my sister"*.

Similarly, there was a family in Havelock Close unusual in that they actually had a black Ford motor car. The two daughters were instructed not to play with the Ali children because their father was a 'blackie'. When my sister started

---

[196] School Photographs

Personal Story of Sylvester M. Chisembele

her teacher training course, the mother came to our flat and asked my mother if Sheila would give her younger daughter, Maxine, lessons. My sister refused not from pique but because she was very active studying and also involved with the Labour Party youth wing. In later life I found it amazing that some incidents in life which, at the time, seemed to me to be unfair or discriminatory, somehow, somewhere along the line are unexpectedly challenged.

In her grammar school days my sister had a Saturday job in Woolworths, Notting Hill Gate and later she arranged for me to join her. I was put on the biscuit counter, but caught eating a chocolate finger biscuit which I had taken from one of the near empty biscuit tins, I was moved away to a counter selling miscellaneous shoe cleaners, whiteners, etc. One Saturday before the store opened someone dropped a case of liquid on the floor, and I was told by the supervisor to clean it up. I was kneeling on the floor with a bucket and floor cloth when my sister walked by. She ordered me to put down the cloth and get up. The supervisor called over the floor manager and my sister told him that I had not been employed as a cleaner but as a counter assistant. After some exchange of views between the floor manager and my sister, I was told to leave it, wash and go back behind my counter. I was sure we would both be sacked, but we weren't and I continued with this Saturday job even after I left school at 15; by that time my sister had already stopped working in Woolworths because she was away in college. My elder brother was also absent for he was in the compulsory National Service.

During my last school year, my mother was already very ill. My younger brother and I came home from school one day to find her lying on the floor, unconscious. My brother rushed to the surgery to get help. Dr. Seager, whose practice was within the housing estate, came and he said that my mother had had a heart attack. She was immediately admitted into hospital. A next door neighbour, Mrs Waite, accepted to look after us. My mother was at that time working in the staff canteen of Woolworths in Kensington High Street, but this was the end; she was never able to work full time again, and thereafter she took part-time employment with the Hammersmith Hospital once more in the staff canteen.

In addition to my Saturday job in Woolworths I was baby-sitting for mothers in Havelock Close and through a friend of my mother I was also baby-sitting for a couple who lived off Kensington High Street. The husband was a reporter and he would sometimes sit at their piano and play the beautiful but somehow saddening tune 'Rustle of Spring'. Both were active members of the Communist Party. I met some very interesting people in their home, among them students from Africa studying in the UK They took me to some meetings and although I did not join the Communist Party, I was too young in any case, I did on Saturdays after my stint in Woolworths sell *The Daily Worker* [197] standing outside the Notting Hill Gate tube station. I had been doing this for some months when a neighbour, who was in the area, saw me, and on arriving back to the housing estate, she immediately informed my mother. When I returned home, it was to find my mother angrier with me than I had ever seen her before. She forbade me any further contact with the couple and that was the end of my time with them. However, my experience with this family, who were unlike any other that I had ever met, entrenched in me a sense of the injustices and wrongs that so many people suffered in the world.

My best subject at school was science and in 1951 through a job placement officer who came to advise pupils about to leave school, I was found a job in what we were told was a laboratory attached to a company in Hammersmith. The laboratory turned out to be in a small building within the

---

[197] A Communist Party newspaper

grounds of Vitamins Limited and was more in the nature of a small factory, in that it was staffed by women wearing white overalls and head covering standing around a conveyor belt on which moved along tiny glass ampoules filled with a vitamin substance; checked; and then packed into small boxes.

Although I was shy and tongue-tied in the presence of adults, I had the good fortune to come to the attention of Dr. Baker who was the controller of this vitamin ampoule department. She thought I was unsuited to this work and she arranged, through her sister who also worked for Vitamins Limited to have me transferred to the offices. I was placed under the care of Mrs Gladys Ball who was the personal secretary to the Company Secretary, Miss Jenkins.

Mrs Ball encouraged me to take evening classes in Pitman shorthand, typewriting and Business English, and this I did. Later I included courses on English Language and English Literature. My younger brother also attended evening classes. Mrs Ball and her husband, Fred, ran the Young People's Fellowship attached to the Rivercourt Methodist Church, which was at the top of the road leading down to the premises of Vitamins Limited. We were not a church-going family, but Mrs Ball brought me to the YPF (Young People's Fellowship) and into the Church. Mrs Ball became my mentor and our friend up to the time of her death in November 1999.

One day I was called for an errand into Miss Jenkins' office. Seated in a chair in front of her desk was a man who had been my regular customer when I was on the biscuit counter in Woolworths. I instinctively jerked. When the visitor left, Miss Jenkins called Mrs Ball into her office and shortly after I was also called in. Miss Jenkins asked me if I was still working in Woolworths and when I told her that I was, but it was only on Saturdays, she asked how much I was being paid. I told her that I received 10 shillings. At that time I was receiving two pounds ten shillings wages from Vitamins Limited. Miss Jenkins told me that she would instruct the personnel department to increase my wages by ten shillings provided I left the Woolworths Saturday job immediately and concentrated my spare time on night school studies. I did.

Vitamins Limited was the manufacturer of Bemax which in its day was a very well-known vitamin wheat-germ supplement, and it was also the parent company of Agricultural Food Products Limited. Both organisations were situated within the same complex. One of my duties was to man the till in the canteen which provided for the factory workers and office staff during the luncheon period. I was also entrusted with the task of receiving rent payments from the owners of barges that were moored in the River Thames alongside the Vitamins Limited riverside boundary. The positioning of the company enabled staff members, including me, to watch the Oxford and Cambridge Boat Race from a privileged position either on the quayside or on the company riverside barge which housed the personnel department.

Three years later, I took a job as personal assistant to a Mr Doernberg who was Sales Manager for Bailliere, Tindall & Cox a publisher specialising in medical and scientific books, situated in Henrietta Street, Covent Garden. Mr Doernberg was Jewish and had escaped from Germany just before the outbreak of the Second World War. He had suffered internment here in Britain. His wife told me of an unpleasant incident when the group of prisoners, in which he was placed, had been taken out for exercise in the barbed wired grounds of the internment camp; a spectator threw oranges over the boundary wire, which the prisoners instinctively caught, whilst another person took photographs. These photographs later appeared in the press purporting to show how prisoners were receiving luxuries when the British people were experiencing hardship. They were a cultured couple and invited my sister and me several times to their home in Southgate, North London and it was he who introduced me to the music of Mozart and Beethoven.

Personal Story of Sylvester M. Chisembele

I have been extraordinarily fortunate to have had many experiences in several walks of life. I have been extremely privileged in my parents; and to have met good and kind people who have taught and influenced me.

Chapter Notes

PART ONE: The Freedom Struggle 1948 – 1964

Chapter 1 (1948 – 1959)   1

1948 – 1951
    Chisembele: backdrop: entry into political activism.
1951 – 1956
    Imposition of Central African Federation:
    Growth of ANC throughout Luapula Province:
    Attempt to involve Catholic Church.
1957 – 1959
    Assassination attempt on Chisembele:
    Fateful tour of ANC leader Harry Nkumbula:
    Genesis of UNIP:
    Paramount Chief of Barotseland misgiving re validity of Treaty:
    Declaration of State of Emergency:
    Arrests of freedom fighters and trade union leaders:
    Disquiet in British House of Commons.

Chapter 2 (1960 – 1964)   29

1960 – 1961
    Detainees: release from rustication:
    Visit of British Prime Minister:
    Luapula decides to boycott Monkton Commission:
    'Wind of Change' speech in South Africa:
    Visit of The Queen Mother to Barotseland:
    Promise of Lord Dalhousie to Paramount Chief of Barotseland of treaty protection:
    Paramount Chief of Barotseland visit to London.
1961 – 1962
    Treason charges move against Luapula leadership:
    Cha Cha Cha campaign:
    Differences between Luapula and Northern Provinces:
    Magoye Conference – Luapula stands alone.

Chapter Notes

1963 – 1964
>British Government race to burn documents:
>Kenneth Kaunda agrees British drawn-up Constitution:
>Last minute wrangling for mineral rights:
>INDEPENDENCE ACHIEVED.

PART TWO: The Kaunda Era 1965 – 1991

Chapter 3 (1965 – 1969)   59

1965 – 1967
>Early Days:
>President Kaunda's Economic Policy/Promise.

1968 – 1969
>Personal Relationships:
>Government involvement in 'engagement':
>Deportation of Sophena Baptiste:
>Political intrigues and changes:
>Chisembele, appointed Minister of Barotseland.

Chapter 4 (1970 – 1972)   99

1970 Barotseland - Problems and achievements:
>Catholic Church early days in Fort Rosebery:
>Luapula leaders' decision to control own affairs:
>President Kaunda ban on Committee of 14:
>Referendum to change Zambian Constitution.

1971 Kuomboka Ceremony:
>Committee of 14 actions against and ban on former leaders:
>Political changes and Chisembele suspension from office:
>Chisembeles return to Lusaka and acquire Chisamba farm:
>Simon Kapwepwe resigns:
>Alliance between Kapwepwe and Harry Nkumbula:
>Detention of several UPP officials:
>Chisembele and TAW International connection.

1972 Unrest in Copperbelt and Northern Provinces:
>Simon Kapwepwe detained and UPP banned:
>Chisembele suspension lifted but refuses appointment:
>Chona Constitution Review Commission appointed:

Chapter Notes

Chisembele farm progress.

Chapter 5 (1973 – 1977)   119

1973   Chona Commission presents recommendations:
          One Party State declared by President Kaunda:
          General Elections:
          Paulina Milambo, former wife, opposes Chisembele:
          Chisembele hospitalized for suspected food poisoning:
          President's preferred candidates in Luapula defeated.
1974 – 1975
          Luapula and Copperbelt work to consolidate leadership:
          Chisembele embarks on poultry farming project:
          Chisembele appointment Minister Eastern Province:
          Move to Chipata.
1976 – 1977
          Chisembele exempted from Leadership Code:
          Kapwepwe and Nkumbula 'forgiven' by President and rejoin UNIP:
          Underground campaigns:
          Copperbelt serious disturbances:
          President Kaunda transfers Chisembele to Copperbelt:
          Rumours and plots abound:
          Attempt made to implicate Chisembele in fabricated plot to overthrow Kaunda.

Chapter 6   (1978 – 1979)   133

1978   Member of the Central Committee ["MCC"], Ananias Chongo, informs Chisembele that President indicates Chisembele will never be a MCC:
          Kaunda informs Chisembele he will appoint him MCC:
          National Council Conference; Kapwepwe and Nkumbula outmanoeuvred in attempt to challenge for presidency:
          President announces new Members of Central Committee Chisembele excluded:
          General Elections; Luapulans Valentine Kayope and Peter Chanshi vetoed by Central Committee.

Chapter Notes

1979   Chisembele not included in new Cabinet:
       Move back to Chisamba:
       A word on Chisembele farming programme.

Chapter 7 (1980 – 1983)   147

1980   My mother dies in England:
       Simon Kapwepwe dies:
       Outbreak of Newcastle Disease on our farm:
       Chisembele still under harassment:
       Chisembele rents shop and moves into trade.
1982   I am diagnosed in UK with heart condition:
       Chisembele in serious car accident when returning from
       constituency tour and meetings with Luapula leaders:
       We attend Commonwealth Parliamentary Conference.
1983   Managing Director of Lonrho calls Chisembele to meeting:
       Kaunda informs Chisembele of intended appointment:
       Chisembele declines Cabinet appointment:
       On campaign Chisembele again involved in car accident
       caused by sabotage:
       Chisembele loses seat and rejects pressure to contest result:
       Retirement from politics:
       Chisembele converts retail shop into a restaurant:
       President adopts IMF economic restructuring programme.

PART THREE: Retirement and Events 1984 – 2009

Chapter 8   161

       Some Words on Youth and Character of Chisembele.

Chapter 9 (1984 – 1990)   175

1984 – 1985
       Restaurant difficulties and successes:
       Political climate worsens in the country:
1986   We experience activities of paramilitary police/soldiers:
       President shocked when food-riots break out:

Chapter Notes

Tense and dangerous situation exists fuelled by ferocious activities of paramilitary police, people killed, shops looted.

1987 Chisembele declines calls to return to political organisation: Chisembele works on document for Constitution change: President Kaunda forced by circumstances - strikes and rapidly fading support to sever relations with IMF: Arrests follow including Trade Union leader Chiluba: ZCTU May Day rally banned replaced by procession of civil servants and UNIP cadres:
Chisembele nearly run off road by an unmarked lorry: Chisembele takes over The Garden Restaurant from Lusaka businessmen Theo Bull and Gaudenzio Rossi, and wins International Tourist Award for 1990.

1988 Situation in the country explosive with brutality and repression now the methods of ruling party, UNIP: President Kaunda outraged by corruption in United Church of Zambia; but challenged by graft in Government: Chisembele's restaurants and farming so successful that mistake is made in clearing mortgages:
Animal husbandry introduced on the farm.

1989 – 1990
Dangerous situation in the country moving towards anarchy: Calls grow for return to multi-party democracy:
President announces Referendum but too late, situation beyond Government control:
President Kaunda forced by circumstances to announce intention to restore multi-party politics:
Mvunga Constitution Review Commission appointed: Chisembele submits a written document to the Commission and emphasises need to remove sole-power given to one individual under present Constitution.

Chapter 10 (1991 – 1995)   187

1991 Mvunga Commission issues report on recommendations: Several political parties are formed and registered the frontrunner is the Movement for Multiparty Democracy headed by Chairman of ZCTU, Frederick Chiluba:

Chapter Notes

Frederick Chiluba comes to Garden Restaurant for advice from Chisembele who emphasises need to keep out corrupt leaders:
UNIP delegations solicit Chisembele's support:
Rumours within UNIP that Chisembele is behind-the-scene organiser for Chiluba:
Historic election of Movement for Multi-Party Democracy brings euphoria in the towns and high-hopes rekindled:
President Chiluba calls Chisembele for meeting but fiasco with security officials at State House prevents meeting.

1992 Chisembele receives unofficial, verbal invitation to a meeting with President, but does not accept due to previous debacle:
Corrupt practices already emerging in new Government:
Attempts to form regional Parties said to be financed and organised by ex-President Kaunda:
Rumours of Zero Option plot to overthrow Government.

1993 Chisembele called to meeting regarding reports of a planned coup d'état:
Government accuses Iraq and Iran of coup plot involvement:
Ex-President's son, Wezi Kaunda, and others detained:
State of Emergency declared:
Nation shocked when plane carrying Zambia National Soccer Team crashes:
I have heart attack and return to UK:
Chisembele returns from UK to find farm wrecked and son ill:
The Garden Restaurant repossessed by the Christian Council:
President Chiluba appoints Mwanakatwe Constitution Review Commission.

1994 – 1995
Tragic death of son, Mwale Finbar Chisembele:
President Kaunda in all-out effort to regain power:
Groups from UNIP visit to solicit support from Chisembele:
MMD officials continue calling Chisembele to meetings for advice in spite of corrupt moves against him:
Mwanakatwe Constitution Review Commission recommendations:
Kenneth Kaunda barred from contesting presidency by citizenship clause.

Chapter Notes

Chapter 11 (1996 – 1999)   199

1996 Chisembele's remaining restaurant removed by the
      Zambia National Building Society:
      Presidential and Parliamentary Elections:
      UNIP boycott elections, MMD successful:
      Rumours begin that President Chiluba is not a Zambian:
      Reuben Kamanga, Zambia's first Vice-President dies.
1997 President Chiluba calls Chisembele to meeting and asks his
      plans:
      Commissioner of Lands threatens Chisembele with farm re-
      entry and reallocation:
      Coup attempt by 'Captain Solo':
      Opposition leaders arrested:
      Ex-President Kaunda arrested.
1998 Ex-President Kaunda charged with involvement in coup plot:
      Ex-President Kaunda released and announces intention to
      resign UNIP presidency:
      Petition brought before High Court to nullify President
      Chiluba's election:
      High Court throws out Petition.
1999 Petition now brought against ex-President Kaunda:
      High Court declares ex-President stateless:
      Chisembele receives 'Notice to Re-Enter' his farm:
      Murder of Major Wezi Kaunda:
      High Court reinstates ex-President Kaunda's citizenship:
      Visit to Chisembele from MD of Dar Farms & Transport who
      exposes corruption behind intended seizure of farm:
      Chisembele informs Minister Kayope of corruption details:
      Actions begin to fight for farm:
      Chisembele cold-shouldered by Government:
      Promised appointment with President Chiluba fails to
      materialise:
      Chisembele given the 'run around'.

Chapter 12 (2000)   209

2000 Ex-President Kaunda resigns as UNIP President and is first
      replaced by Francis Nkhoma then ousted by Tilyenji Kaunda:

Chapter Notes

Chisembele receives 'Certificate of Re-entry':
Provocative tactics used by Ministry officials cause
Chisembele loss of composure:
Next day Chisembele called to State House:
Certificate of Re-entry' cancelled:
Chisembele receives letter from President Chiluba regretting "psychological torture and anxiety":
Chisembele begins meetings with Ministers for farm and restaurants compensation:
President Chiluba tries to remove two year limit on presidential office.

Chapter 13 (2001 – 2003)   217

2001   President Chiluba accepts failed bid to extend presidential term:
        Levy Mwanawasa appointed successor:
        Michael Sata resigns from MMD and forms Patriotic Front:
        Levy Mwanawasa wins election but EU Observation Mission fail to sanction result:
        Dissidents arrested:
        Opposition parties unsuccessfully challenge Presidential election in High Court.
2002   Mwanawasa removes Chiluba's immunity from prosecution:
        Rumours of corruption surrounding Mwanawasa emerge:
        Chisembele tries and fails to make appointment with President re his static compensation claim:
        We hear on BBC of actions for restitution by victims of atrocities and dispossession suffered at the hands of various governments.
2003   Chisembele decides to make a claim on British Government:
        Extensive requests for assistance from Zambian Government, organisations and Human Rights lawyers unproductive:
        Reports of widening corruption appear in the press:
        President Mwanawasa asked to explain his acquisition of property:
        President challenged by previous MMD Ministers re UNZA land:
        Zambian Constitution disquiet:

Chapter Notes

President appoints Constitution Review Commission.

Chapter 14 (2004 – 2005)   231

2004   Chisembele's claim against British Government submitted to ECHR who accept to hear the case:
Minister of Foreign Affairs tells Chisembele the claim will "open the floodgates" Chisembele replies "that is their right":
Zambia Attorney General refuses to assist in claim against British Government:
Judges of ECHR find claim against British Government inadmissible by time limit:
Chisembele circulates widely farm and restaurants issue to expose Government corruption:
Chisembele refuses offer of Independence Day honour:
Media reports of Chisembele accepting Award which is gazetted:
Secretary to the Cabinet says he has been misinformed.
2005   Chisembele ill but cause undiagnosed:
Broken promises of appointment with President Mwanawasa:
Chisembele submits paper "Constitution Contribution for Public Awareness" to Mung'omba Commission:
Chisembele speaks at forums and Yatsani Radio reporter queries effectiveness of Committee of 14.

Chapter 15   (2006 – 2009)   255

2006   Chisembele very ill admitted to hospital where conditions are appalling:
All efforts and requests to Government for assistance ignored:
Sylvester Mwamba Chisembele dies under traumatic circumstances:
I write to President Mwanawasa to say I will continue the fight for justice for my husband:
Newspaper carries Obituary and article detailing Government neglect:
Strong reaction from public with treatment of freedom fighters brought to the fore:

Chapter Notes

President Mwanawasa and former President Kaunda argue about neglect of freedom fighters:
Newspaper editor informs me they are blocked from printing anything further written by me:
I begin distribution of copies of Chisembele's "Constitution Contribution for Public Awareness":
Telephone call from State House informing me an appointment will be granted:
President Mwanawasa suffers a stroke and flown to London:
Copperbelt business man invites me to meeting:
Anderson Mazoka, leader of UPND dies:
I have hostile meeting with Secretary to the Cabinet re 'Award' which is still not degazetted:
Chisembele's "Constitution Contribution for Public Awareness" serialised in newspaper:
General Elections:
Mwanawasa re-elected, riots follow.

2007 President Mwanawasa reacts with threats to critics of his views on adoption of any amendments to the Constitution:
We are approached by the Anti-Corruption Commission on farm issue.

2008 We fail to arrange a re-burial of Sylvester Mwamba Chisembele in Cathedral grounds:
President Mwanawasa dies.

2009 Dominic Chisembele dies:
President Kaunda, Government Ministers, Michael Sata attend funeral for Dominic Chisembele:
Extensive distribution throughout Zambia of Chisembele's paper "Constitution Contribution for Public Awareness":
I am attacked and threatened at home:
Six months later I leave Zambia.

Footnotes

Footnotes specific to this book are available to researchers at: The Bodleian Library, Oxford University; the Centre for African Studies, Cambridge University; the SOAS Library, London University; various Africana University Libraries.

1. Hansard, HC Deb 21 November 1951 vol 494 cc392-7.
2. Hansard, HC Deb 24 March 1953 vol 513 cc658-801, HC Deb 06 May 1953 vol 515 cc407-30.
3. "The Lion and Albert" and "Cuckoo in The Nest", courtesy Robin B. Clay.
4. Folder "Documents Submitted to ECHR 29.4.04" - Claim Reports 1-5 p 2; Chisembele "Struggle History note", scan.
5. Ibid. Fn.4 Folder "Documents Submitted to ECHR 29.4.04" - Claim Reports 1-5 p 3.
6. David C. Mulford, "Zambia The Politics of Independence" (Oxford University Press, 1967). p 163.
7. CMS Chiwama, history note, April 2011, scan.
8. Hansard HC Deb 27 November 1958, vol 596, cc563-697.
9. Hansard, HC Deb 04 June 1957 vol 571 cc1085-211.
10. The Hon. Mrs Betty Clay, Diary 25th October 1957, scan, courtesy of Robin B. Clay.
11. "Chembe Pontoon" circa 1958, photograph courtesy Ian Singer.
12. Ibid. Fn. 4 Folder "Documents Submitted to ECHR 29.4.04" - Claim Reports 1-5 pp 13, 4.
13. Hansard HC Deb 15 May 1959 vol 605 cc1571-91.
14. Postcard received in detention, September 1959, scan.
15. "The Litunga, British Prime Minister", January 1960, photograph courtesy Robin B. Clay.
16. Barotse Kuta", The Litunga, Federation Governor-General and British Resident Commissioner"; The Litunga with Lord and Lady Dalhousie, September 1958 Photographs courtesy Robin B. Clay "Kariba Dam, 1958" newspaper cuttings, courtesy Robin B. Clay.
17. Kariba Dam, 1958" newspaper cuttings, courtesy Robin B. Clay

Footnotes

18. "Drum-beat Welcome for The Queen Mother", May 1960; "We Value Status Barotse", The Queen Mother visits Kuta, May 1960, photographs courtesy Robin B. Clay.
19. "Visit of the Paramount Chief & Party to England for Talks with the Secretary of State, April 1961", Gervas Clay, Resident Commissioner, 28 April 1961. NB I am grateful to Robin B. Clay for the use of some footnoted (copyright) material and pictures from his family archives.
20. HC Deb 21 March 1963 vol 674 cc93-4W; HC Deb 25 July 1963 vol 681 cc218-9W.
21. "The Barotseland Agreement 1964" Secretary of State for Commonwealth Relations, May 1964.
22. Ibid. Fn.6 David C. Mulford, "Zambia The Politics of Independence",
23. Ibid. Fn.6 David C. Mulford, "Zambia The Politics of Independence", p 138.
24. Hansard HC Deb 03 April 1958, vol 585, cc1377-8.
25. Hansard, HC Deb 19 October 1961 vol 646 cm366.
26. www.bbc.co.uk/history/worldwars/wwtwo/colonies_colonials_01.shtm; HC Deb 01 June 1956 vol 553 cc656-80; HC Deb 01 August 1958 vol 592 cc1815-58, HC Deb 04 June 1957 vol 571.
27. Recording of Ms Agnes Mumba singing freedom songs, sound file October 2014; Ms Agnes Mumba, Mutale Sunkutu and Steven Kalande have given me permission to use the quotation and anecdotes attributed to them.
28. "Africans 'Strike' After Death Threats in Luapula Province" *Northern News* (Ndola) 20.08.61.
29. Zambia, National Assembly Daily Parliamentary Debates, First Session of the Seventh National Assembly 4.12.91, column 109, excerpt, scan.
30. "Chisembele, China 1962" composite photographs; "Chisembele Visiting Chiefs on Campaign".
31. The *Guardian* newspaper, 29.11.2013 "Revealed: the bonfire of papers at the end of Empire".
32. Chisembele, "Constitution Contribution for Public Awareness", 2005, pt 2 p 16.

Footnotes

33. "Zambia, National Assembly Parliamentary Debates, Fifth Session of the Seventh National Assembly", 07.05.96, column 127, excerpt, scan.
34. "Republic of Zambia, Government Gazette", 28.06.1966, scan.
35. Zambia, National Assembly Daily Parliamentary Debates, First Session of the Third National Assembly 30.1.74, column 689, excerpt, scan.
36. Background of move to Zambia: see Appendix B.
37. Letter from John Muchengwa, circa 1967, scan.
38. Michael Filalo Chisembele, diary, 1917 - 1945 original in Bemba, scan (with English translation).
39. Chisembele, "Statement of the Circumstances Leading to the Engagement", 20.03.69, scan.
40. "Minister engaged" *Times of Zambia* (Ndola) 10.03.69; News "Summary Dressings:" ZANA (Lusaka) 11.3.69; Passport, Sophena Baptiste, scans.
41. "1945 Xmas Card from L.A. Y.M. Ali", scan.
42. "Muslim War Graves, Shah Jahan Mosque".
43. "Brookwood Military Grave of Yusuf M. Ali", photographs; Opening of Peace Garden, 12.11.2015, scans; Sophena Chisembele, speech; http://www.964eagle.co.uk/news/localnews/1791694/prince-edward-unveils-new-woking-peace-garden/ http://www.exploringsurreyspast.org.uk/themes/places/surrey/woking/woking/woking_muslim_burial_ground/; ww.bl.uk/learning/images/asiansinbritain/larg124395.htm
44. "Prime Minister of India, Indira Gandhi - Card 1976", October 1976.
45. Statement of Arrest Sophena Baptiste, 13.03.69.
46. Chisembele letter to President Kaunda, 19.03.69, scan.
47. "Minister's fiancée told to leave" *Times of Zambia* (Ndola), 12.03.69; "Reprieve for Minister's fiancée" *Times of Zambia* (Ndola) 14.03.69.
48. Folder, "1969 Issue".
49. Michael F Chisembele letters to Chisembele, circa 1969, 15/2/70 and 25.5.70, scans.
50. "Excerpt Luapula MPs letter to President Kaunda, 21.4.69", scan.

Footnotes

51. "Chisembele letter to President Kaunda, 29.04.69", scan.
52. Statement of Chisembele, 20-21.05.69, scan.
53. "President Kaunda's Money", 3.06.69, photograph.
54. S. Baptiste letter to President Kaunda, 3.06.69, scan.
55. President K.D. Kaunda letter to S. Baptiste, 3.06.69, scan.
56. "Miss Sophena can stay on" *Times of Zambia* (Ndola) 4.06.69, scan.
57. Sophena Baptiste, diary excerpt, 4.6.69, "We were both very upset. I was booked to leave for London but after another defamatory statement in the press, I cancelled the flight and Sylvester announced his resignation. KK telephoned at 11pm saying he wanted to see us both tomorrow at 2 pm".
58. Chisembele letter to President Kaunda 5.06.69, scan.
59. Statement of Chisembele 17.06.69, scan; S. Baptiste letter to The Crown Agents, 4.6.69, scan.
60. "Sophena's name cleared" *Times of Zambia* (Ndola) 6.06.69, scan.
61. Ibid. Fn.59 Statement of Chisembele, 17.06.69.
62. "LONDON Fly-away Sophena" *Zambia News* (Ndola) 8.06.69, scan.
63. Chisembele letter to Secretary General, 18.06.69; Secretary General letter to Chisembele, 24.6.69; Permanent Secretary, Establishments letters to S. Baptiste, 23.6.69 scans.
64. President Kaunda, letter to Central Committee and Ministers, 18.06.69, scan.
65. Luapula MPs' letter to President Kaunda, 3.7.69, scan.
66. *Times of Zambia* (Ndola), 15.08.69, scan.
67. UNIP Mufulira Representatives letter to SM Chisembele, 26.6.69, scan.
68. Chisembele letters to S. Baptiste, 1.08.69; 2.08.69; and 10.08.69, scans.
69. Ibid. Fn. 7, Chiwama, history note, April 2011, scan.
70. Chisembele letter to Vice-President., 29.10.03, p 6.
71. Chisembele, letters to S. Baptiste, 13-14.08.69 and 25.8.69, scans.
72. Dingiswayo Banda letter to Chisembele, August 1969, scan.
73. Sophena Baptiste, letter to family, 24.11.69, scan; I was young and sufficiently naive to be a little astonished by the fact that in the Government Residency in which we now

Footnotes

lived, I was sleeping on a bed which had engraved on the headboard a British Royal Coat of Arms. I was informed by the head house servant who had served in the house for years going back to Colonial times when the house was the Residency of the British Resident Commissioner, that the bedroom and certain other furniture in the house (the dining room chairs carried the same insignia) had been especially brought in from the UK for the visit made by Queen Elizabeth The Queen Mother in 1960.

74. Excerpts S. Baptiste family letters, June and July 1970, scans.
75. "Interview with Yatsani Radio" sound file, 22.11.05 (please note that Chisembele was already very ill when this interview took place. His normal voice and fluency are absent and he died some few weeks later).
76. Chisembele "Agenda Jottings", 1969.
77. Comment: Dr. Mwewa was a parastatal chief as Managing Director of the National Building Society previously known as First Permanent Building Society; he originated from Chief Milambo's area in Mansa. ("Parastatal" State owned and run company in Zambia usually taken over from a private concern).
78. Valentine Kayope, "Eulogy for Chisembele", 9.2.06, scan.
79. John Muchengwa letter to Chisembele, 27.11.69, scan
80. "The Queen Mother boarding the Nalikwanda", May 1960, photograph courtesy of Robin B. Clay; Sophena Chisembele, letter to family, 9.03.70, scan.
81. Sophena Chisembele, letter to family, 13.08.70, scan; "President Kaunda visit to Mongu". Zambia Information Services, photograph.
82. Sikota Wina telegram to Chisembele, 17.08.70, scan; Secretary, Credit Organisation of Zambia letter to Chisembele, 7.04.70, scan; Jonas Mwambwe letter to Chisembele, 12.08.70 with reply 19.08.70, scan.
83. "The Litunga – Petitions Court – 1970" Zambia Information Services, photograph; "Mrs E Ali – Home Chiswick, London", photograph.
84. Chisembele, "Constitution Contribution for Public Awareness", 2005, pt 2 p 17.

Footnotes

85. Chisembele excerpt of letter to Sophena Chisembele, 21.06.70, scan.
86. Ibid. Fn.74 Excerpts from family letters June and July 1970, scan.
87. Sikota Wina, telegram to Chisembele, 4.09.70, scan.
88. Ibid. Fn.82 Jonas Mwambwe letter to Chisembele, 12.08.70 with reply 19.08.70, scan.
89. Chisembele, "Points to Remember", 21.09.70, scan.
90. President Kaunda's Address at Mulungushi Hall, 6.10.70, scan.
91. Chisembele letter to Stalin Kaushi, 7.10.70 and reply October 1970, scan.
92. Chisembele letter and attachments to Peter Chanshi, 8.10.70, scan.
93. Chisembele, "Speech at Blue Gums Rally", 15.11.70, scan.
94. Chisembele letter to President Kaunda, 13.11.70, scan.
95. President Kaunda letter to Chisembele, 17.11.70, scan.
96. Unfortunately, I cannot locate a copy of this letter but it will be on government files. The quotation, however, is accurate.
97. "Kuomboka The Litunga, Chisembele and Kapwepwe" Zambia Information Services, photograph; Sophena Chisembele letter to Family, 19.03.71, scan.
98. *The Zambia Daily Mail*, Zambia 21.04.71, excerpt "KK announced suspension from UNIP of leaders from various parts of the country in the second crackdown this week on indiscipline in the Nation. The latest move follows the suspension of Mr Sylvester Chisembele, the Cabinet Minister for Western Province, announced by the President on Sunday".
99. Sophena Chisembele letter to family, 23.04.71, scan.
100. Mrs E Ali family letter to Sophena Chisembele, 30.07.71, excerpt "...also if Sylvester sees the Litunga will he tell him that I will answer his last letter which I received last April as soon as I am better", scan.
101. Cabinet Office letter to Sylvester Chisembele, 7.7.71, scan.
102. Folder "Filalo Farm" correspondence, photographs and scans.
103. "Chisembele Statement of Events 1971 to 1975", 19.7.75, scan.

Footnotes

104. Governor of Bank of Zambia, B.R. Kuwani, letter to President Kaunda, 3.10.75, scan.
105. Grindlays Bank Int (Zambia) Ltd. letter to SM Chisembele, 5.02.73.scan.
106. Ibid. Fn.70, Chisembele, letter to Vice-President, 29.10.03, p 7; Cabinet Office, letter to Chisembele, 7.02.72, scan.
107. Zambia, National Assembly Parliamentary Daily Debates, First Session of the Third National Assembly 30.1.74, column 692, excerpt, scan; Valentine Kayope, "History note", 18.9.10, scan.
108. Ibid. Fn.105 Grindlays Bank Int (Zambia) Ltd. letter to Chisembele, 5.02.73, scan; Ibid. Fn.104 Governor of Bank of Zambia, B.R. Kuwani, letter to President Kaunda, 3.10.75, scan.
109. "Chisembele, in Eastern Province". Zambia Information Services, composite photographs.
110. President Kaunda, "Exemption letter", 3.3.76, scan; UNIP Secretary General, "Exemption letter" 12.3.76, scan.
111. Comment: - allowance claims for travel and tours, internal and external, were allowed but even at the time of leaving government service in 1983 the government never fully honoured this commitment in as far as Chisembele was concerned. He left office with nothing and outstanding allowance claims remained unpaid.
112. Ibid. Fn.104 Governor of Bank of Zambia, B.R. Kuwani, letter to President Kaunda, 3.10.75, scan.
113. Sophena Chisembele, letter to my mother, 13.12.76, scan.
114. Sophena Chisembele, letter to my brother-in-law, John Ahern, (New Zealand), 22.1.77, scan.
115. "President Kaunda and others – Copperbelt Rally" Zambia Information Services, photograph.
116. Sophena Chisembele, excerpt of letter to Mrs E. Ali, 6.12.78, scan; D.M. Chisembele, telegram to Mansa District Governor, 21.11.78, scan; Kayope, letter to Chisembele, 30.11.78, scan.; Stalin Kaushi, excerpt of letter to Chisembele, 30.11.78, scan.
117. Sophena Chisembele, letter to my brother (E. Alison), 5.7.79, scan.

Footnotes

118. "Maize Building Collapse", photograph. Ibid. Fn.102 "Filalo Farm"; Ibid. Fn.104, Bank of Zambia Governor, letter to President Kaunda, 3.10.75, scan.
119. Sophena Chisembele, excerpt from a letter to my sister (Dr. Sheila Ahern), 3.11.80 "Business-wise we are doing very little, but we have rented a shop in Lusaka and when a trading licence is granted we shall sell jewellery and groceries, So I shall go to UK to select some stuff for the shop which is called Ethel Ali City Shop. I bet you are wondering at the combination of groceries and earrings! But here that would not be an improbable combination. The farm is more or less at a standstill. We are getting chicken houses reconstructed and chickens will again be kept but in a smaller unit."
120. Chisembele and Mwale Chisembele letters to Sophena Chisembele, 28.5.82 and 19.6.82, scans.
121. Sophena Chisembele, letters to Dr. Sheila Ahern, 20.3.83 and 11.4.83, scans.
122. Comment: I have no note on the reason in my diary, but from memory the reason was that counting had been delayed several times and candidates were told to leave and return later, but when Mr Chisembele and Mr Noah Type did return at the given time they were told counting had already begun and they could not be allowed to enter.
123. Fr. Jan Wessels, M.Afr. excerpt letter to Chisembele, 27.10.83, scan.
124. Fr Jan Wessels, composite photographs.
125. "Fr. Jan Wessels with Chisembele", photographs and correspondence, February 1981, scans.
126. Hansard HC Deb 04 June 1957 vol 571 cm1108; Ibid. Fn.38 Michael Filalo Chisembele, diary; Bishop of Mansa, René-Georges Pailloux, M.Afr. letter to Chisembele, 20.5.73, scan.
127. Ibid. Fn.6 "Zambia The Politics of Independence", David C. Mulford, (Oxford University Press, 1967), excerpt scan; ibid. Fn.78, Kayope, "Eulogy for Chisembele", 9.2.06, scan.
128. Ibid. Fn.29 "National Assembly Debates 4.12.91".
129. Ibid. Fn.4 "Documents Submitted to ECHR 29.4.04" - Claim Reports 1-5 p 2.

Footnotes

130. Ibid. Fn. 84 Chisembele, "Constitution Contribution for Public Awareness", 2005, pt 2 "Corruption and Moral Decay of 1980's".
131. The Garden Restaurant, "Tourist Award, Trade Leaders Club" 24.11.89; Zambia National Tourist Board, 4.1.90, scans; Comment: We were unable to collect the trophy as our application for travel and existence allowance was refused.
132. "History of Farm ZSIC loan"; "History of Buckley Township", scans
133. Ibid. Fn.84 Chisembele, "Constitution Contribution for Public Awareness", 2005, pt 2 "Corruption and Moral Decay of 1980's".
134. Sophena Chisembele, excerpt of letter to my sister, Sheila Ahern, 1.08.91, scan
135. *Times of Zambia* (Ndola), 24.1.91, scan.
136. Letters from Valentine Kayope to President Chiluba 16.3.92, SMC 17.3.92; Diary excerpt, scans
137. Letter from ex-Ministers Mambwe and Mumba re New Political Party, 18.06.1992 scan
138. Sylvester M Chisembele, "A Brief History 1991 – 2000", p 1
139. Letter from John Ahern, 5.04.93, scan.
140. Ibid, Fn.102 Folder "Filalo Farm Destruction & Seizure", documents and photographs;   Ibid. Fn.138 Chisembele, "A Brief History 1991 – 2000"; "Sequence of Events".
141. Comment: - Mrs Monica Chitoshi has read this paragraph and has given me permission to quote her name.
142. Ibid. Fn.138 Chisembele, "A Brief History 1991 – 2000".
143. K.D. Kaunda Citizenship documents, scans
144. Comment: - In 1989 the exchange rate was K21 to the £1 sterling; by 1997 the exchange rate was K2200 and rising to the £1 sterling.
145. Ibid. Fn.84 Chisembele, "Constitution Contribution for Public Awareness", 2005, pt 2, p 28.
146. "Judiciary Not Free", *The Post* newspaper, 6.5.2002, scan.
147. Diary entry page 21st- 26th February 2000, scan
148. Letter from President Chiluba to Chisembele, 31.3.2000; "Summary & Comments on the Brief History 1991 - 2000", Chisembele, 2002
149. BBC News, 16th January 2002, scan

Footnotes

150. Folder, "BHC – Claim Correspondence" : - British High Commissioner, Lusaka letter to Chisembele, 29.10.2003, 20.08.03, scan
151. Ibid. Fn.70, Chisembele, letter to Vice-President, 29.10.03.
152. *The Post* newspapers, 17.11.2003; 25.11.2003; 22.12.2003, scans.
153. Ibid. Fn.4 Folder, "ECHR – Claim Correspondence".
154. "Some Important Diary Notes & BBC Quotes - 2003 & 2004", Sophena Chisembele – 2004
155. "Minister of Foreign Affairs – Meeting Notes" 18.3.04; "Letter from Minister of Foreign Affairs", 05.08.04; Chisembele "General Comments on Freedom Fighters", July 2004
156. "Letter of Ruling from European Court of Human Rights", 25.10.2004.
157. Ibid. Fn.154 "Some Important Diary Notes & BBC Quotes - 2003 & 2004", Sophena Chisembele – 2004.
158. "Solicitor General – Meeting, 5.3.04"; Ibid. Fn.102 Folder, "Filalo Farm": "Commissioner of Lands", correspondence.
159. Letter from Solicitor General, 5.4.04, scan; Letter to Solicitor General GRZ, 16.5.04.
160. Ibid. Fn.102 Folder, "Filalo Farm: Distribution Cover Letter – 2003".
161. Letters from "Zambia Congress of Trade Unions – 23.9.04, 15.11.04 and 6.12.04"; "Speaker of National Assembly - 25.8.04"; "Archbishop James Spaita, 11.10.04", scans; various other letter scans in Folder, Ibid. Fn.102 "Filalo Farm".
162. *The Post* newspaper 10.09.04, scan.
163. Letter from Big. Gen. Miyanda, 21.10.04, scan.
164. Folder, "Award Issue".
165. "Sakala S - Diary Notes 2004-5"
166. Ibid. Fn.164 Folder, "Award Issue" "Rebuttal Letter – 27.10.04".
167. Letter from Deputy Minister, Office of the Vice-President, 9.12.04, scan; Letter from Minister of Sport, Youth & Child Development, 21.1.2005, scan.
168. "The Vitality of Constituent Assembly" the *Weekly Angel* (Lusaka) serialised between issue No. 0069. 10.04.2006 to

Footnotes

issue No. 0083, 25.10.2006, scans; Ibid. Fn.84 "Constitution Contribution for Public Awareness", 2005.

169. Ibid. Fn.75 Yatsani Radio, sound file "S.M Chisembele interview with Yatsani Radio" 22.11.05; *Sunday Post* (Lusaka), 20.11.05; Letter from. Kayope April 2012; National Assembly Debates 30.1.74, col.691, 692, scan.

170. Letter from W.V.C. Kayope, 29.6.12, scan

171. Sylvester M. Chisembele, "Funeral Mass", 05.02.2006, composite photographs

172. Letter to President Levy Mwanawasa, 6.03.2006; Folder "Obituary Documents".

173. The *Weekly Angel* "Death of a Hero", 13.3.06, Issue 0066, The *Guardian*, "Other Lives", 8.12.06.; The *Weekly Angel* "VJ Lets Down Politician's Wife", Issue 0067, scan; The *Weekly Angel* "Editorial", 20.3.06, Issue 0067, scan

174. Sophena Chisembele, "A Brief History – 2006 onwards", Shadreck Banda was shown this document when written in 2008 and gave permission for references to himself to be included; Sophena Chisembele, Diary Excerpts for 2006, scan; Dr. M.W.C. and Mrs B. Barr, emails to and from Sophena Chisembele, April 2006.

175. *The Post* newspaper, excerpt March 2006

176. *The Post* newspaper, excerpts March and April 2006

177. Chisembele correspondence with Simon Sakala, December 2004 and March 2005; Letters from Simon Sakala to President Mwanawasa, Commissioner of Lands and Sophena Chisembele, April 2006, scans

178. "Account of Meeting with Cabinet Secretary – 26.04.06".

179. Ibid. Fn.152, *The Post* newspapers, 17.11.2003, 25.11.2003.

180. Comment: - Ex-President Fujimori fled Peru in 2000 but five years later he was arrested in Chile, extradited to Peru and sentenced to prison for 6 years for corruption. Some years on, other charges including violation of human rights were brought against him, for which he was found guilty and given further sentences of imprisonment.

181. Ibid. Fn.174 Sophena Chisembele, Diary Excerpts for 2006, scan.

182. AJ Lungu, Notes re Meetings, 2006

183. "ACC. DM Chisembele and Pikiti & Co." folder

Footnotes

184. "GRZ Gazette Notice No.... of 2006".
185. Letter from President, FFTUZ – 12.01.07, scan
186. Anti-Corruption Commission – Meeting 9.04.2007
187. "Treason charge threat in Zambia", scan BBC News, 10.10.2007, scan
188. Letter from Fr. Lazarous Mwansa, Secretary/Chancellor of the Archdiocese of Lusaka, 8th May 2008, scan.
189. Comment: - Dominic Chisembele had for a long time a respectful relationship with President Kaunda; his wife, Mary Katongo, for years had been employed as personal nurse to President Kaunda and remained for some time working for President Kaunda after the lost election in 1991.
190. Ibid. Fn.174 Sophena Chisembele, "A Brief History – 2006 onwards".
191. Zambia Police, "Police Statement", 11.3.09
192. Comment: - Dr. Michael Barr and his wife Beryl Barr, friends I had met in Zambia in 1968; both working for the British Crown Agents; Beryl my fellow stenographer and Michael working for the Geological Survey Department of the Zambian Government.
193. The corruption surrounding the seizure of our farm was so blatant that it defied belief: Ibid. Fn.102 folder "Filalo Farm".
194. With friends I had joined protest marches outside the Belgian Embassy in London during the period of the arrest, imprisonment and later assassination of the first elected Prime Minister of the Democratic Republic of the Congo, Patrice Lumumba. I had taken part in a mass protest rally outside the Belgian Embassy in London in February 1961 which was described as a riot but, in fact, was not as far as we demonstrators were concerned; rather the disturbance was instigated by mounted police who charged towards us causing panic and injuries. At this rally one of the speakers was Kenneth Kaunda who had taken refuge in London in 1960-1961. In Northern Rhodesia at that time there was a freedom fighter held in prison, named Sylvester Mwamba Chisembele, I never imaged then that I would one day meet and marry this imprisoned freedom fighter in a free Zambia or live in a house in Ndola, Zambia in which at one time the hero whose murder we had protested in demonstration,

Footnotes

Patrice Lumumba, had taken refuge; "Christian Ogbu – Farewell Party, 1962", photograph. Christian Ogbu on returning to Nigeria became involved in the Biafran civil war in Nigeria (1967-1970) and lost his life.
195. Brighton photographs, 1939 and others, scan
196. School Photographs
197. A Communist Party newspaper

INDEX

Anti-Corruption Commission
   ACC, 273, 274
African National Congress, ANC, 3, 8, 9, 10, 11, 12, 13, 19, 20, 21, 22, 93, 102, 112, 286, 291
Anglo American Corporation, Oppenheimer, P., 31
Banda, Dingiswayo, 26, 62, 78, 92, 95, 108, 110
Banda, Rose, 244
Banda, Rupiah, 276
Banda, Shadreck, 260, 261, 263, 264
Barotseland, 17, 18, 27, 28, 29, 30, 31, 32, 61, 63, 92, 94, 96, 100, 101, 102, 104, 107,110, 124, 131, 132, 259
Barotseland Agreement, The, 32, 33
BBC, 84, 86, 220, 232, 234, 275, 298, 312
Belman, Security Officer, Fort Rosebery, 9, 10, 12, 13, 167
Benson, Sir Arthur, former Governor of Northern Rhodesia, 17, 25, 26
British Government, 3, 4, 13, 15, 29, 32, 37, 38, 40, 50, 51, 52, 53, 69, 91, 103, 220, 221, 223, 225, 231, 232, 233, 235, 267, 306, 313
British High Commission, 67, 69, 74, 75, 224, 225, 226, 231, 260, 277
British South Africa Company, 52, 53
Butler, R.A., First Secretary of State, 32
Butungwa Choir, 37, 43
Callaghan, James, British Prime Minister, 16, 17, 36
Captain Solo, 203, 204, 311
Castle, Barbara, 35
Catholic Church, 8, 10, 11, 14, 56, 59, 61, 78, 162, 163, 164, 269, 305, 306
Chakulya, Wilson, 120, 288
Changufu, Lewis, 81, 268
Chanshi, Peter, 135
Chembe, Luapula, 20, 23, 25, 119, 120, 136, 166, 259, 271, 288
Chikwanda, Alexander, 268

INDEX

Chiluba, Dr. Frederick, President of Zambia, 181, 187, 188, 189, 190, 192, 193, 196, 201, 202, 204, 205, 207, 213, 214, 215, 216, 217, 218, 221, 222, 223, 224, 228, 244, 267, 276, 287, 292

Chiluba, Victoria, 188, 189, 214, 271

Chilupe & Co., Lungu, A.J., 207, 245, 270

Chimba, Justin, 26, 108, 110, 287, 291

Chimese, Chief, 44, 163

Chinsali, 37, 42, 43, 282, 291

Chipata, 21, 63, 64, 65, 127, 169, 171, 307

Chipili, Webby, 228

Chisembele, Dominic, 14, 111, 112, 114, 121, 122, 124, 136, 137, 165, 271, 273, 274, 276

Chisembele, Dr. Christina, 62, 178, 184, 194, 240, 241, 270, 271, 273, 274, 281

Chisembele, Michael Filalo, 62, 156, 162, 163

Chisembele, Mwale, 62, 154, 194, 195, 310

Chisembele, Sylvester, 1, 2, 7, 8, 9, 10, 14, 15, 19, 20, 22, 23, 27, 29, 33, 34, 35, 36, 38, 41, 42, 43, 44, 45, 48, 49, 50, 51, 53, 54, 59, 60, 61, 62, 63, 64, 65, 66, 67, 68, 69, 72, 75, 76, 77, 78, 79, 80, 81, 82, 83, 84, 85, 86, 87, 88, 89, 90, 91, 92, 93, 95, 96, 97, 99,100, 101, 102, 103, 104, 106, 107, 108, 109, 110, 111, 112, 113, 114, 115, 116, 117, 118, 119, 120, 121, 125, 126, 127, 128, 129, 130, 131, 132, 133, 134, 135, 136, 137, 140, 152, 155, 156, 157, 161, 162, 163, 164, 168, 169, 170, 171, 172, 173, 174, 175, 181, 184, 186, 187, 188, 189, 190, 191, 192, 194, 195, 196, 199, 201, 202, 203, 205, 206, 207, 208, 209, 210, 211, 213, 214, 215, 216, 217, 219, 220, 221, 223, 224, 225, 226, 227, 228, 231, 232, 233, 234, 235, 236, 237, 238, 239, 240, 241, 242, 243, 244, 245, 246, 247, 248, 249, 250, 251, 252, 253, 255, 256, 257, 258, 259, 260, 261, 262, 263, 264, 265, 268, 270, 271, 273, 274, 276, 277, 278, 279, 281, 282, 283, 284, 285, 287, 288, 289, 290, 291, 292, 293

Chishala, Josiah, 205

Chitambala, Frank, 114, 137

Chitambo, Chief, 9, 12, 13

Chitimukulu, Paramount Chief of the Bemba People, 44

INDEX

Chitoshi, Mrs Monica, 196
Chiwama, Christopher M.S., 15
Chona Commission, 117, 119, 307
Chona, Mainza, 22, 107, 131, 260
Chongo, Ananias, 133
Chongwe, Dr. Rodger, 224, 225, 237
Churchill, Sir Winston, 39, 40, 73
Chuula Commission, 92, 105, 106, 107, 117
Clay, Gervas, Resident Commissioner of Barotseland, 6, 18, 27, 31, 32, 93
"Committee of 14", 81, 95, 96, 97, 104, 108, 109, 117, 225, 249, 250, 251
Constitution, 5, 16, 30, 32, 40, 48, 52, 53, 60, 81, 86, 91, 92, 95, 96, 103, 105, 117, 119, 130, 134, 157, 186, 187, 189, 196, 216, 228, 244, 247, 248, 250, 252, 263, 264, 265, 266, 267, 268, 273, 274, 276, 277
Copperbelt, 1, 2, 10, 14, 17, 23, 36, 37, 44, 47, 49, 51, 59, 62, 64, 65, 66, 77, 78, 79, 80, 84, 87, 88, 90, 91, 92, 106, 111, 115, 116, 117, 118, 121, 122, 124, 127, 128, 129, 130, 131, 133, 134, 137, 154, 156, 185, 228, 246, 247, 249, 250, 259, 265, 266, 271, 282, 283, 284, 287
Creech Jones, Arthur, 40
Dalhousie, Lord, Governor-General of the Federation of Rhodesia & Nyasaland, 30, 305
David, Tim, British High Commissioner in Zambia, 221, 226
Eastern Province, 21, 42, 63, 72, 117, 123, 124, 126, 128, 129, 168
European Court of Human Rights, ECHR, 231, 313
Federation of Rhodesia & Nyasaland
   Federation, 3, 4, 5, 6, 7, 8, 11, 16, 29, 30, 39, 40, 305
Fenner Brockway, Archibald, 27
Fort Rosebery, 1, 2, 8, 9, 10, 11, 12, 14, 15, 21, 23, 24, 25, 26, 29, 34, 35, 38, 43, 47, 161, 162, *See* also Mansa
Gandhi, Indira, Prime Minister of India, 72, 73
Gandhi, Mahatma, 72, 73
Griffiths, James, Secretary of State for the Colonies, 3, 5

INDEX

Hammarskjold, Dag, Secretary General of the United Nations, 129

Hone, Sir Evelyn, Chief Secretary later Governor of Northern Rhodesia, 22, 23, 24, 34, 283

Horizon, 1

House of Commons, 4, 5, 16, 27, 35, 36, 40

Huggins, Godfrey, former Federal Prime Minister, 4

International Monetary Fund, IMF, 157, 176, 180, 308, 309

Iqbal, Dr. Zafar, 71

Johnson, James, 40

Kalande, Steven Chalwe, 44, 46

Kalasa Mukoso, Senior Chief, 23

Kamalondo, Chikako, 120, 196, 288

Kamanga, Reuben, Zambia's First Vice-President, 50, 78, 80, 81, 85, 95, 108, 112, 113, 137, 201

Kamayanda, Protasio, 8, 10, 11, 13, 14

Kanganja, Dr. J.L., 242, 243, 263, 268, 272

Kapijimpanga, Judith, 228, 264, 273

Kapwepwe, Simon, 26, 42, 50, 80, 81, 88, 91, 92, 97, 107, 109, 110, 112, 116, 127, 128, 129, 130, 134, 147, 282, 283, 285, 287, 288, 289, 291

Kasoma Bangweulu, Chief, 8, 283

Katontoka, Amos, 126, 171

Kaunda, Dr. Kenneth, President of Zambia, 3, 21, 22, 23, 31, 33, 42, 48, 49, 50, 53, 54, 55, 99, 59, 60, 63, 64, 66, 67, 69, 76, 77, 79, 80, 81, 82, 83, 84, 85, 86, 87, 88, 89, 90, 91, 92, 94, 96, 101, 102, 103, 104, 105, 106, 107, 108, 109, 110, 111, 112, 115, 116, 117, 119, 120, 121, 122, 123, 125, 126, 127, 128, 129, 130, 131, 132, 133, 134, 135, 136, 137, 147, 154, 155, 157, 170, 171, 172, 173, 179, 180, 181, 183, 185, 186, 187, 188, 189, 191, 192, 193, 196, 197, 200, 201, 204, 205, 206, 209, 216, 219, 220, 221, 222, 224, 240, 249, 250, 251, 256, 259, 260, 261, 276, 279, 282, 283, 285, 286, 287, 288, 289, 290, 291

Kaunda, Major Wezi, 193, 204, 206, 209, 311

Kaunda, Tilyenji, 209, 311

INDEX

Kaushi, Stalin, 120, 289
Kavindele, Enoch, 252, 261
Kawambwa, 23, 38, 152, 284, 285
Kayope, Valentine W.C., 120, 135, 136, 187, 189, 190, 192, 196, 207, 213, 221, 222, 223, 224, 251, 256, 257, 268, 281
Kekana, James, 240, 241
Kenya, 220, 232
Kolala, Cuthbert M., 239, 240, 241
Kunda, G., 234
Kuwani, B.R., Governor of the Bank of Zambia, 125
Labour Party, 16, 27, 35, 298, 300
Larmer, Dr. Miles, 281, 282, 283, 285, 288, 292
Lembalemba, K.R, 192, 215, 219
Lennox-Boyd, Alan, Secretary of State for the Colonies, 17, 40
Lewanika I, Lubosi, Litunga of Barotseland, 17
Lewanika II, Mbikusita Godwin, Litunga of Barotseland, 93, 99, 100, 101, 102, 110, 111
Lewanika III, Mwanawina, Litunga of Barotseland, 29, 31, 32, 100
Liboma, Fines, 102
Lisulo, Daniel, 78, 132
Luapula Province, 1, 3, 8, 9, 14, 17, 18, 19, 20, 21, 22, 23, 29, 30, 33, 34, 36, 37, 38, 42, 43, 44, 47, 48, 49, 50, 51, 53, 54, 55, 62, 66, 67, 76, 77, 78, 79, 80, 81, 86, 87, 88, 89, 90, 91, 92, 94, 95, 96, 103, 104, 106, 107, 111, 115, 117, 118, 120, 121, 122, 124, 127, 128, 130, 134, 135, 151, 152, 162, 172, 191, 249, 250, 251, 259, 271, 281, 283, 284, 285, 286, 287, 288, 289, 290, 291, 292
Lubushi Seminary, 1, 14, 15, 61, 165, 166
Lubwe Mission, Samfya, 8, 11, 63, 162, 163
Lumumba, Patrice, Prime Minister of the Democratic Republic of Congo, 128, 220
Lusaka, 14, 19, 22, 23, 25, 26, 29, 31, 35, 43, 60, 63, 64, 65, 66, 68, 75, 76, 78, 81, 82, 83, 85, 88, 89, 90, 91, 94, 99, 101, 104, 106, 108, 109, 111, 112, 116, 122, 126, 128, 131, 135, 136, 138, 148, 149, 152, 153, 172, 175, 178, 181, 191, 193, 194, 203, 221, 224,

INDEX

228, 231, 232, 239, 246, 266, 270, 271, 272, 275, 283, 285, 306, 309

Lyttelton, Oliver, Secretary of State for the Colonies, 4, 5
Machel, Samora, President of Mozambique, 127
Macleod, Iain, Secretary of State for the Colonies, 48, 51
Macmillan, Harold, British Prime Minister, 29, 30
Magoye UNIP Conference, 48, 49, 50, 54, 55, 103, 173, 287, 288, 291, 292
Malawi, 8, 21, 22, 68, 124, 200, 205, 206
Mansa, 1, 45, 46, 47, 65, 67, 75, 88, 89, 104, 120, 126, 136, 151, 155, 156, 157, 162, 205, 284, 288, *See* also Fort Rosebery
Mazoka, Anderson, 218, 269, 270, 314
Mbilishi, S.C., 103, 120
Mbozi, E.B., 63, 65
Middleton, Col., District Commissioner, 19, 29
Milambo Chilyapa, Senior Chief, 8, 283
Milambo, Chamalawa, Senior Chief, 61
Milambo, Kaole, Paramount Chief of the Ushi, 44, 90
Milambo, Myelemyele, Senior Chief, 282
Milambo, Paulina, 61, 62, 119, 120, 283, 288, 307
Miyanda, Brig. General Godfrey, 242
Mmembe, Chisembele, Bwalya Matilda, 43, 62, 178, 240, 241, 248, 255
Mongu, 26, 27, 95, 96, 101, 104, 108, 126, 168
Monkton Commission, 30, 305
Movement for Multiparty Democracy, MMD, 121, 188, 189, 190, 192, 193, 196, 197, 200, 201, 206, 207, 211, 212, 216, 217, 237, 239, 242, 244, 252, 261, 267, 269, 292, 310, 311, 312, 313
Muchengwa, John, 63, 75, 97
Muchengwa, Sylvester, 8, 9, 10, 11, 13, 14, 63
Mudenda, Alfred, 247
Mulakwa, Chief, 8, 283
Mulemba, Humphrey, 94, 95
Mulenshi, Evans, 41, 45
Mulford, David C., 20, 33, 34, 35

INDEX

Mulungushi, 87, 92, 106, 134
Mulwe, Aran, 78, 79, 287, 292
Mumba, Agnes, 42, 43
Mumba, Dr. Nevers, 226, 227, 238
Mung'omba Commission, 228, 244, 247, 248, 274, 313
Mung'omba, Dean, 201, 204
Mutale Sunkutu, 44
Mutemba, Andrew, 42
Mutesa, Love, 219, 252
Mutti, Jethro, 95
Mvunga Constitution Review Commission, 186, 187, 309
Mwamba, Senior Chief, 44
Mwanakatwe Constitution Review Commission, 196, 197, 200, 201
Mwanakatwe, John, 63, 65, 66, 67, 78, 82, 87, 94, 196, 310
Mwananshiku, Clement, 104, 120, 289, 292
Mwanawasa, Levy, President of Zambia, 217, 218, 219, 221, 222, 227, 228, 236, 237, 238, 239, 240, 242, 243, 244, 245, 246, 252, 256, 257, 260, 261, 262, 264, 267, 272, 274, 275, 276
Mwanga, Vernon, 256, 257, 269
Mwansa, Dr. K.T., 233, 256
Mwansa, Fr. Lazarus, 275
Mwansakombe, Chief, 9, 12
Mwewa, Dr. Simon, 96, 97
Ndola, 10, 14, 26, 65, 67, 68, 69, 75, 76, 78, 81, 83, 88, 91, 128, 134, 135, 138, 156, 205, 224, 287, 292
Ngambela, Barotseland, 31, 99, 100, 101, 110
Nkanza, William, 103
Nkole, A., 210, 214, 215, 223
Nkhoma, Francis, 209, 311
Nkonde, S.B., 235
Nkrumah, Dr. Kwame, President of Ghana, 51
Nkumbula, Harry Mwaanga, 3, 19, 20, 21, 112, 127, 129, 130, 134, 291
North, A.C., District Commissioner, 2, 8, 9, 10, 12, 13, 14

INDEX

Northern News, 47

Northern Province, 1, 21, 37, 42, 48, 49, 54, 61, 76, 77, 78, 80, 81, 87, 88, 90, 91, 94, 97, 107, 112, 127, 128, 130, 162, 165, 216, 250, 257, 285, 286, 288, 291, 292

Northern Rhodesia, 1, 4, 5, 6, 13, 15, 16, 17, 19, 23, 27, 29, 30, 32, 33, 36, 40, 41, 52, 55, 91, 283, 291, 295

Nyalugwe, Crispin, 60, 75

Nyasaland, 3, 4, 5, 6, 7, 16, 29, 39, 288, 291

Nyerere, Dr. Julius, President of Tanzania, 51

Nyirongo, Rev. Gladys, 245, 264

Oasis Forum, 244, 266

One Party State, 86, 106, 107, 117, 119, 127, 130, 186, 187

Pailloux, Rene-Georges, Bishop, 8, 9, 11, 13, 163

Philip Gomani, Chief, Nyasaland, 8

Phiri, Amock, 95, 225

Prokoph, Fr. Max S.J, 99

Queen Elizabeth, The Queen Mother, 30, 31, 100, 305

Roberts, John, United Federal Party, 34

Sakala, Simon, 240, 243, 245, 246, 247, 248, 252, 258, 259, 262

Sakulanda, J.C., ZHRC, 221, 223, 224, 226

Sata, Michael, President of Zambia, 216, 217, 246, 259, 268, 271, 272, 276, 285

Sha Jahan Mosque, 71

Shamabanse, Henry, 95

Shapi, Alex, 8, 12, 20, 45, 115, 116, 196, 290

Sikatana, M., 215, 219

Sikota, Sakwiba, 228

Sipalo, Munukayumbwa K., 94, 109

Soko, Ackson, 95

Soko, Shadreck, 116, 117, 128

South Africa, 7, 29, 30, 52, 53, 112, 126, 220, 270, 305

Southern Rhodesia, 3, 4, 5, 6, 16, 17, 30, 35, 39, 282

Spaita, James, Archbishop of Kasama, 14, 238, 247, 252, 257, 275

INDEX

State House, 66, 67, 69, 76, 77, 79, 82, 83, 85, 96, 108, 117, 122, 129, 131, 133, 134, 137, 139, 154, 189, 190, 192, 205, 207, 210, 213, 219, 236, 237, 238, 242, 260, 262, 267, 274, 276, 285
State of Emergency, 23, 24, 25, 34, 193
Swingler, Stephen, 27
Tembo, Lt. Gen. Christon, 207, 227
Tembo, Nephas, 26, 42, 78, 110
The Guardian, 51
The Post, 109, 227, 239, 249, 258, 261, 264
The Weekly Angel, 248, 258, 259, 260, 261, 263, 264
Thomson, E.C., Senior Colonial Provincial Commissioner, 14, 23, 24, 90, 285
Times of Zambia, 76, 135, 258
Type, Noah, 136, 155
United National Independence Party, UNIP, 21, 22, 23, 33, 34, 35, 36, 37, 38, 42, 45, 46, 47, 48, 49, 50, 67, 77, 87, 88, 92, 93, 94, 101, 102, 104, 105, 110, 112, 114, 116, 119, 120, 121, 124, 127, 129, 130, 134, 135, 180, 183, 187, 188, 191, 192, 193, 196, 197, 200, 201, 204, 209, 249, 261, 272, 286, 287, 288
University Teaching Hospital, 136, 193, 255, 277
Vangelatos, MD of Dar Farms & Transport, 206, 207, 208, 209
Wina, Sikota, 104, 200, 286
Welensky, Sir Roy, Federal Prime Minister, 6, 7, 16, 17, 43
Wessels, Fr. Jan, M.Afr., 135, 156, 157
Zambezi, 6, 7, 26, 30, 99, 104, 131
Zambia African National Congress, ZANC, 21, 22, 23, 35
Zambia Congress of Trade Unions, 181, 187, 189, 238, 252, 273, 324
Zambia National Broadcasting Corporation, ZNBC, 117, 135, 203, 216, 240, 263, 264, 269, 273, 275
Zambia Daily Mail, 76, 110, 258
Zero Option, 191, 192, 193, 205
Zukas, Simon, 228
Zulu, Grey, 77, 82, 261, 291
Zulu, Solomon, 264, 265, 266, 268, 269

www.ingramcontent.com/pod-product-compliance
Lightning Source LLC
Chambersburg PA
CBHW050527300426
44113CB00012B/1983